"*Swimming in the Sacred* brings the stories of women who serve as underground psychedelic guides into the brilliant light of day. With gratitude and openheartedness, Rachel Harris honors their wisdom and commitment, without shying away from the potential for harm. The diverse practices cultivated by women over the decades, which span the distance between the psychedelic emergence of the 1960s and the current reemergence, contribute an invaluable perspective to the field of psychedelic care."
— Jamie Beachy, PhD, MDiv, assistant faculty in wisdom traditions and director of education, Center for Psychedelic Studies, Naropa University

"*Swimming in the Sacred* is an astute set of observations by a seasoned psychonaut, trained in psychology (but well aware of traditional perspectives), on the pressing questions of today's psychedelic movement. Rachel Harris offers enormous insight into the possible nature of entity encounters, psychedelic therapy (and who's best qualified to offer it), scientific and traditional metrics for assessing such matters, and other issues. This is a must-read for psychedelic explorers, coming at exactly the right moment in our collective journey."
— Dana Sawyer, professor emeritus of philosophy and world religions, Maine College of Art & Design, and author of *Aldous Huxley: A Biography* and *Huston Smith: Wisdomkeeper: The Authorized Biography of a 21st Century Spiritual Giant*

"Rachel Harris takes readers on a personal journey to meet women of the psychedelic underground, and along the way she reveals how women have been quietly but persistently nurturing a therapeutic renaissance that is not reflected in the scientific headlines. Beautifully written, this is a compelling and intimate look at some of the unsung heroines building a sustainable psychedelic future."
— Erika Dyck, University of Saskatchewan, author of *Psychedelic Psychiatry* and *Women & Psychedelics*

"I would like to offer my heartfelt endorsement of *Swimming in the Sacred*. In this insightful and timely book on women psychedelic elders, Rachel Harris weaves together her wide-ranging interviews with fifteen women who have, for decades, at the risk of incarceration, been skillfully guiding medicine journeys with others as part of the psychedelic underground. These courageous women, impelled by the keen desire to help others to grow spiritually, were willing to share their compelling stories with Harris, who in turn crafted this lucid, vivid, and often wryly humorous text as a way to honor the wisdom and heart of these gifted women."

— **G. William Barnard**, professor of religious studies, Southern Methodist University

"A luminescent light shines onto shadow aspects of the psychedelic renaissance in *Swimming in the Sacred*. Rachel Harris provides a long-overdue recognition of women's hidden contributions to psychedelic healing, research, and sacred wisdom. Harris astutely navigates the paradox of shadow and light in the current explosion of collective interest in psychedelic medicines in the US by recounting the experiences of women healers who have traversed healing realms for decades, some underground and some in the open light. Through a Jungian lens, Harris weaves her personal experiences with the life experiences of psychedelic medicine women, including Harris's healing through indigenous Shipibo healers of the Peruvian Amazon, writing with humor, clarity, and easy-to-read flow. Her book exposes vulnerable moments in the unfolding of psychedelic healing in her life, juxtaposing her intellectual skepticism of the nonmaterial realms with her curiosity and reverence for these same invisible yet real realms accessible through psychedelic medicines and the healers. Harris shares her personal process impacted by psychedelic medicines, revealing her individuation process, while deeply honoring the lives of scantly recognized women healers."

— **Jerome Braun, MA, LMFT, IAAP**, Jungian analyst; diplomate of C.G. Jung Institute, Zurich; and author of "Impact of Personal Psychedelic Experiences in Clinical Practice" in *Psychedelics & Psychotherapy*, edited by Tim Read and Maria Papaspyrou

"As with the women she describes, Rachel Harris's gift is her ability to straddle different worlds. Weaving together academic research, a discerning psychologist's intuition, and a deep belief in the transformative power of mystical experience, she highlights the critical importance of listening carefully to the spiritual wisdom of the underground healers among us whose work stands resolutely outside the Western therapeutic model."

— **Mark Woodbury Brown**, author of *The Headless Vase*

"This is an important and wonderful book. It's full of surprises and revelations, facts and stories, humor and wisdom. Rachel Harris gives us an immensely helpful and necessary guide for anyone interested in the transformative traditions that emerge in all cultures from the essential symbiosis between human beings and the plants and fungi that make life on earth possible. It's the fruit of a long life lived with courage, curiosity, compassion, and a wise and critical intelligence. The voices of these shadowy figures of the sacred underground are so important for us to hear now. The lives and practices of these women provide essential context, grounding, and cautions for everyone hoping to explore the powerful healing potential of our mysterious and elusive life-giving companions."

— **Tom Cheetham**, author of *Imaginal Love*

"I've spent twenty-six years in the Amazon jungles apprenticing with one of the last of the traditional ayahuasquero shamans. As a gringa in that machismo society, it was no small feat. Now Rachel Harris proudly brings to light the wisdom of modern women in modern settings who are keepers of the psychedelic mysteries of the feminine."

— **Connie Grauds**, author of *Amazon Medicine Woman*

"Ever so carefully, Rachel Harris leads us into the deep end. Her storytelling pulses with life, illuminating treasures that have been overlooked for far too long. In gratitude, she reveals the untold stories of some of our bravest navigators. *Swimming in the Sacred* takes us on a delightful journey through the underground of this psychedelic renaissance and brings us back to the surface, for a much-needed breath of fresh integrity."

— **Joe Tafur, MD**, author of *The Fellowship of the River:*
A Medical Doctor's Exploration into Traditional Amazonian Plant Medicine

"What an opportunity! Fifteen wise women with hundreds of years of experience guiding psychedelic life-changing journeys share their stories. Rachel Harris has deftly woven their opinions, concerns, reservations, and reflections into a book-length conversation. Her own additional observations, personal experiences, and pertinent research expand the value of every other contribution. The result is a feast of wisdoms to guide the next generation, emphasizing putting healing others above all else to develop their hearts as well as their skills. This book is a treasure box of guidance and support."

— **James Fadiman**, microdose researcher and author of
The Psychedelic Explorer's Guide: Safe, Therapeutic, and Sacred Journeys

"Rachel Harris has become an important voice in psychedelic studies. Her perspective is compassionate, balanced, informed, and pragmatic. *Swimming in the Sacred* is full of wisdom, experience, and nuance — a necessary contribution to the field."

— **Jeremy Narby**, author of *Plant Teachers* and *The Cosmic Serpent*

"The space of psychedelic ceremony is vast — a sacred ocean. This remarkable book is a narrative distillation of knowledge and insight informed through extensive conversation with women ceremony leaders from the psychedelic underground of contemporary Western society. It is a skillfully woven pedagogical treasure for present and future generations of healers — a sourcebook of wisdom jewels from medicine women who operate with intuitions cultivated over decades and thousands of hours of immersive practice. A true gem!"

— David E. Presti, University of California, Berkeley, author of *Foundational Concepts in Neuroscience: A Brain-Mind Odyssey* and *Mind Beyond Brain*

"Rachel Harris has delivered a singular book, inspired by in-depth interviews with fifteen elder underground guides, women with 'more experience with the process of working with entheogens than any of the academic research teams' involved with psychedelics today. The author brings her psychology and research background, and her study of the history of psychedelics, together with insights grounded in her own encounters with visionary realms. In doing so, she connects the wisdom of these guides with scholarship from multiple disciplines that the reader can explore for further learning. Articulating the ineffable conditions of nonordinary states — and the unique expertise of women engaged in 'lifelong learning with entheogens' — is no small task. With deep respect and admiration, the author interprets for the reader stories, wisdom, and guidance from these remarkable women, 'silent and unseen,' who have been 'in relationship with these medicines for decades.' Harris invokes the 'existential reassurance' that can benefit clients who work with medicine guides and therapists connected to 'a much larger and more subtle world,' who have centered their own healing in service to others."

— Sylvia Thyssen, senior editor, Erowid.org

"Now that the transformative potential of psychedelic exploration is once again spoken of openly, many curious but inexperienced seekers recognize that they would prefer not to make the journey alone. For the past half century, those who have had a wise teacher or mentor to support them have been remarkably fortunate, since our social environment has made it difficult to find this kind of guidance, and dangerous to provide it. *Swimming in the Sacred* explores the work of a group of women whose skillful presence in the

psychedelic underground perpetuates an ancient spiritual and cultural tradition that has been carefully concealed during fifty years of reprehension and suppression. Without pulling away the protective cloak of discretion, this inspiring book reveals the work of these priestesses in a way that is respectful, factual, and instructive."
— Mariavittoria Mangini, PhD, FNP, Women's Visionary Council

"An invaluable account of medicine women, working at the edges of consciousness and societal consensus, in deep relationship to the unseen, in service and allyship to the healing forces of life. Rachel Harris has captured their voices with her exquisite narrative that draws us into the very essence of the felt sense, the tactile, the delicate, the mythopoetic worlds such work emerges from. As we are navigating the process of mainstreaming psychedelic medicines in the Western world, these voices bring a depth and wisdom that are essential for informing our ways forward."
— Maria Papaspyrou, MSc, coeditor of *Psychedelics & Psychotherapy: The Healing Potential of Expanded States* and codirector of the Institute of Psychedelic Therapy

"In this poignant, inspirational, and heartfelt book, Rachel Harris takes us on a fascinating journey exploring the compassionate and dedicated work of women elders of the psychedelic community. Drawing from her life as a psychologist and a commitment to spiritual practice, Dr. Harris beautifully weaves together stories of the compassion, courage, and wisdom of these women, along with remarkable tales of the early history of psychedelic research. In these often bewildering times, this book reminds us of the essential human capacity for transcendence, meaning, and the awareness of our interconnectedness with each other and with nature, all of which are available through spiritual experience, potentially generated by psychedelics administered in safe, trusted, and supported relationships and settings. Harris elegantly reveals the ineffable wonder of human consciousness, including worlds of joy and suffering and the transformative wisdom within. *Swimming in the Sacred* is a gift and a refreshing delight, arriving at the right time."
— Anthony P. Bossis, PhD, clinical psychologist and clinical researcher

"Rachel Harris shows deep admiration and respect for the powerful and accomplished women she has come to know: the underground guides who connect with the plants that are the source of psychedelic medicines for our age, as they were long before the culture of modern medicine. This book, while it may be dense to read, carries the understanding of wise women who have lived at the center of the psychedelic plant world and have made their healing powers accessible. Here you will find the experiential complement to rule-bound academic studies that cannot acknowledge spiritual dimensions. *Swimming in the Sacred* is an antidote to the medicalization of psychedelics that risks losing this spiritual core."

— Dr. Roger D. Nelson, director of Global Consciousness Project

SWIMMING

IN THE

SACRED

Also by Rachel Harris, PhD

Listening to Ayahuasca: New Hope for Depression,
Addiction, PTSD, and Anxiety

20-Minute Retreats: Revive Your Spirit in Just Minutes
a Day with Simple, Self-Led Practices

SWIMMING
IN THE
SACRED

Wisdom from the
Psychedelic Underground

RACHEL HARRIS, PhD

New World Library
Novato, California

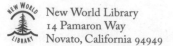 New World Library
14 Pamaron Way
Novato, California 94949

Text design by Tona Pearce Myers

Library of Congress Cataloging-in-Publication Data

Names: Harris, Rachel, date, author.
Title: Swimming in the sacred : wisdom from the psychedelic underground / Rachel Harris.
Description: Novato, California : New World Library, 2023. | Includes bibliographical references and index. | Summary: "A revelatory look at the previously unseen world behind today's psychedelic renaissance: contemporary Western women who have long guided people on shamanic, visionary journeys of healing and self-discovery"-- Provided by publisher.
Identifiers: LCCN 2023000812 (print) | LCCN 2023000813 (ebook) | ISBN 9781608687305 (paperback) | ISBN 9781608687312 (epub)
Subjects: LCSH: Women healers--United States--Interviews. | Women psychologists--United States--Interviews. | Hallucinogenic drugs--United States. | Hallucinogenic plants--United States.
Classification: LCC RZ407 .H37 2023 (print) | LCC RZ407 (ebook) | DDC 615.7/883--dc23/eng/20230228
LC record available at https://lccn.loc.gov/2023000812
LC ebook record available at https://lccn.loc.gov/2023000813

First printing, May 2023
ISBN 978-1-60868-730-5
Ebook ISBN 978-1-60868-731-2
Printed in Canada on 100% postconsumer-waste recycled paper

 New World Library is proud to be a Gold Certified Environmentally Responsible Publisher. Publisher certification awarded by Green Press Initiative.

10   9   8   7   6   5   4   3   2   1

This book is dedicated to the women who have practiced the sacred art of guiding journeys despite great legal risk to themselves. They are the true heroes of the psychedelic renaissance.

CONTENTS

PREFACE

I live on a small island off the coast of Maine, a rock six miles out to sea. We have little topsoil, and the spruce grow spindly and then blow over when winter winds and spring rains hit them hard. Walking through the woods, I see there are many blowdowns where a tree has fallen and the root system is exposed, torn from the mossy earth. Sometimes there's an opening in the ground right at that spot, inviting curiosity and exploration. It's almost as if I could crawl into the shadows there, under the web of disconnected roots, and enter another world.

The dark is darker on the island. We have no ambient light, and when the moon is waning, the Milky Way is a cloudy streak across the sky. The darkness descends, envelops me. I melt into the night. The me and not-me are one and the same. When I return to myself and my fears, I sweep my flashlight across the landscape, on the lookout for wild eyes that glow in the dark.

When the wind is up and the sea is rough, the waves crash into Boom Beach, which is not a sandy beach but a cove filled with granite boulders. The surf bounces these boulders like marbles, and the ground booms and shakes the quarter mile to my cabin, where I feel the rumble in my bones.

I came home one afternoon to see an eagle perched on a log floating in the pond about ten feet away from me. We looked at each other and hesitated. Both of us. The eagle made the first move, spreading its wings, talons up. Then I saw the half-eaten seagull drifting in the water, bloody and bloated. And the circle of white feathers on the bank of the pond. *Evidence*, I thought at first, *a murder*. But no. The kill is about life — the eagle flies high.

Some nights I hear the coyotes sing their song of "red in tooth and claw" — their sound carries across the pond. I know they're by their lairs in the rocky ledges up in the hills of the island interior. It's a choral celebration that chills my bones. I stay inside my cabin and watch the moon move across the sky until the river of light is reflected in the water. Then, as in a dream, I follow the silvery pathway.

On summer mornings, I walk along the road that cuts through the forest to encircle the island. I pause where the road allows a view of Head Harbor and the ocean rolling into the granite shore. The day after a storm, I can hear the surf, arising from different directions, echoing around the island. Spring water in the brooks tumbles over rocks. The island is always speaking; I have to be quiet to hear.

I went out with a neighbor in a fourteen-foot aluminum skiff around the southern end of the island. The small outboard motor was remarkably quiet, and we didn't talk much. We were hoping to see one of those gigantic sunfish that swim on their sides and make eye contact when you come upon them. But we didn't. It's a big ocean, and I guess they had other things to do. What we did see were different shades of granite along the rocky shoreline, acres of spruce trees, and no signs of civilization. No houses, no wires, not even an adventurous hiker spotting us on the water. We saw the island as it has been for centuries, eons, since a volcano burst it out of the sea. We are quite temporary in the history of this world. And small.

A clear day, early in summer, and the azure blue sky expands forever — a celestial dome. We take the sky for granted, forget that it's as ethereal as light. It's the expansiveness of the sky that somehow reaches down to the physicality of earth and the center of my chest. I take a big breath to stretch the boundaries of my heart but reach the limits way too soon. Not quite "as above, so below." I yearn for the spaciousness of the sky to enter into my heart and carry me into the celestial realms.

Nature speaks to us in myriad ways, sometimes through weather, starry skies, other-than-human beings, and medicine plants, inviting us into unknown worlds. The women psychedelic guides you'll meet in this book have responded to such invitations, whether from inner or outer worlds, by following entheogenic pathways that led deep into mystery.[1] They are warriors who thrive with the velocity of shamanic journeys, revel in the chaos that is inevitable, and return renewed. They have worked with all the medicines in small and heroic doses. They live in communion with the spirits, and healing happens in their presence. I still don't know how they do it, but I have asked them many questions and written down our conversations and hope to share their words and wisdom in a way that inspires awe, cultivates humility, and embraces love.

Chapter One

OUT OF THE SILENCE

My mother had her own idea about how to celebrate her children's birthdays. She would walk me and my older brother past the neighbor's flower garden, where I remember the hollyhocks in full bloom, taller than I was at five years old. Whether it was their standing in the world, their brilliant colors, or the delight I took in the sound of their name, these plants had a presence I recognized as we walked by, trespassing on our neighbor's lawn to cross the street and climb the hill to reach the broad meadow. That's where the birthday present was.

Small airplanes lined up along the side of the meadow. I know in the memory of my jostled bones that there was no airstrip. My brother and I climbed into a plane for our birthday flight. This was the early 1950s, and airplane rides for civilians, especially children on their own, were a rather exotic idea. Only fifteen minutes flying over a small town changed me.

I learned for the first time that there was something I could do that my brother, almost four years older, couldn't. I could enjoy the adventure, unafraid. My brother, not so much. Part of what fascinated me with the whole experience was the new perspective. I looked down past the wings and propellers to see the white, stucco house where we lived on one floor, and the neighbor's garden with the hollyhocks. I saw familiar landmarks but from an entirely new viewpoint. That was my mother's real present and, surprisingly, the gift of the entheogens decades later.

Like most children, I was a serious observer of my mother during my earliest years. I watched her learn how to drive a car for the first time when she was almost forty. A native New Yorker who'd lived in the city all her life, she was terrified. She spent years backing up and moving forward along our fifty-foot driveway, never venturing onto the street. I stood on the running board, going for a free ride, as she inched along the driveway. After years of this, she worked up to driving in traffic and eventually driving across a small bridge over a river. Gradually, she developed confidence, but I don't think she ever drove over fifty miles an hour or more than twenty miles from home. She wanted me to have bigger adventures.

And I have — adventures of the psyche and spirit that open up new ways of perceiving, of being in the world in a different way, of shifting perspectives from an earthbound view to one above the clouds.

After the publication of *Listening to Ayahuasca*, an opportunity arose for me to interview women who have been sitting with people on psychedelic trips for the past twenty or thirty years or more. These women are elders within the psychedelic community and have a long history of strict confidentiality about their work. They are part of the silent psychedelic underground.

When I began the interviews for this book, I thought I would be very similar to these women. Certainly, I had been in many of the same places they'd been — such as Esalen Institute in Big Sur, California, during the late sixties when drugs were readily available and mostly used for psychospiritual development. I knew a number of the mentors who trained these women guides. I had been around during those early psychedelic years; I thought I could've gone in their direction. Certainly, I shared the same enthusiasm for these mind-blowing trips that expanded and deepened the spontaneous peak experiences I had known from when I was a child. I had no way of talking about those moments in my life, but I knew they formed the core of my being, and I'd been pursuing them since those early plane rides opened up new vistas.

I thought the women guides represented my unlived life, the road not taken. I thought they'd be as enamored as I was with the therapeutic potential in these psychedelic medicines. I thought their work would look somewhat like my private psychotherapy practice, albeit with illegal drugs and far greater confidentiality and secrecy. I cannot believe how wrong I was...about everything.

The women of the psychedelic underground are priestesses, shamans. I didn't know that when I started to interview them. I thought they were therapists, like me. They're not. When I asked Mary about integration after a ceremony, she explained, "If a client asks, I will offer a brief check-in by phone a day or so after the ceremony."

"What if the person wants to talk with you more?" I persisted.

"I can schedule time on the phone or in person," Mary explained, "but that's an extra fee, and I'm very clear that I'm not available for ongoing psychotherapy. If the person wants more, they can do another ceremony. I'm very supportive but I'm not working as a psychotherapist."

Our culture doesn't exactly have a role for what Mary does. Calling these women priestesses or shamans is our culture's best approximation. My exchange with Mary was the turning point for me — when I realized these guides are doing something completely different from what I'd imagined.

Based on this exchange, I said to Medridth, "I assume you see people once?"

"No," she replied emphatically. "Two-thirds of people I see are in my life — I'm sitter, guide, big sister, friend, gossip." But even though she uses Gestalt therapy in her weeklong retreats, she said, "I'm not a psychotherapist. I'm about self-discovery. The answers are inside and will emerge. I have certainty about the spiritual process."

If someone has questions or difficulties after a ceremony, the women guides often tell them to do another journey. The guide points the person back to their relationship with the medicine and away from an ongoing therapeutic relationship with the guide. This is not done in an uncaring way. Rather, it's a statement of faith in the psychedelic process and that healing comes through the journeys themselves.

I also interviewed other women with extensive psychedelic experience but with no history of working underground. These women provided additional perspectives and had the advantage of being able to speak publicly and allow me to use their names. For instance, Connie Grauds is a pharmacist who apprenticed for twenty-six years in the jungles of Peru with one of the last of the indigenous shamans of the old ways. He initiated her as a "shamana," and because she straddles two worlds, she's very clear about the distinctions between the Western psychological viewpoint and indigenous healing. Connie gave me permission to use her name and she spoke freely about her own training and experiences. In honor of transparency, we're good friends with years of sharing life stories.

Connie and I were standing in a home kitchen of a friend of mine, chatting casually about shamanism. I was asking my usual, therapeutically oriented questions. Connie drew close to me, face to face, and shouted with great intensity, "We don't care about the family history. We don't even want to hear about it." Connie was repeating words she'd heard from her maestro during her apprenticeship. All of a sudden, the kitchen seemed very small and way too close.

There's no question in my mind that Connie did a shamanic intervention using her maestro's words to shock me out of my usual way of thinking. Later that same day, I asked my friend, who had witnessed this exchange, "Did Connie yell at me?" I needed a reality check, as I was sure she had yelled at me at the top of her lungs. My friend said, "No, she didn't yell at you."

I had to think about this for a long time. It still *felt* as if Connie had yelled at me, and it does even now as I remember this situation. I do realize, though, that this wasn't the case. Connie had focused her energy on me to make a very important point: This is *not* psychotherapy. She blasted me out of my assumption with a shock of energy.

The underground guides might be therapeutic but they are not therapists. They travel to other worlds, cultivate unseen allies, guide journeys, and bring their clients home safely. Their primary relationship is with their personal healing spirits, plant teachers, ancestors, unseen forces of nature. Not many therapists would describe their work in quite this same way.

My First Psychedelic Experiences

I landed in San Francisco during the infamous summer of love, 1967. I saw the Diggers serve food to thousands in Golden Gate Park, heard Stephen Gaskin inspire his followers to form a cavalcade of vans driving to Tennessee to start "the Farm" commune, saw drugs everywhere, and took nothing. I've always been on the serious side and have never taken anything for fun...well, other than marijuana, which still makes me giggle during the rare times I indulge. I was in search of the Great Mystery and my own personal healing, not unlike many of the psychedelic guides I've interviewed.

The following year, I lived at Esalen Institute as a fellow in their six-month residential program. Again, drugs were all around but I was cautious. When I finally decided to "trip," I planned with a few friends to spend a sunny afternoon on a ridge above the fog line in Big Sur. We each set spiritual intentions, fasted, and meditated. Big Sur is a glorious setting, and as the LSD came on, the landscape grew ever-more saturated with golden light. After the onset, I began to notice unusual physical sensations, and after a totally unknown amount of time, it finally dawned on me that I was hungry. I'm embarrassed to admit this, but I spent what might have been the peak of an acid trip frying bacon in the kitchen of a Big Sur homestead. I can't remember much of what else happened the rest of the day, but my body retains that warm glow of basking in the sunshine, like a babe with a satisfied stomach, sprawled out in the bassinet of the mountain ridge, empty sky above and warm earth below.

There's a consensus that an inward focus supported by an experienced guide is essential for a therapeutic outcome. A focus that does not usually include frying bacon, I might add. Change is not inherent in the drug itself. Healing depends on how the medicine is used, the support of the guide, the intentions. Think about it — if all the people who had tripped during those sixties music festivals had experienced a psycho-spiritual wake-up call, the baby boom generation would not have exploited the natural world and one another in pursuit of profits the way they have during the last half century.

One experience with MDA (similar to but different from MDMA) remains vivid in my memory because it proved to be a turning point that has stayed with me my whole life. I was still living at Esalen and planned to swallow the pill and head to the lodge where a few hundred people were gathered for dinner and conversation. I was under the impression that this medicine was mostly a social experience of openhearted communion. What better place than a buzzing lodge filled with kindred spirits? I lasted maybe half an hour. What sent me reeling back to my cabin was watching myself in conversation — I saw quite plainly that I wasn't really *in* the conversation, I was role-playing the conversation. I was totally on a people-pleasing, feminine script. This reminds me now of a *New Yorker* cartoon where a professorial-type older man is talking and talking through eight panels to a young woman who just listens intently, saying nothing. In the last panel, the man exclaims to her, "You're a very intelligent little woman, my dear."

This cartoon is a perfect illustration of my 1950s cultural programming, and MDA showed me how I was caught in this outdated conditioning. I don't remember anything else from this experience, and perhaps one insight that lasts a lifetime is enough. I spent the rest of that trip alone, never talked with anyone about it, and never took that drug again until...I was researching this book, over half a century later.

My Own Underground Journey

Since I had never experienced a psychedelic in the manner of the underground guides I was interviewing and the current studies I was researching, I arranged to do so. The standard protocol for both underground sessions and psychedelic research studies includes safe, comfy surroundings, eyeshades, earphones for music, setting of intentions, and at least one guide or sitter. I can't explain why it took me a year of researching the hidden world of medicine journeys to realize that I was writing about something I hadn't yet experienced, but suffice it to say, once I realized my lack, I corrected it immediately.

The underground guide lovingly tucked me in, and I was cozy under blankets with earphones and eyeshades in place just as I entered the vastness of inner space opened by the MDMA. Not only was this already completely different from the social experiment of my youth, but it differed from my almost two decades of drinking ayahuasca in traditional ceremonies. Committed to that muddy brew, I often bemoaned the fact that I hadn't fallen in love with a more fun medicine like MDMA.

Ayahuasca is a challenging medicine, and for me, every ceremony has been an ordeal. Even my personal shaman, who has witnessed my suffering, has expressed surprise that I have persisted in drinking the concoction. Yet I crave the afterglow, the golden hours, days, and weeks of heightened self-reflection, insight, and rejuvenation. My connection with the mysterious plant spirit, Grandmother Ayahuasca, has become essential to who I am, especially in relation to the wilderness where I live for most of the year. How could I stand on a granite ledge overlooking the ocean and not feel her coursing through my body? Feel her presence in everything green and alive? I feel this even months after a ceremony.

I didn't expect MDMA to be present in this same way, but I did have hopes my journey would be more fun, heart opening, and maybe even cosmic. As the journey began, I wandered somewhat lost through the realms of the living and the dead. I realized I was in the realm of ayahuasca and not in the empathic, social, heartfelt world usually associated with ecstasy. *Oh shit*, I thought to myself and then succumbed to my fate. The inevitability of my mortality was zooming toward me through a black sky. I didn't have the will to resist so I surrendered, not quite an elegant surrender, closer to giving up. Then, as death approached, I heard a voice separate from death, *You won't be alone. We'll be with you.* I felt immediate relief and reassurance.

Since then, this message has been "working me," a phrase I picked up from Arielle, one of the psychedelic guides I interviewed. She uses it to refer to an idea, event, thought, or experience that is moving around in her psyche. She isn't just thinking about it — she's osmosing it, mulling it over, experiencing a felt sense of it. Whatever is working on her is alive in her body, requiring attention, moving the furniture around in her psyche. Writing about it now, that's how I still feel about *You won't be alone.* To me, it means more than I won't be alone when I die, but rather, I am never alone. This idea continues to work on me, chipping away at my materialistic belief system. In my previous book, *Listening to Ayahuasca*, I describe how I somehow made an exception for my relationship with Grandmother Ayahuasca, accepting her spirit presence in my lived experience without that upsetting my entire belief system. Now, if I'm "never alone," I must accept that I live in a world of the unseen, in the swirl of the Great Mystery I've been yearning for all my life.

In the moment, I didn't think all this. Instead, during my MDMA experience, I mentally wandered who knows where until I eventually returned to an issue that had arisen a few years before during a previous ayahuasca journey. At that time, I'd had a screaming debate with Grandmother Ayahuasca regarding the existence of evil. While I thought I was so loud that I was disturbing the people around me, evidently this was one time when it truly was "all in my head." My position was, I don't believe in evil. But I was up against a plant teacher with seemingly unlimited sources of information, and needless to say, I lost the debate: Exhausted, I had to admit that, yes, evil exists.

Now my problem was how to differentiate evil intentions from unintentional harm related to narcissistic behavior. With the help of MDMA I refined my understanding. This medicine quiets the amygdala, the part of the brain that recognizes danger. MDMA is a treatment for PTSD precisely because it tones down the amygdala and allows people to view their traumas with less reactive fear.[1] I believe that is part of what happened with me. I reviewed the people in my life who had harmed me and discerned the differences between evil and narcissism. Evil is when people cause intentional harm. Narcissists typically do harm unintentionally, without any empathy for the damage they inflict on others. That's not the same as being evil. Further, I was learning to see the complexity in people — how the same person can sometimes have evil intentions to do harm without any concern for collateral damage; how they can also be damaged themselves; and how they can also at times be charming and kind, doing volunteer work helping others. Each of us can encompass all these wildly divergent, seemingly contradictory aspects.

Still in the journey, I asked, *What's the life lesson I need to learn?* The answer was clear: I need to know how to recognize people who are dangerous so I can protect myself, which is something I hadn't learned to do in my family of origin or in relationships.

During the waning hours of my MDMA journey, my guide did extensive shamanic clearing throughout my aura or energy field. I asked her to place crystals on my heart center, and that quickly grew into requests for pretty much every injury or surgery I've ever had — abdomen, C-section scar, arthritic knee, neck surgery, broken shoulder. I felt like the old, scarred dolphin I once encountered decades ago while sailing on the intercoastal waterway. The dolphin swam alongside the boat while I perched at the bow. We played sort of a hide-and-seek game. Every time the dolphin surfaced, we made direct eye contact, and then she (I was sure she was a female, though I couldn't know) would dive back under the water, and I could see all the scars along the whole length of her back. It was almost as if she were showing me the history of the traumas in her life. I felt myself soften with every meeting until I entered into such communion with her that my eyes filled with tears. In my MDMA journey, I felt some of that same compassion for my own scars, a written history across my body.

As for the crystals, it was unusual for me to ask for them. I appreciate crystals for their beauty, but even though I'm immersed in these mysterious realms, I don't really embrace them. I think they arose in my mind because I had just been reading James Cowan's *Mysteries of the Dream-Time: The Spiritual Life of Australian Aborigines*.[2] Crystals figure prominently in the Aborigines' ritual initiations. The initiate's skin is scored in order to insert crystals permanently into the body. I don't know if this is a literal practice or if it's a metaphor, but the association readily came to mind in my expanded state. My guide chose specific crystals that are particularly helpful for healing broken bones and wounds, and I pressed them into my body as she placed them. The weight, coolness, and sharp edges of the crystals were somehow very reassuring.

My guide told me later that she could see dark places in my aura or energy field. She could see into my body, even under a blanket, and she targeted specific areas as she sprayed me with an essence of infused herbs to support my healing process. At the same time, she feathered the whole length of me with her eagle wing fan, and then she did the same with smoke from burning cedar and sweetgrass. She said she generated concentric circles with her fan to loosen up and then pull out the dark energy. I felt like I was floating on the wind as she repeatedly cleared me from head to toe. This went on for quite a long time.

I don't know how this shamanic clearing, or what I call "vacuuming my energy field," relates to the more psychological work I did in the journey, but I have no doubt it's all connected. My guide explained that the sweetgrass called in ancestor spirits who helped to reinforce the experience that I was not alone. And I can only hope that all that clearing helped to lift me out of my karmic patterns so I could find new ways of protecting myself. Certainly, I felt very cared for and protected as my guide again and again feathered me with smoke and sprayed me with flower essences.

There was a world of difference between my earliest psychedelic experiences, when I was essentially on my own, and my more recent journey with an underground guide. On my own, I wandered somewhat randomly in both inner and outer worlds. I had life-changing experiences, but mostly I was just plain lucky that those journeys went well. Traveling with a guide, especially one who knows the shamanic territory, created a much richer container for energetic clearing and protection.

Michael Pollan understood the importance of working with a guide when he began his foray into psychedelic territory, culminating in a handful of journeys. He interviewed a number of underground guides, not for their stories, but for his own personal safety as he began his psychedelic explorations.[3]

Conversely, I want to know who these underground guides are, these women who provide medicine journeys with illegal substances for people seeking spiritual and psychological healing. These women are so grateful for their own healing with entheogens and so impressed with the powerful possibilities that these experiences offer that they are willing to risk incarceration and all the commensurate losses in order to provide this kind of healing to others. They have been guiding journeys secretly for decades, long before the current psychedelic

renaissance opened up research into entheogens and researchers began to discover what these women have known all along.
In this book, I present their stories — how they came to these
medicines in the first place, how they use them as part of their
own healing, and how they came to be trained to work with
others.

Herstory: One Woman's Experience

Kendra Smith, wife of the famous religion scholar Huston
Smith, was the first woman I interviewed for this book, though
she has never worked as an underground psychedelic guide.
That means I started this study by breaking my own rule about
the criteria to be included, which is perhaps a perfect trans-
gressive start to an exploration of illegal guides.

I sat with Kendra in her sunny living room in Berkeley.
We were surrounded by Tibetan thangkas and other artifacts,
reminders of the Tibetan family who shared the house with
her and who helped to take care of her husband, Huston, over
the last years of his life when he was bedridden. At ninety-six,
Kendra is as bright and clear as ever except for her knees,
which are a source of pain and frustration. In some ways,
Kendra has reached a time of life when she is finally coming
into her own, not as a daughter of an esteemed philosophy
professor or as the wife of an esteemed religion professor, but
as a lifelong spiritual seeker and intuitive. She was born a mere
three years after women were first given the right to vote; she
was not sent to college because...of the usual reasons; she was
a 1950s wife who went into therapy as soon as she got a job to
pay for it herself; she completed college and a master's and a
doctoral program to become a therapist; and she raised three
daughters, losing one to cancer and losing a granddaughter to
murder. Kendra is the matriarch of an extended family that

includes six doctoral-level physicists who don't understand her nonmaterialistic view of the universe.

I wanted to interview Kendra because she participated in an important historical event in 1960s psychedelic history. At the start of the decade, "long before they became *the sixties!*" as Huston once wrote,[4] he arranged for Aldous Huxley to be a visiting scholar at MIT, where Huston was a professor. In turn, Huxley suggested that Huston meet a new researcher at Harvard who had just returned from a summer in Mexico where he had taken magic mushrooms. That new researcher turned out to be Timothy Leary, who was already on a mission to explore the therapeutic potential of psychedelics. At their very first meeting with Leary, they arranged for Huston and Kendra to experience a psychedelic trip.

Around noon on January 1, 1961, Huston and Kendra arrived at Leary's large house in Newton, Massachusetts, where an array of little pink pills was laid out on the table. Huston wrote that they were mescaline; Kendra remembers them as psilocybin. Huston wrote: "One capsule was a mild dose, Tim said; two, average; and three would make a walloping helping."[5] Huston took one; Kendra took two and then a third later on. She told me, "I wanted to go for it — a full monty."

Kendra had been suffering with memories of childhood trauma, depression, and life-crushing social anxiety. She was painfully shy and even fearful around people. She was desperate for change.

"Terror and fear came up," Kendra said, but she finally let go and experienced going through evolution from slime in the ocean to emerging onto land — "all so tiring." She remembers this as symbolic of giving birth. "In fact, at one point on that 1961 day, I asked myself whether I was being born or giving birth."

Around midnight, Huston and Kendra drove back home

to Belmont, still slightly under the influence. A few days later, Kendra realized that she was no longer depressed. She felt more open to people, even having a friendly chat with her car mechanic, something that would have been impossible before. "I wished life could be more like this," she said. "I realized *I could be different. I could enjoy being with people.* This was the *big difference* after the trip." She felt hopeful for perhaps the first time in her life. These feelings faded after about three weeks, but Kendra remembered the possibility.

After this initial experience, Kendra entered psychotherapy. It took her a few tries to find a good therapist but she persevered. Kendra took other psychedelic drugs, never for recreation, always as part of her psychospiritual path, and of course, illegally. She feels they may have opened her up and increased her sensitivity to paranormal experiences and a non-material reality, which changed her worldview forever. Her last psychedelic experience was about ten years ago when she was in her mid-eighties. Besides being on the cutting edge of the psychedelic sixties, Kendra's a good example of how these medicines can be woven throughout life, instilling a practical and spiritual acceptance of death and the mystery beyond.

Kendra remembers telling Tim during the trip that she heard glass breaking and a baby crying. In the moment, Tim told her she was hallucinating, but later on, it turned out that a mirror had broken and there was, in fact, a baby in the house. Almost sixty years later, Kendra remembers this with all the clarity and intensity of a psychedelic experience as yet "another example of a man not listening to a woman," or what we might call gaslighting. Evidently, Tim did not yet appreciate the value of setting to ensure a safe space, and Kendra didn't have the advantage of a guide to protect her.

I asked Kendra if anyone else had ever interviewed her about her early experiences with Leary. She said, in a rather matter-of-fact manner, "No, no one seemed interested." Kendra's story, herstory, if you will, allows a glimpse into the cultural context surrounding the entry of psychedelics into the public sphere. Women had achieved the vote but they still didn't have a voice, not even within the psychedelic subculture undergoing a cultural and spiritual "awakening."

Women of the Psychedelic Underground

As the sixties came to an end, psychedelic drugs were demonized by the press and co-opted by rock concerts. It became more and more difficult to find reliable sources of pure medicines. Eventually, the federal government classified all the psychedelics as illegal and dangerous with no medical benefits. Yet some people continued to work in a sacred way with these medicines, quietly and below the radar. The decision to go underground, to continue to access newly illegal drugs, and to guide people, often strangers who were screened and ultimately trusted to be discreet on the basis of their word alone, is quite a leap of faith.

I decided early in the planning of this project to interview only women. I feel that the women doing this work have a different quality to their relationship with the medicines. They seem to have a more subtle, energetic connection with the spirit world that the medicines open up. One example is when I was developing my questionnaire for a research paper entitled "A Study of Ayahuasca Use in North America."[6] Based on the intuitive wisdom of one of these underground women, I included the question "Do you have an ongoing relationship with the spirit of ayahuasca?" This turned out to be an important aspect of the study. Almost 75 percent of study participants responded yes, and this has continued to influence my understanding of how the relationship with a plant spirit can help heal attachment issues from childhood.

I know a male underground guide who has almost forty years of experience, and he agreed with my decision to focus on women. He said:

> I think women make better guides than men. They have menstruated and suffered, and they're better at suffering than men. Their timing is more sensitive. When you're involved with the deepest part of a person's psyche, women are more careful than men, including me. Women tend to trust and respect the person's process and don't push them one way or the other. You can stop someone from crying by simply handing them a box of Kleenex. Women are less likely to get in between the person and their experience.

These women guides don't have a public voice — they are still working underground. Working outside the legal structure requires silence and anonymity, which is why I've used pseudonyms for all the underground guides in this book. However, even when it's freely chosen, remaining invisible is not so easy. Being silent and unseen triggers the cultural experience of being mansplained or just plain ignored, not unlike Kendra Smith who said "no one seemed interested" in her experience. It's as if these women are twice silenced — by both gender issues and drug laws. I identify with having no voice in a myriad of smaller ways, and I very much want them to have their say, even though they must remain anonymous.

Also, there's a historical precedent for women working with medicine plants. It's now accepted that, in ancient Greece, it was women at Eleusis who knew the Secret of Secrets, the recipe for mixing psychoactive plants with beer for the long night of traveling through mystical realms.[7] The same holds true, according to Brian Muraresku, for "all the Indo-European sacraments — the *soma*, *kykeon*, and even Dionysian wine."[8] Later on, herbalists, midwives, and witches were predominantly women, and there's even evidence that the first shaman was a woman.[9] All silenced by the patriarchy.

Even now, men dominate the university research teams studying the therapeutic potential of psychedelics, and they are most often the presenters at psychedelic conferences and the authors of psychedelic books.[10] Even when woman are acknowledged, their roles are often downplayed. The authors of one research paper admitted that they themselves fell "prey to the same misogynistic assumptions" when they failed to acknowledge that "Gordon Wasson's wife, Dr. Valentina 'Tina' Pavlovna Wasson, had as much if not more influence in bringing the psilocybin mushroom to the attention of North America."[11] In *Psyche Unbound*, a 2022 book honoring Stan Grof, only three of the twenty contributing authors are women, and of those three, one is a second author and one is long dead.[12] Perhaps this reflects the long-standing gender imbalance in doctorate degrees — only in the last few years have more women earned doctorates than men in subjects related to psychedelic research. Women's voices are on the rise, but it will take some years before a gender balance is established.

This imbalance persists even when womens' contributions are public. Requa Tolbert and her husband George Greer were the first people to study MDMA and report on their findings in a professional journal.[13] Their description of how to conduct therapeutic sessions with MDMA provided part of the foundation for the MAPS treatment protocol.[14] Although Requa is the second author in these two articles, she had her own voice when she wrote about her experiences at psychedelic conferences, describing "our complaints about 'the men's macho attitudes' about psychedelic use and inquiry: taking heroic doses, mixing agents that do not even grow on the same continent, trivializing ethnobotanical lore, and either ignoring voices of wise women or ghettoizing them onto a single panel such as 'Women and Psychedelics.'"

Elsewhere, Requa wrote:

> In my life, it has usually been females who have taught me the lessons of attending to emotion and spirit in the course of healing work....My girlfriends coached me in my early efforts to relate to the spirits of the plants and to the elemental forces holding us all up. Of course I know men who think about these things, but it was women, who were not scientists, who were the most energetic in crafting space and ritual to address the spirits of the various Medicines.[15]

These observations were published in 2003, and I daresay not much has changed since then. In addition, the women I interviewed describe a far more intimate relationship to the plants, their allies, and ancestors. They live more closely with these unseen others even when not in ceremony. The relationships transcend their state of consciousness and are part of their everyday lives.

Women's Experiences

For all these reasons and more, I limited my interviews to women guiding medicine journeys. In addition, I set a criteria of at least twenty years of experience. I knew from my years as a therapist in private practice that this type of work is an art. It's not just about expertise; this work requires wisdom that only comes from decades of experience and personal maturity.

I interviewed a total of fifteen women who fully met this criteria. Two of them had guided Michael Pollan after he had rejected a number of other guides for varying degrees of strangeness, one who was famous within the psychedelic community. A few interviews lasted one to two hours. Some interviews went on for days, with subsequent conversations many months later. Given the legal risk these women live with, I decided not to ask if I could record the interviews. Instead, I wrote down everything by hand, filling up four traditional school notebooks.

I also conducted auxiliary interviews with women who hadn't worked underground for twenty years. Three women only had ten years of experience. These women tended to be slightly younger than the more-experienced group, but they had the same passion and commitment to the medicines. This younger group gave me a glimpse into how women grow into being elders — they weren't quite there yet with the same confidence and maturity.

Another reason I set a twenty-year criteria is because I didn't want to interview self-appointed guides, those with no lineage in their training who had decided on their own that they were ready to lead journeys. People regularly come up to me at conferences to tell me how they were called by Grandmother Ayahuasca after just a few ceremonies to start leading ceremonies themselves. Ego inflation is alive and well in the psychedelic world.

One woman I met via emails and a few telephone calls is a good example of what I mean by a self-appointed guide. There were so many problems with her story, and they all serve as warnings. First, she described guiding her own mother on an MDMA journey, and she did so with an ulterior motive: She hoped that her mom would come to the realization that her second husband was abusive and that she would end the marriage. On top of this, she overdosed her mother with MDMA. The daughter thought she was giving her mom the same dose that MAPS (the Multidisciplinary Association for Psychedelic Studies) uses in their PTSD studies, but she was wrong and gave way too high a dose. This was her mom's first experience with any kind of entheogen, and she was nauseous and vomiting most of the journey. Surprisingly, the mother was interested in trying it again. The so-called guide was considering a journey where they would both take MDMA in order to become "closer." When I told her she shouldn't be serving as a guide for her own mother, she became defensive and told me that she had consulted with her elders. I rather strongly told her, "Get new elders!"

Training to lead medicine journeys begins with one's own healing. Then it involves entering into a mentorship with an elder, assisting that elder to guide others, receiving feedback and supervision, and finally, years later, working on one's own, hopefully with colleagues available for consultation and support. In fact, two of the women guides told me that when their mentor told them they were ready to guide others or sing in ceremony, they resisted, not feeling quite ready yet. They both reported that it took about a year longer for them to feel ready to lead.

Connecting to Underground Guides

I wrote *Listening to Ayahuasca* as a result of my personal relationship with the spirit of the plant, which has given me an inkling of how the women psychedelic guides experience their work. Every woman I interviewed talked about her relationship with plant spirits or plant teachers, with the medicines, or with unseen helpers. That said, while I know about this world, and I've experienced it, I don't live there. I still suffer with not quite accepting the unseen world of communicating with plant teachers even as I write about it.

Nevertheless, my ayahuasca book opened up connections for me in the psychedelic community, and in time, those relationships allowed me to meet with many underground psychedelic guides who granted me permission to share their stories, wisdom, and guidance.

It helps that my therapeutic roots grew out of the soil between the ocean cliffs and the Pacific Highway at Esalen Institute during the late sixties and early seventies. For years I lived at Esalen, first as a residential fellow and then as a staff member. I heard Stan Grof explain his cosmological map more than a decade before he wrote his first book. I learned how to stay with the process during countless hours of somatically oriented group therapy sessions. I sat with Suzuki Roshi at Tassajara, and even though I didn't understand what he was talking about, I traveled into an expanded state of consciousness as I listened to him. I had the perfect foundation to become a psychedelic guide. But I didn't.

Instead, I went to graduate school and pursued my academic ambitions. But that's not the real reason I didn't become a guide. First of all, I wasn't called. The medicines, and I took a few, didn't call me. Or at least, I didn't hear them. Second, I'm a wimp. The medicine women I've interviewed, each very unique, are all spiritual warriors. Alas, I'm not.

They have journeyed far beyond my capacity. They have certainty in their connection to unseen sources of guidance. They have physical and spiritual stamina and fearlessness. I have questions and anxieties. I am not of their ilk. Trust me, I am not belittling myself or presenting a fake modesty. I know my limits and where my gifts lie. These women who swim in the sacred are beyond me.

Yet we recognize each other. One of my earliest referrals, from three different sources, was to Medridth, the eldest of the guides. I sent her a cold email, even though I knew Medridth never agrees to this sort of inquiry. All my referral sources had warned me this was probably a hopeless request. However,

the woman Medridth called to check on me was the person
who was mentoring me through this process of contacting
underground guides. I could not have even begun this project
without her support. So naturally Medridth got a good recom-
mendation and responded to my email.

Then we had to arrange an interview. I told her that I
could fly out to meet her the last week of March, but Medridth
said she was traveling then to a town that, serendipitously,
happened to be about forty miles from where I was spending the winter. I figured fate was on my side and we made
arrangements. As I parked my car in her driveway, Medridth
was already at the garden gate waiting for me. We recognized
each other immediately. We had both been at Esalen at the
same time but hadn't hung out together, just seen each other
around. We knew lots of the same people from that era half a
century ago.

This meeting was unique; the other interviews did not
start like this, but there was always a connection. With Cedar,
a retired academic, I almost felt like we were sisters or at least
cousins, coming from the same genetic heritage. I don't usually
feel that way with someone new. I later found out that our
family backgrounds had absolutely nothing in common, but
my sense of connection continued. Further, interviews are not
a normal way of getting to know someone. I dove immediately
into intense, intimate questions about each woman's life and
personal healing.

Also, the issue of safety and discretion was of immediate
concern. Some underground guides don't want the word *psychedelic* sent to them in an email, so I had to somehow ask
permission to even send my request for an interview without
using it, even though the project description (which appears
below) starts with the word *psychedelic*. I had to respect each
woman's sense of privacy while inviting her to reveal her

underground work with a total stranger. A delicate beginning. Once I received permission, I sent each woman the following project overview and interview request:

Interviews with Women Guides of the Psychedelic Underground

For decades women guides have been working with psychedelics, healing themselves, deepening their own wisdom, and in turn, helping others to do the same. These women have stories of how they came to do this work and what they've learned in the process.

Current psychedelic research is laying a foundation for how these medicines will be used therapeutically with a limited number of counseling sessions to prepare, support, and minimally integrate the experience. These research protocols may be significantly different from the best practices developed over decades of work by guides in the underground psychedelic community. Without the constraints of cost-effectiveness, psychedelic women can follow the path of healing that's specific to each client seeking to journey. It's very important that we don't lose their hard-earned knowledge.

My intention is to interview the *Women Guides of the Psychedelic Underground* so that their expertise can be preserved. These women carry the other story of psychedelic healing, the story that won't be published in research journals. Their voices need to be heard while their identities are protected. The best way I know to honor these women is to only write about what they're willing to share and to let them review and edit anything that goes public. The power will always be in their hands to determine what gets published.

Here are the kinds of questions I'll be asking, although all conversations will depend upon what the woman wants to share.

How did you begin to work with others?
Were you mentored, guided?
What is the story of your personal healing with these medicines?
What is your relationship to these medicines?
How do you see your relationship with the client?
How do you feel about the inherent risk of this work?
What are the big issues that arise for people over time in this psychospiritual process?
Do you see any patterns or stages that people tend to pass through?
What are your best and worst healing stories?

Meeting the Women

The fifteen women I interviewed who fit my full criteria — having worked as guides in the psychedelic underground for at least twenty years — range in age from fifty to eighty-seven. A list of the women, using their pseudonyms and including a brief description, appears at the end of this chapter. Most are Caucasian, two are Native American, one is a Peruvian-born US citizen, and one is African American. A few of the guides have indigenous, shamanic lineages from apprenticing in South America and elsewhere for extended periods of time. A number are experienced in Stan Grof's Holotropic Breathwork, his strategic approach to working legally with expanded states of consciousness, or Ralph Metzner's Alchemical Divination Program.[16]

Most of the women guides have worked in the so-called real world as teachers, government administrators, business executives, professors, legal advocates, and holistic healers. Two are therapists but keep their underground practice very separate from their professional lives. The women live all over the United States. Many of them know each other, and most referred me to my next interview. Of course, a few women did not want to be interviewed, but for those I spoke with, I promised to send everything I wrote so they could change whatever they want. All the women wanted to remain anonymous, but they had different requests regarding protecting their identities. All continue to work with the medicines, guiding journeys.

The best explanation for why the women are willing to risk everything to work underground with illegal medicines came from Janet, one of the therapists:

> The illegality adds a lot of stress that I sure could do without. But then I find myself asking, how can I not do this? There's a risk, but it helps people so much. I've heard from clients over and over that it's given them freedom from suffering and a quality of life they hadn't dreamed of. I've had several tell me, "I wouldn't be alive today if we hadn't done this work." These are precious people now living full lives. It would be legal but unethical not to offer the help that is possible.

I don't think this is an overdramatization. Each woman I interviewed expressed the same level of gratitude to the entheogens for their own healing. Their own healing was the gateway to working with others, and they all acknowledge that their process of healing never stops.

I have come to think of this group of women as a dying breed, or perhaps more delicately, the women represent an archeological layer in the history of entheogenic practice. The current crop of people, both underground and working in research settings — sitters, psychedelic therapists, guides — will not have the depth of experience that these women have. They won't have the years of initiation and mentorship that these women have lived through. Recent psychedelic therapists may have graduate degrees and some years of clinical experience, but that's not the same as sleeping on the jungle floor and being attacked by chiggers or working side by side with the Secret Chief, the pioneering psychedelic therapist Leo Zeff.[17] They won't have been adopted by a Native American medicine man or studied with shamans worldwide.

Dr. Rosalind Watts, a psychedelic researcher and therapist, recently admitted, "My final session [in a research study] was with a participant who during the session 'became' his grandfather whilst his grandfather was drowning at sea....I had many more questions than answers. We needed input from the 'elders,' those who have been through all this before....We were like parentless children feeling our way in the dark."[18]

The women I've interviewed have lived unusual lives, most of them don't have children, some are married and some not. One woman describes herself as a nun, not in the usual religious sense, but in her dedication to the mushrooms she serves. I came to feel these women are most like the ancient Greek priestesses from the Eleusinian Mysteries, those who prepared the psychotropic elixir and communed with the realm of spirits. R. Gordon Wasson, who originated the theory of a pre-Christian psychedelic sacrament at Eleusis, wrote, "If our Classical scholars were given the opportunity to attend the rite at Eleusis, to talk with the priestess, what would they not exchange for that chance?"[19]

This book is a chance to talk with these women, to travel with them in conversation through their stories, their training, and their work. They want to be heard, if not identified. They want their perspectives included in the psychedelic renaissance.

I spoke with most of the women more than once, following up with additional questions. Relationships grew — I was a weekend guest at Arielle's home when she arranged for me to speak at a local psychedelic conference. I spent all day with the two Native American medicine women. After twelve hours of conversation, two meals, and many stories, I felt overwhelmed but didn't want to admit it.

When I was ready to drive home, an hour's drive, one of the Native American women asked me if I needed to use the bathroom before I left. I answered, "I don't know." The two women immediately recognized that I was in an expanded state and took charge. They sent me to the bathroom, which it turned out I did need, and then they brought me into their prayer room to clear my energy field with eagle feathers. Somehow they hadn't invited me into this room despite our twelve hours of spiritual conversation and sharing. I had remained at the dining room table the whole time, not knowing that the door to the prayer room was just a few feet behind me. If I hadn't allowed myself to become vulnerable entering into the spiritual reality these women described, I would've missed this room filled with power totems and shamanic tools. After they cleared my energy field, I felt much better and drove back to where I was staying with no problem.

Before this, I had fallen into an expanded state of consciousness after an all-day interview with Maureen, but I hadn't realized that this would become a pattern. That conversation went from ten in the morning to four in the afternoon, and when I left, I knew I was not quite safe to drive. I stopped at a nearby gas station, filled up the tank, and bought some peanut M&Ms, which I immediately devoured. That mix of protein and sugar got me home, but still I couldn't calm down.

I paced around my small rental apartment for about an hour and finally called a good friend, who understood right away that I needed to ground myself. This is not usually an issue for me, and I was able to do so during our phone conversation.

The next time I saw Maureen, she mentioned that, as I was leaving that day, "You looked like you'd seen a ghost." In a way, I had. Just talking about these unseen realms had left me in an expanded state, almost like a contact high but without any medicines involved. She thought it was hilarious. Thank goodness I managed to take copious notes because all I can remember is that I kept asking her, "Four days and nights on a mountain with no food *or* water?"

"Yes," she nodded, "many vision quests."

These women have much to teach us about other worlds, about prayer, about medicine journeys. I've read the research studies on the new psychedelic medicines. They don't cover the same territory.

Women of the Psychedelic Underground

ELDER UNDERGROUND GUIDES

Alyana is Diné (Navajo) and works with peyote.

Arielle trained with Stan Grof in Holotropic Breathwork.

Audrey trained long-term with Stan Grof in Holotropic Breathwork.

Cedar is a cultural anthropologist who apprenticed with Ralph Metzner.

Charlotte has specialized in working with well-functioning people.

Darlene is Diné (Navajo) and Ash:wii (Zuni) and works with prayer.

Debbie has worked long-term with Medridth.

Janet is a master's-level licensed therapist and one of the early supporters of MAPS (Multidisciplinary Association for Psychedelic Studies).

Jessica is a PhD psychologist in private practice who apprenticed with Ralph Metzner.

Mary apprenticed with Ralph Metzner.

Maureen apprenticed with her adopted Native American grandfather.

Medridth is the eldest of the elders. She apprenticed with the Secret Chief, Leo Zeff.

Radha apprenticed with a Shipibo shaman in Peru.

Radianthawk is Peruvian by birth with Quechua lineage. She is now a US citizen.

Rose apprenticed with a Peruvian shaman.

YOUNGER UNDERGROUND GUIDES

Carmen apprenticed with a Shipibo shaman.

Klara apprenticed with a Shipibo shaman.

Sarah works directly with the mushrooms.

ABOVEGROUND ELDERS

Connie Grauds apprenticed twenty-five years with a shaman in Peru and has written many books.

Kendra Smith is the widow of religion professor Huston Smith. She was interviewed about her trip at Tim Leary's house in 1960.

Ann Shulgin was a lay therapist who used MDMA when it was legal. She was the widow of Sasha Shulgin and died in 2022.

Chapter Two

VISIONS FROM CHILDHOOD

The first question I pondered after spending time with the women guides was "What do they have in common?" The most obvious answer is that they all work secretly. Some of them know each other and a few don't. In conversation with one of the women guides, I casually mentioned the first name of another. "Who's that?" she immediately asked, anxious to learn about a kindred spirit engaged in the same secret calling. Realizing I had broken confidentiality, albeit with just a first name, I stammered an apology. Needless to say, I was apologizing to the wrong person, but I figured a breach of confidentiality with one is a breach with all.

The strongest theme that emerged is that many of the women guides are unusually open to expanded states of consciousness and have been this way from childhood. They have a fluidity in the way they talk about themselves and their experiences. I often had a hard time following their stories, which were not always presented in a chronological way. At first I thought they were disorganized in their thinking. My notes after an interview often looked more like a mind map for brainstorming than a linear narrative.

I have to admit to a certain amount of judgmentalness on my part, especially after trying to clarify what happened and when, asking them, Was this before? How did you meet? Where were you? Even with such pointed questions, I often failed to grasp the timeline of stories. I thought, *These women are not coherent in their life narratives.* Such disorganization may indicate a history of trauma, need for therapy, or just plain muddy thinking. In *The Mindful Therapist: A Clinician's Guide to Mindsight and Neural Integration*, psychiatrist Daniel Siegel wrote about the clinical importance of developing a coherent life narrative, or how you come to be who you are.[1] I even wondered if the extent of their psychedelic use had interfered with their thinking — a traitorous thought.

Finally, I realized the women have a far more flexible relationship to time than I have; they aren't internally organized around cause-and-effect the way I am, almost to a fault. As a therapist I'm trained to see how this caused that; I'm attached to understanding current problems in terms of past history. The women guides are more spontaneous in their thinking; yes, they are often a bit dreamy, but they describe unfolding life stories full of synchronicities, coincidences, and unexpected happenings. This was my first clue that the women live in a different world from me, a world that is far more magical and surprising.

Psychologically, these women would score high on the personality factor "openness to experience," which is one of the variables from the five-factors model of personality. This factor has six dimensions: active imagination, aesthetic sensitivity, attentiveness to inner feelings, preference for variety, intellectual curiosity, and broad-mindedness. Research has shown that these personality factors have an equal genetic and environmental influence. Theoretically, scores on the openness to experience factor are not supposed to change over a lifetime. However, psychedelic research has overturned that assumption. A study at Johns Hopkins found that after one high-dose psilocybin session, people scored higher on openness than before, and this increase remained stable more than one year after the psychedelic journey.[2]

It could be argued that this group of women guides is more open due to their extensive use of psychedelics, but after hearing their life stories, I maintain the opposite view. They found their way to the entheogens because they had always been open, permeable to a larger, unseen reality beyond this material world.

This quality of being sensitive to other realities appears in children, but in our culture, it's discouraged. Even very young children know not to speak of such things, since if they do, adults will squash their experience, explain it away, or give advice like, "Just ignore it." One of the underground guides told me, "When I was little, I thought I could talk to trees. Then later I was told, 'No, you can't talk to trees.' I never mentioned it again, and now, of course, I know I can talk to trees." Our culture doesn't take seriously what children say, especially when their comments don't fit our materialistic concept of reality. It's possible that the women guides have been silenced from the very beginning of their lives.

Other cultures don't silence their children in the same way. In India and countries where reincarnation is part of the worldview, young children, most often at ages between two and four, talk about their past lives. Psychiatrist Ian Stevenson, now deceased, founded the Division of Perceptual Studies at the University of Virginia. He spent his career investigating children who claim to remember a previous life, where they lived, who they were, and how they died. Stevenson collected over twenty-five hundred such cases and matched the child's memory with actual data from the previous life.[3] Birthmarks or other physiological manifestations have been found to relate to experiences of the remembered past life, particularly when there's been a violent death. In some cases, children have been born with scars that relate to past-life injuries, or they recognized family members, homes, or personal items from a past life.

A few psychologists have studied childhood mystical experiences by asking adults about their memories. Tobin Hart turned to autobiographical accounts of historical figures to explore how their worldview, ethics, and spiritual development were shaped by early mystical experiences.[4] For instance, Black Elk had visionary dreams at ages five and nine in which elders offered him a medicine, a spiritual power, that would help him lead his people. He said, "I did not have to remember these things; they have remembered themselves all these years."[5] The experiences remained alive and active in Black Elk's psyche — they worked on him, as Arielle described.

A colleague of Hart's, psychologist Kaisa Puhakka, wrote about an authentic way of knowing developed from her childhood experiences that involved a merging of knower and known. With adult reflection, she said, "These experiences were the major mileposts on my spiritual journey."[6] After reviewing hundreds of first-person reports from adults remembering their childhood spiritual experiences, psychologist Michael Piechowski concluded that these experiences are "often the foundation for the unfolding of a person's spiritual development" throughout life.[7]

It seems almost fated that Albert Hofmann, the researcher who first synthesized LSD in 1938, also had such an experience in his childhood. In *LSD: My Problem Child*, Hofmann wrote:

One enchantment of that kind, which I experienced in childhood, has remained remarkably vivid in my memory ever since. It happened on a May morning....As I strolled through the freshly green woods filled with bird song and lit up by the morning sun, all at once everything appeared in an uncommonly clear light....It shone with the most beautiful radiance, speaking to the heart, as though it wanted to encompass me in its majesty. I was filled with an indescribable sensation of joy, oneness, and blissful security....These experiences shaped the main outlines of my worldview and convinced me of the existence of a miraculous, powerful, unfathomable reality that was hidden from everyday sight.[8]

Did the young Albert Hofmann tell anyone? No. Did this childhood spiritual experience prepare him for his discovery? Perhaps. After all, Hofmann didn't realize LSD's psychedelic properties at first. Only five years later, based on an intuitive hunch, "a peculiar presentiment," did Hofmann produce LSD-25 again to see if "this substance could possess properties other than those established in the first investigations."[9] In 1943, after being accidentally exposed, Hofmann took a famous bike ride under the influence, and we all know the result of that trip.

Pioneering psychologist Gordon Allport, one of the first to study personality, described the openness to spiritual experience as "the portion of personality that arises at the core of the life and is directed toward the infinite. It is the region of mental life that has the longest-range intentions, and for this reason is capable of conferring marked integration upon personality, engendering meaning and peace in the face of the tragedy and confusion of life."[10]

Such statements regarding the long-lasting and integrative influence of spiritual experiences are reminiscent of the Johns Hopkins questions from their psilocybin studies. After their entheogen experience, subjects were asked: "How personally meaningful was the experience? Indicate the degree to which the experience was spiritually significant to you? Do you believe that the experience and your contemplation of that experience have led to change in your current sense of personal well-being or life satisfaction?"[11] Research subjects consistently reported that their psilocybin experience was one of the five most personally meaningful and most spiritually significant experiences of their lives, which is similar to how people describe the lifelong impact of early spiritual experience.

I recently did an autobiographical exercise that built on the central role of spiritual experiences throughout a lifetime, starting with childhood. I wrote down every mystical, numinous experience I've had over the course of my life. Looking over the list, I realized these experiences told a personal story quite different from my outworn narrative of all the traumas and abuses I've experienced, mostly from men. I think the latter is precisely the kind of story that my dear friend Connie Grauds was referring to when she "yelled" at me in my friend's kitchen, "We don't even want to hear about it."

Questions Describing Childhood Spiritual Experience

Researchers Peter Nelson and Tobin Hart developed a questionnaire for adults to reflect on any memories they might have of spiritual experiences from childhood.[12] These twenty-one questions cover a wide swath of possibilities, and they help to clarify the range of experiences children have had.

1. Have you ever had the experience of receiving guidance from some source that is not part of our usual physical world?

2. Have you ever encountered a time in your life, either precipitated by crisis or good times, which led you to adopt a new or different spiritual practice?

3. Have you ever experienced a personal crisis which led to questioning your very identity only to have this process lead you to a new and profound awareness?

4. Do you feel that you have ever been directly aware of or influenced by the presence of God?

5. Have you ever had an accident and, at the moment it was happening, someone or something seemed to appear from nowhere and intervene to help you?

6. Have you ever had memories that felt like they were about you, but at the same time seemed to be about someone else of a different time and place?

7. Do the presences and/or feelings of others seem to enter into you without any verbal or physical contact as if you are a receiver and they are transmitters?

8. Have you ever had an experience during a life-threatening event — such as an accident, major surgery, or other physical trauma — in which you had an intense experience of a nonordinary light or darkness and/or experienced meeting deceased loved ones or other disincarnate beings (beings in nonphysical form)?

9. Have you ever seen, physically felt, smelled, or heard something or somebody that you realized in retrospect was not really there in the same way as ordinary everyday objects, people, and events?

10. Have you ever felt a presence of someone who was not there in a physical way?

11. Have you ever had a vivid experience of "flying" to a remote location without any physical means and/or have you had the experience of actually seeing your physical body from a perspective "outside" of yourself?

12. Do you ever feel that at times you know about events before they happen and/or you know about past events without having heard or read of them but later learn they actually happened?

13. Do you ever feel that at times you know people's thoughts/feelings unusually accurately without being told or shown in any direct, physical way?

14. As a child, did you have times when you experienced life as an illusion and unreal, but one in which most people, including grownups, seemed to be caught up? (Perhaps it appeared to be like a play in which everyone was just acting but didn't know it.)

15. Have you ever found yourself knowing and/or saying something that seemed to come through you, rather than from you, expressing a wisdom you don't feel you usually have?

16. Have you ever felt as though you were very close to a powerful spiritual force that seemed to lift you out of or take you beyond your ordinary self?

17. Have you ever had an intense experience of attaining union with the "cosmic," divine, or ultimate ground of being in which you felt yourself "dissolve" or merge with the ultimate and after which you felt as though the encounter had changed your life?

18. Have you ever had an experience in which you perceived that all was really connected together as one?

19. Do you sometimes feel a sense of awe and wonderment inspired by the immediate world around you?

20. Do you sometimes purposely "tune in" to a special quality of the world that seems to underlie everything around us?

21. While awake, have you ever suddenly been cast into a strange new world or reality which had a vividness that made the whole experience appear to be absolutely real although in retrospect you realized that the entire episode may not have physically happened?

Remember, these are questions adults were asked about their childhood spiritual experiences. They could just as easily be questions asked of someone after a psychedelic journey. Did you tune in to a special quality in the world, have extrasensory perception, or encounter beings other than human?

Because our culture doesn't pay attention to children who report such experiences, these question may appear exotic or fantastical. But they are the norm for the women guides I interviewed, and these childhood experiences may have foreshadowed their affinity for expanded states of consciousness via entheogens.

The Guides Remember Their Childhoods

A similar distant look came over a number of the guides when describing an elder woman in their family who was connected to other ways of being. Even though each story was unique, there was something in the nonverbal descriptions of their experiences that signaled a connection with mystery. Somehow these elder women in their families held a door open to other worlds, unseen vistas. As children, the guides recognized that these family elders were important to them above and beyond whatever the relationship was. It's almost as if the older women planted a seed in the guides as children that eventually opened and grew at a later time in life. The women I interviewed reflected back on these early influences as affirmations of their early spiritual experiences.

Usually this kind of energetic transmission was nonverbal but a few women described more specific influences. "My maternal great-grandmother, a tall black woman, was a witch," Medridth explained. Her lineage was clearly along matriarchal lines — Medridth proudly told me how her mother kept a garden and was very connected to her plants. "She was vegetarian and trained in massage therapy with the Mayo Clinic." It's interesting that Medridth understands her purpose in life is to work with women, continuing in that matrilineal tradition. In her words, "I model being a good sister."

Radianthawk, a woman guide from a Peruvian family, knew her grandmother, a Quechua native, was a *curandera* (traditional healer or shaman) even though she was a remote figure in her life. They shared a bedroom, and her grandmother was, she said, "always clearing the house of bad energy. I was surrounded by the culture of the natives. When ceremonies and healings took place, the elders never kept the children away from these occasions. It was the normal thing to do. I was very aware and curious, not realizing I was going to come back to my culture as a Westernized adult to find out what they were doing during these ceremonies. They were passing the knowledge without any ties." The impact of these family elders did not seem to depend upon the amount of contact or even closeness. It was enough that there were such elders in

Radianthawk's early life, and that energetic connection blossomed when Radianthawk was ready to move through that open door into other realms.

About Radianthawk, the Quechua natives said, "There's something special about her." Early on, Radianthawk knew she came from another life, and she had vivid dreams about that life. "I wanted to know what mind was, who's doing the thinking." She left the Catholic Church when she was seven years old and said she "always felt different."

Feeling alone in childhood emerged as a theme among the women guides. They felt set apart from their peers and the "regular world" from a very early age. Maureen said, "I grew up outdoors — that's where I found solace," and she described her experiences of being at one with things. "Everything I do now is based in nature." Maureen trained with a Native American medicine man. Things sometimes have a way of working out perfectly; especially when there's help from the other side, people seem to find each other.

Another guide, Janet, described a different type of experience from her adolescence. "I was out late one night on my first psychedelic experience and got caught driving in a blinding snowstorm. I saw, heard, and felt, *God takes care of his children* — and made it safely home. Later, my mother told me, 'I had the strangest dream — you were out in the night and in danger, but then I heard a voice say, *God takes care of his children*. I knew you'd be all right.'"

These examples are not exactly numinous experiences but, rather, describe spiritual influences. Another guide, Rose, reported a clearly spiritual experience:

I had my first spiritual opening at age six. As a teen, I already knew there was so much more than this state of consciousness. I was a lone wolf — heard my own celestial music. Was meditative and quiet....My first medicine experience was in nature — got opened up to the Great Mystery, awesome beauty of nature. Always sacred. I was uncomfortable with recreational use — like it was a fix.

Rose's adolescence was in the sixties in Los Angeles, a period famous for teenagers experimenting with psychedelics, so Rose's spiritual path was already far from the madding crowd.

Arielle is very clear about the connection between her childhood spiritual experiences and her life's work. "I had a rich, inner world as a child, and it's connected to my adult life and work." Here's the best description of a young child's experience of journeying: "I was aware of other realms — called it Going Out the Window at Night. I had access to other worlds in my dreams — not a fantasy. Never had conversations about it…until now. Hadn't thought about it until you asked."

By age seven, Arielle had a new phrase to describe her journeying, "Going Up Past the Clouds." She told me:

I encountered huge beings, like Greek gods and goddesses — robed, fully formed, and transparent. They were sitting around a table playing a game like chess and laughing, playing chess by moving people around on earth. I got up there a few times and flew around, observing. Very real dream. Seemed natural to me to travel.

In those dreams, other states — that felt like the real world. Being there felt real, I was in a heightened state of awareness, I felt very alive. I belonged there. I was better suited for that world than this. I never told anyone.

I don't know if these experiences were actual night dreams or meanderings during that hypnagogic state right before one falls totally asleep. As a child, Arielle might not have made such a concrete distinction between being asleep and awake, but as a psychologist, I want to know. However, it seemed intrusive and disrespectful to bluntly ask her, "Were you literally asleep when you had that experience or were you awake?" In the moment, I felt the most important thing was for me to honor the child in her who was sharing these delicate experiences for the first time.

Arielle told me about her favorite white oak tree, which was 450 years old. "I would climb up and lay on top of the limbs way up high. I was small and could fit. I carved a niche where I kept a candle and my favorite stones. I'd talk to the tree. Never thought about it before." Sharing this, she realized the connection between her childhood ritual and her life of leading ceremonies.

Arielle described a long-ranging pattern of numinous experiences, not just a few outstanding moments of peak experiences, and said she moved fluidly between this world and other worlds as a child: "I learned to navigate in expanded states of consciousness back then. I use these same skills now to teach the next generation working with psychedelic studies."

Speaking to Arielle helped me clarify my differences with these women guides. I had spiritual experiences as a child but certainly not a pattern of intentionally returning again and again to expanded states, of moving between worlds with such ease and familiarity. Arielle also said, "I never needed a belief system because I had an inner knowing that came from my own experiences." I, on the other hand, continue to struggle with believing my own experiences. My old belief system has fallen away and turned to dust, but I don't have the certainty in my own experiences the way these women have in their very bones.

I asked Arielle how she knew her favorite tree was that

old. Her voice changed into her adult, practical tone: "The tree was cut down one day, and someone from the extension service came to count the rings. That's how I knew how old." Continuing in her practical voice, she said, "I moved to another tree."

This shift in Arielle, from her dreamy description of other realities during childhood to a very concrete matter-of-factness, reflects the ease with which she moves between states of being. Her boundaries between worlds are remarkably permeable, and yet she, and many of the guides, has a demanding career that requires strong executive skills — planning, organizing, strategizing. It's almost as if they can code-switch between states of being, living in both worlds, consensual reality amid invisible realms.

Later Spiritual Initiations

Not all of the women guides described childhood spiritual encounters. Audrey described how she experienced a transformational spiritual initiation when, in early adulthood, both her parents died of independent causes within a six-month time period. She said this initiation grew into a "passion for end-of-life work." Audrey followed this calling into Buddhist meditation and hospice work with children, perhaps the most challenging of death and dying work. She feels these experiences prepared her for her training in Holotropic Breathwork with Stan Grof. Later on, when Audrey encountered ayahuasca, she felt like she was in "familiar territory." She describes herself as "constitutionally able to meet people in deep waters and maintain my own equilibrium."

This capacity is a prerequisite for a psychedelic guide, one that I don't have, I might add. Not only do I get scared, but I lose my center, my equilibrium, by overempathizing with the person in a psychedelic crisis. My boundaries are too porous, too open. This is a real asset as a psychotherapist but not for traveling in deep psychedelic waters. The theme for my life is all about healing, but not the same kind of in-depth journeying with all kinds of entheogens that the women guides have experienced.

I remember an interview with Medridth — who was about eighty-seven at the time — when she exclaimed with enthusiasm that, with all the current interest in ketamine, she wanted to try it again. I was amazed at her passion for exploring expanded states of consciousness at her age. But journeying is the theme of her life, and she has no fear.

Al Hubbard: Another Childhood Vision

Al Hubbard was the very first guide in the Western psychedelic world, and he was also strongly influenced by his childhood spiritual experiences. I include him here as a historical figure because his insights, arising from those early mystical experiences, are built into the very soil of the psychedelic underground. The psychedelic practices Al Hubbard developed form the foundation for the underground women guides as well as for current research protocols.

Al Hubbard got his start in psychedelics in 1951, almost as soon as Sandoz Laboratories in Switzerland, where Albert Hofmann worked, began distributing Delysid, their original name for LSD-25. Hubbard was the "Johnny Appleseed of LSD,"[13] distributing this new miracle drug with a missionary zeal throughout the fifties. He seemed to know everyone — in 1955 he was the psychedelic guide for philosopher and author Aldous Huxley, who said that his LSD experience with Hubbard surpassed the mescaline trip he described in *The Doors of Perception*.[14]

Hubbard was born in Kentucky in 1901 to a poverty-stricken family. He claims he didn't wear shoes until age twelve[15] and dropped out of school by eighth grade. But it seems he had help from other sources. In his own words, "I always had a mystical turn of mind."[16] As a teenager, Hubbard had angelic visions that guided him to build a radioactive battery, which he sold for seventy-five thousand dollars in 1919.[17] Thus began his rags-to-riches-and-back-to-rags personal story, which includes all sorts of unverifiable intrigue, ranging from his possible participation in the CIA's MK-Ultra program to bootlegging to international spying to psychedelic research. As enticing as his story is, the focus here is on how his "mystical turn of mind," consistent from childhood, influenced more than half a century of work in the psychedelic underground and led to the scientific protocols still being used in psychedelic research today.

According to Willis Harman, Stanford University professor of engineering and past president of the Institute of Noetic Sciences, "Al was desperately searching for meaning in his life." Then, on a hike in the woods, an angel appeared to him. "She told Al that something tremendously important to the future of mankind would be coming soon, and that he could play a role in it if he wanted to. But he hadn't the faintest clue what he was supposed to be looking for."[18]

Much later, here is how Hubbard himself told this story:

> I had a place back in the mountain, where I used to go as a kid. So I went back there, and what seemed to me — and I only say "what seemed to me" because that was what it was, an image of a person, that conveyed to me the idea there would be something new coming into the world. It was very old but new to our kind of people, and there would be a place for me. Well, when [John] Smythies [a British psychiatrist studying psychedelics] showed up with the mescaline, as far as I was concerned that was it.[19]

Hubbard had a special lifelong relationship with this angel, whom he understood to be the Virgin Mary. In the documentary *Hofmann's Potion*, psychologist Duncan Blewett remembers that Hubbard "had a religious vision that he was working on behalf of the Virgin Mother and giving people a key to the religious universe."[20]

Laura Huxley, Aldous's wife, described a Hubbard visit when he arrived with a tank filled with some kind of gas. He offered to share it, but she and Aldous declined. Hubbard went into the bathroom and breathed it in for just ten seconds. When he came out, he was energized, talking about a vision he'd just seen of the Virgin Mary.[21]

In 1951 Hubbard read about an experiment in a scientific journal that described giving LSD to rats. "He knew that was it," said Willis Harman. LSD was what the angel said was coming. Hubbard tracked down the scientist who was working with LSD and who was evidently willing to share some of this new drug with Hubbard. Hubbard's early experience with LSD was what inspired him to travel to Sandoz in Switzerland, where the drug was manufactured. He returned triumphantly with ten thousand doses of LSD-25.[22]

Over the ensuing years, based on his own personal psychedelic journeys and his experiences guiding six thousand people, Hubbard was considered to "know more about LSD than anyone."[23] He was the first to recognize the therapeutic value of an LSD-inspired mystical experience, which in 1962 the *Journal of Neuropsychiatry* called "a new concept in psychotherapy."[24] Would Hubbard have developed this approach if he hadn't had those childhood spiritual experiences?

Hubbard's Method: The Origin of Psychedelic Protocol

Hubbard was the "unpublicized father of the American psychedelic therapy movement."[25] From his point of view, the transcendent experience was the whole point of a medicine journey. In 1957, his underground influence reached the Canadian medical establishment, where psychiatrist Humphry Osmond was treating alcoholics. Hubbard had extensive informal experience with giving high doses (500 micrograms) to alcoholics as well as to a large number of nonalcoholics, and the results were encouraging. Without an academic degree — his PhD was from a Kentucky diploma mill — Hubbard shifted Osmond's therapeutic approach from an analytically oriented psycholytic (low dose) to a mystical psychedelic (high dose). This was a significant therapeutic shift that continues to be a theoretical foundation for the current psychedelic research renaissance. Although the mechanism is not yet clearly understood, the conceptual framework is that psychedelics are therapeutic to the extent that they lead to a mystical, ego-dissolution experience.

Way ahead of his time, Hubbard understood that psychedelics shatter rigid ways of self-organizing personality and identity, opening the possibility of "extensive emotional reeducation," as a 2014 study characterized it.[26] That study includes an illustration showing greater neurological connectivity in brain function when under the influence of psilocybin, and this provides scientific confirmation of Hubbard's intuitive insight. Based on fMRI findings, the authors conclude that psilocybin disrupts the normal organization of the brain and increases novel connections and flexibility. Similar neurological findings were reported for LSD effects — the brain is free to explore a variety of functional connectivity patterns that go beyond those dictated by anatomy.[27] Again, greater flexibility results.

After the peak of the psychedelic experience, Hubbard presented the patient with artwork from world religions. This is the optimum time in the journey when the person is still open and yet able to enter into the archetypal realm of universal symbols and to project meaning onto them. Or as one of the current underground guides explains, the archetypal images "work on the patient," deepening and broadening the transcendent experience. The original therapeutic intention was that this would facilitate the development of a new and healthier personality structure that would become integrated into daily life long after the journey had worn off.[28]

With his spiritual history and underground experience, Hubbard was the first to create an environment designed to cultivate a mystical experience. Abraham Hoffer, research psychiatrist at Saskatchewan Hospital in Canada, heard of Hubbard's success with alcoholics and invited him to demonstrate his approach. Before Hubbard's arrival, "no special effort was made to control the environment of the patient undergoing (psychedelic) therapy. Hospital rooms or psychiatrists' offices were used and there were many environmental distractions which interfered with the patient's experience."[29]

One of the psychiatrists from this early experimental period lost a patient — the psychiatrist left the room briefly and the patient disappeared. The staff looked all over for the patient in the surrounding Los Angeles neighborhood, but the person could not be found. As the psychiatrist was walking slowly and worriedly back to his office, he happened to glance up into a tree and spotted his patient.[30] He talked him down, literally and figuratively.

Hubbard originated the importance of set and setting, even though he didn't call it that, as essential for a psychedelic experience. His focus on setting resulted in comfy treatment rooms decorated with fresh flowers and universal religious symbols, even now a staple of current psychedelic research. He was the first to recognize that the most powerful trips involved turning inward, and he encouraged patients to cover their eyes to deepen their inner experience. Hubbard carefully selected music to soothe the traveler through rocky transitions and to evoke a mystical response. He found that a mirror and family photos could be used to facilitate self-reflection. He said, "You take a mirror and look at it, and you know all about yourself."[31] All these elements are still present in current research protocols as well as underground rituals.

There is, of course, some controversy about what Hubbard contributed, perhaps because he was such a controversial personality. A rascal and a rogue, and certainly not an academic, his contributions are both acknowledged in the scientific literature and downplayed, if not ignored. Eyeshades were not used in the beginning, but a 1953 photo shows a towel draped over a person's eyes during a journey.[32] Jim Fadiman thinks it was Hubbard who first came up with the idea of putting something over the eyes to help the person focus inward.[33] Hubbard's use of eyeshades was also confirmed by Tania Manning, who asked Connie Littlefield, director of *Hofmann's Potion*.[34] Connie interviewed psychedelic pioneer Myron Stolaroff and psychiatrist Oscar Janiger and reported that they credit Hubbard with the introduction of flowers, a mirror for self-confrontation, personal photos, and eyeshades.

Hubbard's method also paid attention to set, asking for a full autobiography and then conducting an interview, though Hubbard questioned more like a policeman than a psychiatrist. He said, "You read his autobiography, then you see if he's lying to ya."[35] Hubbard claimed to be able to evaluate whether a person would be willing to look at "what they're doing" or not. If they're not, then nothing will reach them — "I had feelings at the time that I was not getting through to them." He also recommended that people "lay off the sinning business." But he added, "I avoid condemnation. For anything. I don't want to judge anyone." Hubbard wanted to know how open the person was, how accepting of themselves they could be, and whether or not they were a "searcher," someone interested in spiritual realms. He used all this information to determine dosage (which is explored later).

The Hubbard method is documented in the 1959 "Handbook for the Therapeutic Use of Lysergic Acid Diethylamide-25: Individual and Group Procedures," written by Duncan Blewett, a psychologist, and Nicholas Chwelos, a psychiatrist.[36] This manual opens with an acknowledgment of the "debt which the authors owe to the work of Dr. A.M. Hubbard." That said, the authors credit Hubbard's bogus PhD diploma, which he purchased to facilitate the ordering of LSD from Sandoz. Later, Blewett described Hubbard as "a very strange man," but "he had a whole new way of using LSD for spiritual realization."[37]

Leary is most often credited with the concepts of set and setting: first, because he coined such a catchy phrase, as was his wont, and second, because he presented these terms in a paper presented at the annual meeting of the American Psychological Association in 1961.[38] Hubbard may have had a PhD after his name, albeit purchased, but he was not admitted into the halls of academia from which Leary was soon evicted.

As Jay Stevens describes in *Storming Heaven*, Hubbard "designed a whole experience around Death Valley which he considered an extraordinary power spot."[39] This was considered to be "advanced training" and was done with eyes open to face the barrenness of the desert, an extreme setting perfect for confronting your own life. The desert as a spiritual setting has a long history dating all the way back to the third century and the Desert Fathers. More recently, Aldous Huxley perceived, as Huston Smith recalled, "the boundlessness of its sands....It's a no-thing-ness in which everything is so interfused that divisions are transcended."[40]

As James Fadiman writes in *The Psychedelic Explorer's Guide*,

"The intention of the advanced training was to ensure that you didn't get caught in your personal belief system."[41] Hubbard seemed to have an uncanny understanding of the therapeutic value of a mystical experience and how that allowed for freedom from old beliefs and ways of being. I think this uncanny understanding grew out of his childhood spiritual experiences "seeing" the Virgin Mary. Hubbard said of his own life, "Everything I did was a composite picture of all my lifetime experiences."[42]

However, and there's often a *however* in stories about Hubbard, after the mystical time spent in the desert, Hubbard would shepherd his students to Las Vegas where he hoped their recent journey into the Great Mystery would increase their odds at the gambling tables. Sad to say, this was not the case.

If it's not already obvious, I admit to being enthralled with these stories about Al Hubbard. He's a character beyond imagination, and more importantly, he's a bit overlooked by the current psychedelic renaissance. Somewhat similar to the women guides, he has not been given the credit he deserves. His insight to turn inward during a psychedelic journey, arising from his childhood spiritual experiences, continues to be the basis for the current research protocol. The comfy room with inspirational music, flowers, religious art, and eyeshades is still the setting for psychedelic research sessions almost seventy years after Hubbard's initial explorations.

Hubbard added his unique presence to this early mix in the fifties before the counterculture exploded with psychedelics in the sixties. Things were still fairly quiet — Leary had not yet raised the decibel. Hubbard was having an impact as he guided people on their journeys, including Aldous Huxley; Bill Wilson, the founder of Alcoholics Anonymous; and philosopher Gerald Heard. Hubbard also introduced

LSD to Myron Stolaroff, a senior executive at Ampex Corporation, an early Silicon Valley technology firm. Stolaroff described his first impressions of Hubbard: "Meeting Hubbard was one of the most remarkable things that ever happened to me. He radiated an energy that I could feel. I don't think ever before in my life I'd ever felt anyone. I could feel his energy and I just felt so good in his presence."[43]

As wild as Hubbard's life was, there is a through line that is a central organizing theme for him. As he said, "Everything I did was a composite picture of all my lifetime experiences." This is the story within his story, the spiritual thread of his life: his spiritual visitations with the Virgin Mary as a child in the woods, his early recognition of the cultural significance of LSD, his connection with the Virgin Mary again in the Huxleys' bathroom under the effects of what was probably nitrous oxide. It's his early childhood spiritual experiences that provide a coherence to his life that might otherwise be seen as chaotic. And it's his spiritual vision that provides a through line from the earliest work with LSD to today's psychedelic renaissance.

Psychedelic Underground and Psychedelic Science

While the contributions of the earliest psychedelic guides and explorers led to current research protocols, a huge gap exists between the worldview of the women who risk everything to work in the psychedelic underground and the researchers in university settings. Both groups share a missionary zeal, one that arises from their own healing — from how their own experiences with psychedelics have led to personal psychological and spiritual breakthroughs. But today's psychedelic therapists working in these research studies are relatively new to this world, while the women guides of the psychedelic underground are elders with experiences of the full panoply of psychedelics over the course of decades. These women have dedicated most of their lives to the study and practice of medicine journeys.

Jeffrey Guss is a psychiatrist working with a New York University team using psilocybin with terminally ill patients, and he said, "We're isolated from all the wisdom and knowledge in the underground community. That vast uncollected experience contains details about the medicines' potential and pitfalls, challenges and inconsistencies — the variety of ways psychedelics might wholly, drastically change a life."[44]

Further, researchers conduct their work openly and publish their findings. The underground women guides work discreetly, providing medicine journeys to those who are well connected enough to find them. Referrals work along networks that are filled with serendipity, spiritual searching, and just plain luck. Sometimes the connection is right under someone's nose, and they don't know how to recognize the signs. I trust this to mean they're not ready.

For instance, I had a driver take me from the airport to the home of one of these medicine women. It was a long ride, and the driver and I talked quite openly. He was a burned-out nurse and very interested in my book on ayahuasca. He asked me the most common question, "How can I find an ayahuasca ceremony?" I never answer this question, but instead, I encourage the person's quest. I believe in the tradition that, when the student is ready, the teacher will appear.

When we arrived at my destination, the driveway was lined with very powerful shamanic medicine plants. Large bushes of brugmansia (toé), most of them about ten feet tall, were overflowing with yellow trumpets in full bloom. I was overwhelmed with the lusciousness of the flowers, the scent of the garden, and the obviousness of the medicine plants. The driver didn't recognize the plant or what its presence indicated. I said nothing and he drove off without a clue.

Occasionally, a connection exists between these women guides and the burgeoning psychedelic research training programs, as well as with clinics preparing to open once the research studies lead to limited-access programs. But it's a discreet connection, subtle, and often not recognized by the students in the very same way that the driver missed the significance of the brugmansia garden.

The underground guides are a different breed from the research teams. They are rooted in a spiritual cosmology, an esoteric relationship with the medicines themselves. They live in a different world even when they're not in ceremony. They are in communion with the plants, the medicines, a quality of relationship that goes beyond mere communication. María Sabina, a Mexican *curandera* who died in 1985, was famous for working with psilocybin mushrooms, and she described this quality of being when she sang about herself, "She swims in the sacred."[45]

We would be wise to pay attention to these early pioneers and their explorations into parts unknown decades before modern research protocols arose to try to quantify and define mystical experience.

Chapter Three

BECOMING A PSYCHEDELIC GUIDE

As the psychedelic renaissance explodes, the need for guides and therapists is rising exponentially. Training programs are proliferating that are sponsored by academic institutions, non-profits, and profit-making businesses. This chapter turns to the histories of the underground elders — exploring the personal qualities and experiences that enabled them to learn how to accompany people through psychedelic realms.

Virtually all of the underground women guides I interviewed went through an apprenticeship with luminaries in the psyche-delic world, such as Stan Grof, Ralph Metzner, or Leo Zeff, better known as the Secret Chief.[1] Almost half of the women apprenticed with indigenous healers from Native American tribes or the Amazon basin. Of the three who had been working for only ten years, two are still studying with a Peruvian shaman and the third claims that "the mushrooms are teaching" her. The latter woman also studied with an array of subtle energy teachers but not in an apprenticeship, putting her in a totally different category — experienced but not apprenticed.

An apprenticeship is not a training, no matter how long

the training might be. An apprenticeship is of a whole different order. It's literally sitting at the elbow of an acknowledged elder, learning the craft or art by being present, osmosing the subtle skills to work with energy in the moment. Anthropologist Francis Huxley apprenticed with a Brazilian healer and described the intimacy necessary for the process of transmission: "You have to get their way of seeing into your own system."[2] This characterizes the implicit learning that takes place when the student is in the teacher's energy field as the teacher works.

Radha, a woman guide who trained for many years in the jungle with a Peruvian shaman, described how she learned to sing the *icaros* (healing songs). Her teacher, a powerful shaman, would sing, and "I would sing a nanosecond behind him," she said. She reflected on the kind of synchronicity that arises during this kind of energetic learning process: "The relationship between student and teacher happens on multiple dimensions." She described how she dreamed of the tree one of her apprentices was dieting on, while at the same time her student did a painting of it. There's a subtle merging of images as guides accompany their students through entheogenic realms and track their progress. The teacher tunes in to the student, and the student learns to resonate with the teacher, and information is transmitted nonverbally through this attunement.

Our culture lacks the deep understanding of this embedded approach to learning. Our current use of the term *mentor* in the business world has been reduced to meeting once a week with a boss. Even the leading Psychedelic-Assisted Therapies and Research certificate program at the California Institute of Integral Studies describes the mentorship aspect of their training this way: "The mentors meet with a small group of mentees regularly and once individually during the program."[3]

The program's use of the term *mentor* is more closely

related to networking than to an apprenticeship model: "Our trainees have access to experts in the psychedelic field and in-depth mentoring that enables them to create professional connections not otherwise available among the influencers in this arena." Admittedly, this is a training program and not an apprenticeship, and they are ramping up to meet the field's "rapidly growing demand for psychedelic therapists by training 1,125 graduates over the next three years." My point is that the psychedelic field needs to make the distinction between how the newly hatched psychedelic therapists are being trained and how the elder guides learned in apprenticeships.

Other cultures, at other times, possessed a traditional concept of apprenticeship. For example, consider the rug dyers in twelfth-century Turkey. Their apprenticeship went on for fifteen years, and based on their life expectancy, this was at least half their time on earth. In addition, in order to become a master dyer, the student had to create a color that no one had ever seen before.[4] This seems like a magical request from a fairy tale, yet it illustrates the high standards expected from an apprenticeship.

I recently asked an Academy Award–winning documentary director whether she had a mentor or apprenticeship experience. "No," she reflected, "but I mentored other people." She then described how she worked with a twenty-five-year-old woman for over fifteen years, helped her become a producer in her own right, and then supported her decision to have a child in her early forties. She emphasized that the relationship was about more than the young woman's career: "I considered her a friend of the family — she did my daughters' makeup when they went to proms. And I understood how important it was for her to have a baby." The apprenticeship relationship goes way beyond work or career.

An apprenticeship is more like an adoption, a familial

relationship. For the elder, it's an opportunity to pass on their teachings and practical skills to the next generation. Too often the elder's biological family members are not interested in the old ways, so the elder adopts someone from outside the family. In two instances I know, indigenous elders asked their adopted students to promise to teach any of their family members who might show an interest after the elder passed on. In another case, a dying shaman gave his shamanic power objects to his godson who, in turn, promised to pass them on to any of the old shaman's biological offspring should they decide to enter into training.

Both teacher and student invest enormous amounts of time and energy into the relationship — years and years. The underground guides reported apprenticeships lasting from seven to fifteen to twenty-five years. This doesn't mean that the apprentice didn't begin to work on her own at some point, but this was always, at the beginning, under the eye of the teacher. One woman reported being reprimanded early on by her teacher for offering a combination of medicines she hadn't yet experienced herself. This was evidently a serious misstep. She was told she couldn't guide anyone for twelve months, and she accepted this consequence.

Often the initial meeting of elder and student is a synchronous event, meaning there's a match between outer-world circumstances and the inner-world readiness of the student. Audrey showed up for a lecture and found herself at the first announcement of Stan Grof's initial training in Holotropic Breathwork. He said, "I'm looking for thirty students who want to study with me for the next three years." Audrey raised her hand high and has since been involved in that work for over forty years. She knew immediately.

Medridth was in search of an office to rent, and an Esalen connection referred her to Leo Zeff. I can imagine Zeff

immediately recognizing her easy, elegant grace. He invited
her to assist him at an underground weekend he was doing
in Bolinas, California. This was back in the sixties, and it was
Medridth's first introduction to acid, and then hours later
to ibogaine and ayahuasca in powder form, all in the same
night — remember, this was the sixties. I don't know anyone
doing this kind of mix now. But Medridth said, "I had a strong
intuition to go, not knowing what it was."

Arielle said she went to every lecture, workshop, and
training that Stan Grof conducted for years and years. "Stan's
descriptions of the varieties of expanded states of consciousness matched my inner experiences, affirming my inner knowing. His work is seminal...foundational to my work and
worldview." She also traveled with Stan and a small entou-
rage to various sacred sites in Southeast Asia. Much learning
takes place in personal relationships, just seemingly hanging
out. For instance, Arielle asked Stan, "Why do this work?" His
reply: "It's practice for death, learning how to surrender to the
unknown prepares us for our own experience of dying without
fear."

When Radha discovered that the shaman she was studying with was abusing Western and indigenous women and
girls, she left him. But in this case, the energetic link with this
shaman was difficult to break, and Radha feels that he still
appears in ceremonies in energetic form, although he's unwel-
come. She told me, "When he does show up, I take the opportunity to hone my skills, learn, and be ever more in the light.
So he is not welcome and I thank him as his appearances teach
me." These are powerful relationships on many levels.

Connie Grauds, a dear friend and not one of the underground guides, described her experience of an apprenticeship
to don Antonio, a Peruvian shaman who didn't read or write.
They didn't speak the same language. The apprenticeship

consisted, she said, of her "following, living, resting in ham-
mocks, sharing meals. The process was osmosis, knowledge
washed through me to deliver to the modern world." This she
has done in a myriad of books and presentations.

Don Antonio asked Connie whether she really wanted to
apprentice. "It will kill you," he said. "Make you crazy or heal
you." She understood the risks from the very beginning. He
told her, "My job is to take you to the spirit doctors and bring
you back safely." Don Antonio saw his role as a gatekeeper,
and ayahuasca was the gate. He said only to do it if she followed *dietas* with discipline: no sex, no salt, no sugar, no meat
or spices. You have to be quiet and calm in body, mind, and
spirit. You have to maintain these practices to be pure and fine-
tuned in order to communicate with the spirit doctors. After
Connie had lived like a monk in the jungle for five years, the
spirit doctors finally began to talk to her.[5]

A number of the women elders worked with both Stan
Grof and Ralph Metzner. Angeles Arrien, coming from a
Basque tradition, was a teacher for a few of the underground
guides. The eldest of the elders, Medridth, is still seen as a
teacher for some of the guides, although she prefers to think of
these relationships as part of a sacred sisterhood.

Mary trained with Ralph Metzner after almost twenty
years of extensive study in energy healing work. When she first
attended a training with Metzner, he greeted her by saying,
"Nice to see you again." They had never met before but they
recognized each other from a past life. This kind of past-life
connection is more common in non-Western cultures, including the Tibetan tradition of a student's search for the two-
year-old child reincarnation of his beloved rinpoche.[6]

Although there were thirty people in that initial training, Mary was the only one who apprenticed with Ralph in
an ongoing relationship. They were in regular, close contact

for the last thirteen years of his life. She assisted him in cere-monies, consulted with him about her work with groups, and talked with him at least once a month. Mary knew Ralph was dying and dreamed of him four days before his death. In her dream, she saw him going up in an elevator in a parking garage, dressed in royal colors and fabrics. She walked with him across a bridge.

What It Means to Be an Apprentice

One of the guides was formally adopted into a Native American family of Traditional Medicine Peoples. Her training included peyote ceremonies and focused on ritual, ceremony, prayers, pipe smoke, herbs, nature, and elemental forces. It was quite rigorous and intended to become a way of life. Her full training extended over an eight- to ten-year time period with vows and ongoing practices, including four-day vision quests with no food or water. The purpose was to learn how to work with the subtle realms and to become clear about distinguishing sexual and spiritual energy, a problem even prestigious spiritual teachers seem to have, no matter what their lineage.

As I was listening to this woman's story, I had to ask the question most therapists would want to know: "Was your adopted grandfather ever sexually inappropriate with you, abu-sive in any way?" She was horrified at the suggestion, saying, "No, absolutely not!" I had to ask even though I saw no signs and believed her answer completely. This was a sacred adop-tion, the relationship continuing into the present, years after her grandfather's death.

When she first began this training, she said, "I said yes before I knew what I was saying yes to." She was initiated into a different way of life with rituals, restrictions, and practices that had to be followed on a daily basis. As I listened to her examples, such as ways to work with the elements and tend a fire, I thought the most challenging restriction was not to yell at people.

I had just recently exploded at a good friend I walk with every morning. He was proudly telling me how he uses a have-a-heart trap to catch mice in his house on the island where I live. Then he brings them to the pond and releases them. Well, I live by the pond and have had my share of mice visitations. I didn't reflect or hesitate. "Oh, you bring the mice to *my* neighborhood," I said with raised voice. I continued until he finally said, "How long are you going to yell at me?" That stopped me but I've been resentful ever since.

I lack the mental and physical discipline required to undergo the kind of training this guide was able and willing to endure. All the women underground guides have stories of dedication, discipline, and deprivation in their trainings. Most of them do not have children, and so they have been free to dedicate their lives to their own healing and subsequent training. Radha described sleeping on the ground in the Amazon jungle with bugs crawling over her and chiggers remaining in her skin for weeks. Another guide recounted a history of near-death experiences, including multiple traumatic brain injuries and waking up from anesthesia during two different surgeries.

There is a belief that you follow your destiny or you die. These women had the strength and courage to follow their destiny before they fully understood the entire path. They had faith in their own unfolding. This is the essence of a journey, whether an entheogenic time-limited ceremony or a lifelong destiny.

These apprenticeships are about learning how to navigate expanded states of consciousness, to guide journeys, and to clear and cleanse energy. With an indigenous teacher, the apprenticeship is about becoming a shaman or *curandera*. With a Western teacher, the apprenticeship is more about healing in expanded states, not about becoming a psychedelic therapist, which is what the current training programs promise. One of the elder guides is a PhD academic in anthropology with in-depth training in shamanism. Only four of the women have a master's degree in some kind of spiritual or somatic psychology, and two are now licensed as therapists. The other two have a real track record working in mental health. Another guide is a licensed PhD psychologist with a private practice. The latter three are exceptions. The elder psychedelic guides are not therapists.

In the current psychedelic renaissance, there is no category for these women. They remain underground, a few of them finding ways to contribute to the training of new psychedelic therapists. However, traditions find a way of surviving, and some of these women have adopted an apprentice.

Adopting an Apprentice

Maureen adopted her apprentice after helping her recover from two near-death experiences. The first was from drinking an ayahuasca brew with too much datura in it, and the second, a couple of years later, was from a tobacco purga, where she got nicotine poisoning. Both ayahuasca and tobacco are considered to be master plant teachers that are healing, but in high doses, only tobacco can be deadly.

The young woman suffered with panic attacks, hypervigilance, and nightmares, a full array of trauma symptoms, as well as some kind of lingering, energetic malevolence. Maureen has been working with her for about seven years, and they are a match. Both are strong athletes, although they are almost four decades apart in age; both are fearless about working with many medicines at high doses; and both are dedicated to their journeys. When I arrived to interview Maureen for the first time, her student was there and took notes throughout the long afternoon. When I left, the student stayed, and I imagine she and Maureen debriefed together about how the day went. During a recent medical emergency when Maureen was taken to the hospital, she called her student, who happened to have medical training. An apprenticeship is a familial relationship, not merely a mentorship.

Radha has nine apprentices, but only one is leading ceremonies on his own. Another is leading without permission. Apprentices study with her for years, doing a variety of *dietas* using different plants and restricting diet and activity. Traditionally, this is done in isolation in a *tambo* (a small screened hut) in the Amazon jungle, but Radha and her apprentices live in a large American city, so the *dieta* is done a little differently. For instance, when I saw one of her students, I spontaneously gave him a hug. Unfortunately, I broke a *dieta* rule — no physical contact. The student didn't step back quickly enough, and I was way too exuberant, just one of my many shamanic faux pas.

Mary is currently training ten people — most of them have been attending her group ceremonies for close to ten years. So the training period is on top of those years of working with her on their own healing. Arielle has contributed to the training of therapists working in funded research studies. Other organizations are offering group trainings, but they are not with the same depth as an apprenticeship.

Medridth has the longest history of working with people in what she prefers to call a sisterhood rather than an apprenticeship model. However, the underground guides who have studied with her describe her more maternally as pure unconditional love. Mary said, "She accepted me in a way I've never been accepted before. She helped my natural loving ability to open." Arielle said, "She always had a detached lightness of being about her." Rose has been connected with Medridth for over twenty-five years. Rose said, "She's my guide, teacher, supervisor. Since I wasn't well connected with my mother, it's healing to have a woman elder."

Trust the Process

Medridth's first mentor, Leo Zeff, was a retired psychologist with a Jungian orientation. He was one of the earliest underground guides and introduced over four thousand people to an assortment of entheogens and trained more than a hundred in the therapeutic use of these medicines. Myron Stolaroff interviewed Zeff for his book *The Secret Chief Revealed*, a psychedelic classic that details essential and wise advice about how to accompany people on safe and therapeutic journeys. In this book, Zeff is given a pseudonym, Jacob, even though it was published nine years after his death. Not until a full sixteen years after his death was this man's true identity revealed — an indication of the level of secrecy surrounding the underground guides.

Stolaroff said Zeff "was blessed with an abundance of heart, the most necessary prerequisite for someone accompanying others into the depths of their very souls."[7] Unfortunately, this quality of heart is difficult to operationalize, and current psychedelic therapy training programs only require a professional license. Some training programs to be a psychedelic guide don't even require that, and Oregon is considering "training" people with a minimum of a high school education — a far cry from the psychedelic elders I interviewed and a farther cry from the Eleusinian priestesses.

Due to the illegal standing of entheogens, such programs can't even require or provide experience in the varieties of psychedelic realms. One of Zeff's primary rules was that "the therapist must know the effects of any [such] drugs in themselves, before giving them to anyone else." I would extend this to say that psychedelic therapists should not work with people unless they're experienced with the same medicine the client has taken. Each entheogen has a unique signature and opens portals into different realms. The therapist has to be personally familiar with these territories. Here's how Zeff states this same axiom: "You cannot trip and work with a therapist who hasn't tripped and get any value out of it. You can't relate back and forth."

Another axiom is "trust the process." In the worst moments, such advice can require lots of heart and experience. Ann Shulgin, who apprenticed with Leo Zeff (and who allowed me to use her real name), once asked for his help after a challenging trip left her feeling lost and disconnected. This occurred even though Ann was a seasoned traveler who experimented regularly with a variety of chemical concoctions that her husband Sasha Shulgin produced in his lab. It's humbling to know that no matter how experienced someone is, they can have a disintegrating journey with disturbing aftereffects.

In her book *Pihkal*, Ann described Sasha's invitation to trip. He said, "I've taken up to thirty milligrams. I haven't spotted any activity yet and I thought you might want to take it one more step up — maybe forty milligrams? You almost certainly won't get any effects."[8]

This invitation is a classic warning sign. Anytime someone says, "It's not that strong. Probably won't have a big effect. It's mild," be cautious. There's no way to predict how a psychedelic medicine will affect you. And dosage depends on weight — Sasha towered over Ann.

Ann's crisis extended over days after the ceremony with symptoms of depersonalization, anger closer to fury, and trembling fear. She had never had an experience like this, so she turned to Zeff, who was a member of their private group that experimented with a variety of psychedelics on a regular basis. Ann told him, "I'm living in a universe that is full of some kind of cold intelligence that watches and records everything and has no feelings at all."[9] She described a typical symptom of depersonalization, in harsh contrast to the kind of loving, ecstatic psychedelic experience that is considered to be healing.

Zeff said, "Whatever you're facing is not out there, it's inside you....You're just going to have to accept the fact that some kind of process is taking place which needs to take place and there's only one thing you can do, *must* do, and that is: don't get in its way....I can assure you that you'll be out of it by the end of the week."

Zeff first directed Ann's attention inward, intending to stop the projection. After all, these psychedelics are mind-manifesting, emphasizing what's inside. Ann needed to own that "cold calculating intelligence" as a part of herself, see what she could learn from it, and find a new relationship to it. No matter how strongly we think something is real and out there, it's more therapeutic to take back the projection and deal with it as an internal state.

Because Zeff was so experienced, his prediction that she'd feel better by the end of the week had real power. He was familiar with this territory, both through his own experience and working with others. His positive suggestion reassured Ann and relieved her anxiety, increasing the chance that she would be fine in a few days. These medicines involve so many complex and unpredictable responses that the need for a voice of experience is crucial.

In the Stolaroff book *The Secret Chief*, Zeff described another approach to trusting the process in the exact moment during a journey when things get really scary: "Look at what you're afraid of, just look at it; don't do anything about it, just look at it. Just keep looking at it and just tell me what you experience when you're looking at it."[10] This seems like a simple suggestion, but there's a complexity inherent in his message. The advice translates to "don't resist," but that wording would not be helpful. First of all, it's much harder to stop doing something, to stop resisting, when we've already begun to spiral down into fear. Zeff's suggestion instead redirects the person's attention to something they can do, "just look."

Second, notice how Zeff repeats the word *just* in his suggestion. When I was apprenticed in the Rolf Movement work called Structural Awareness, my teacher was very precise about her use of language to evoke movement. She would say, "Just take a breath up through the top of your head. Just move your knee forward. Just stretch your arm up." When I asked her about this repetition, she explained, "I'm asking for ease of movement, without effort, without trying hard." The teaching was about more than one specific movement — it was about learning to be in your body in a gentle way, about moving from the inside rather than following outside orders. As Zeff said, "Just look." It's that simple. Nothing more is required.

Then he said, "Just tell me about it." Easy. Now the person is lifted out of their experience to connect with the guide and put their experience into words. Zeff knew in his bones, from both his personal journeys as well as his work guiding others, that his suggestion would change the way things were going. Zeff said, "I had them live with [it] and stay with [it] until it became transformed."[11]

The suggestion to trust the process is still standard advice that's often repeated by modern guides in harm-reduction tents at concerts and psychedelic gatherings. It's been good advice for more than half a century of underground use. Even the Beatles offered a version of this advice in the song "Tomorrow Never Knows": "float downstream / it is not dying /...surrender to the void / it is shining." Finally, any advice from a fellow traveler, someone who knows the psychedelic territory, is always reassuring, which is one of the main reasons guides need to be experienced with whatever medicines they serve.

The Basic Rules for Guiding

In *The Secret Chief*, Leo Zeff outlined the agreements he required before he was willing to accompany someone on their journey:[12]

1. They will not leave without my clearance.
2. There will be no physical harm or violence.
3. They will not reveal where or with whom they had the journey.
4. No sex, absolutely no sex.
5. They will do what I say.

Sixty years later and three decades after Zeff's death, his apprentice Medridth described these same agreements in her own words, proving that my mother was correct when she told me, "People live on in the hearts of others."

1. You're putting your life in my hands and I have final say so.
2. We're going to other worlds. I keep you safe in this world.
3. No sex. No danger like standing on your head.
4. Confidentiality.
5. Agreement to do what I say.

I repeat these basic rules for guiding for two reasons. First, Medridth's words illustrate what happens in an apprenticeship — the apprentice makes the teachings her own. She fully integrates what she's learned into her own work. Forty years after Medridth began her apprenticeship and learned these rules, she repeated them to me with virtually the same message.

Second, no sex. And only touch that has been mutually agreed upon with clarification of boundaries before the journey. This might seem obvious, as it's an essential rule for professionals in all the healing arts, medicine, psychotherapy, and religions of all stripes. Unfortunately, we know there is crossing of boundaries and sexual misconduct in all these professions. This is also the case with shamans, psychedelic guides, and psychedelic therapists. In the underground community, there are no professional organizations to enforce ethical standards. This community has to monitor itself, and efforts are being made in this regard.

In 2021, a letter was circulated through the "psychedelic community" in response to abuse allegations. It states this issue clearly:

> [We are] supporting people through their most vulnerable states and darkest moments, and as such, the ethical responsibility of this work cannot be overstated. Because of the vulnerability of expanded states of consciousness, trust that is placed in the hands of a guide or facilitator opens the significant risk of abuse of power. Abuse can take many forms, including therapy abuse, sexual abuse, mental abuse, psychological manipulation, and subtler forms of harm.[13]

The Multidisciplinary Association for Psychedelic Studies (MAPS) has a five-page ethical code with a section on "sexual boundaries" that states, "We do not engage in sexual touch with participants."[14]

There is clear agreement about no sexual contact from both aboveground research and underground psychedelic communities. However, the question remains, what happens when someone breaks this most basic rule? What stops that person from continuing to guide or train others?

I'm especially concerned about the transmission of transgressing boundaries in the training of others. We know that people learn from example, both implicitly and explicitly. The stated curriculum for a training is not the only information being transmitted. When trainers have a history of abuse, that pattern is likely to contaminate the training.

There's been a recent upheaval in the psychedelic community with revelations of sexual abuse and abuse of power. An independent restorative justice team was hired to investigate one case. In their final report, which they made public, they said that their investigation "exposed the deeply disturbing fact that, beyond the direct harm experienced by some, the systems of community accountability have been profoundly inadequate at mitigating harm and holding practitioners accountable."

In the *New York* magazine podcast "Bad Hug," Lily Kay Ross raised a red flag about problems with power inherent in at least one of the psychedelic trainings.[15] She said, "When you are doing therapy that's based on pushing past people's resistance,...if somebody is telling you, 'I don't want to do this,'...somehow it's considered to be therapeutic and part of the method to keep pushing past that." This approach presents an opportunity for abuse given the power differential in the therapeutic relationship and the vulnerability of the client under the influence of psychedelics.

The newly hatched psychedelic professions will have to struggle with these issues just as the other healing and religious professions must, with all the usual pitfalls of secrets, denials, disparagement, outright lies, legal machinations, apologies, financial payoffs, justice, reconciliation, and professional consequences. This is a dangerous landscape, and the use of psychedelics does not protect us from these potential disasters.

This is a wake-up call teaching us that a temporary ego-dissolution experience does not solve all problems. A transcendent experience does not necessarily mean transformation. Or as Charles Stang from Harvard Divinity School said, "Mystical experiences don't translate into ethical behavior."[16]

The Importance of Experience

Learning to say the right thing is not the goal of an apprenticeship, although it's surprising how many people interested in guiding journeys want a recipe for what to say and do. The process is not a recipe. Zeff said, it's "a spiritual trip. What I do and even how I do it is not up to me. I'm guided. I can't define that, I can't explain it. I know that it's true."[17]

The process of guiding someone in an expanded state of consciousness is mostly invisible. Perhaps there's hand-holding. Maybe a brief exchange or quick reassurance. Or a suggestion to turn inward. Mostly the guide is accompanying the journeyer in some mysterious way, sensing the person's energy, entering into their entheogenic dream world, watching for subtle clues. There can be a permeability between the unconscious of the guide and that of the voyager such that the reassuring presence of the guide is felt through blankets, eyeshades, and earphones.

Even in a close apprenticeship over many years, how does someone learn how to be spiritually guided, as Zeff says, to guide? In her apprenticeship, Maureen was told by her teacher, "You ask too many questions — sometimes you [should] just pay attention." Learning happens on many levels, most often without words.

Years later, from the other side of an apprenticeship relationship, Maureen talked about making very small, subtle corrections while working with her apprentice. Exploring her responsibility as a teacher, she asked, "How do we build inner capacity, inner space for rearrangement, to hold change?" Maureen knows that she's planting seeds in her student, nurturing them to grow.

"To grow into what?" I asked.

With a lifetime of entheogenic experience behind her, Maureen answered my question by talking about the invisible nature of guiding people through entheogenic journeys. "Very few people in this work know how to work the subtle realms. The work really begins in the subtle realms. They are the more potent experiences, like water breaking through a rock, trying to find the crevasses."

Looking for a framework or context for learning how to guide in invisible realms, I turned first to Stan Grof's description of the therapist or "sitter" in his 1980 book *LSD Psychotherapy*.[18] He prioritized that the guide must be able to convey a feeling of trust and safety necessary for the voyager to surrender to the experience of ego death. This level of existential reassurance is not cultivated by what the guide says but in their presence. Every client will have their own sense of whom they can trust at this level.

Michael Pollan described the warning signals he experienced with one of the underground guides he interviewed, which made him decide not to work with him, but first he acknowledged, "It's hard to say exactly what put me off working with Andrei."[19] Pollan was undeterred when Andrei described how a "crazy" client had sued him, though that would've been enough for me. I would've left then and there for his disrespecting that client, since things have to go pretty bad in a therapeutic relationship for a client to sue. For Pollan, he was driven away by Andrei's nonchalance about medical risk, life-and-death issues. We each have our unique warning systems.

Grof also focused on transference issues and how projections can go in both directions. The sitter's anxiety can be
triggered by the subject's behavior just as easily as the person
under the influence can project psychological, past-life, and
archetypal images onto the sitter. The guide can be seen as an
angel, a devil, or both, and anywhere in between. In addition,
the psychedelic amplifies all kinds of insights and feelings, so
that many voyagers are, Grof writes, "able to tune in to the
inner feelings of the sitters with great accuracy.... The ability
of the subjects to 'read' the therapist correctly was truly striking
and seemed to border on genuine extrasensory perception."[20]

In other words, the guide cannot hide who they are; they
have to be authentically present. And they have to have had
their own experiences with the medicines they serve in order
to sustain equanimity in the face of existential challenges like
"fear of death, total loss of control, and the specter of insanity,"
Grof wrote. If not, the voyager will see right through them and
realize they are alone and adrift in unchartered waters.

For instance, if the guide tends toward anxiety or fear, the
journeyer is likely to catch it like a virus. There's a loosening of
the boundary between client and guide, so they easily pick up
on one another whether they're intending to or not. In the delicate state midjourney, there are inevitably enough challenging
moments without the client being contaminated by the guide's
emotional state.

Grof expanded on why the sitter's personal development
is critically important: "Unless the therapist deals successfully
with these [existential] issues, the manifestations of the deep
unconscious of the patient will tend to activate her own problem areas and trigger difficult emotional and psychosomatic
responses." If the guide's unresolved issues are stimulated in a
session, this can cloud the experience and exhaust the energy
required to rise to challenges in either person.

Ann Shulgin gave me the same message with a slight variation: "The therapist must have done work on her own shadow. She must know her own territory in order for the journeyer to trust the guide one hundred percent. If not, you can do damage. If the traveler is somewhere you haven't been, it becomes obvious that the therapist doesn't really understand. You can't fool around about this. It's the work of the soul."

The only way to learn how to guide is to be guided by an experienced guide, and so we arrive full circle at the necessity of a long apprenticeship. Not a training, whether over months or a year, whether in person or virtual — an adoption is what's needed, an accompaniment through unknown territories, on low and very high doses, with all of the entheogens.[21] And the women underground guides have done just this, not with the expressed intention to become a guide, but to heal themselves. They originally dove into deep waters in search of their own healing with just enough desperation to be willing to tolerate the long years and challenging trips of an apprenticeship.

Heal Thyself First

Back in the late sixties at the Esalen Institute, the common refrain was "You can't take someone where you haven't been." This translated as "Work on yourself first."

I was recently on a panel with three other therapists talking about integration, and in the last few minutes of the discussion, the lone psychiatrist, who had been relatively quiet, revealed, "I've been in Freudian analysis, behavioral therapy, and am now seeing a Jungian." I chimed in immediately, "Me, too! I'm seeing a Jungian analyst." Later during our debriefing, I told him, "That might've been the most important thing we said." He agreed, adding that he tries to include his own personal experience every time he talks publicly.

Or as Maureen puts it: "No one skips dismemberment, disintegration. This is what creates space. All my old ways didn't work — everything I knew didn't work."

Searching for their own healing fueled the elder guides' personal searches, eventually leading to entheogenic journeys. As a group, they have histories of childhood abuse and trauma, spiritual emergency, great loss, addictions, and serious medical conditions. The quest for personal healing is not the same as yearning for the spiritual experiences they had as children, but they are related. Childhood suffering often opens doors in consciousness through dissociation during abuse when children learn to leave their bodies for their own survival.[22] Alyana told me that Grandmother Ayahuasca said to her in a ceremony, *You were trained for this from a child. We protected your spirit.*

Many of the women guides described how healing continues over a lifetime. It's not like they did a few ceremonies and now are healed. Their process of healing is the story of their lives. They are healers because they continue to work on their own healing. This is a characteristic of these women elders that I think is overlooked when training psychedelic therapists. One of the guides was shocked to learn that not all therapists have had their own therapy. But no, that's not the case, and I don't know how many, if any, of the psychedelic therapy training programs require it.

The underground guides have different ways of describing how healing continues over a lifetime. One said, people grow in "tiers, layers, where they encounter another level of understanding and spiritual access." It's a process of continuous unfolding. Rose described how healing themes unfold over time like a "spiral, issues return at another level as they come up for healing." Mary said how her "cup of healing was filled up" during her many years of apprenticeship, and this was after decades of trainings in energy and family systems work.

With an anthropologist's perspective, Cedar talked about the process of initiations occurring over a lifetime with the traditional three stages:

1. Dissolution, disrepair, coming apart, separation from what was known before.
2. Limbo, liminal stage, ordeals, challenges, requiring perseverance.
3. Integration, movement into new level or status, contribution to the community.

After all these years of my own personal search for healing and transcendent experiences, I have to admit to being in a liminal stage after what I call "my year of dismemberment." I recently underwent a five-and-a-half-hour abdominal surgery in which they removed a rather impressive list of organs and found no cancer. I'm fine and yet struggling with a reservoir of unconsciousness in my body, the blankness of anesthesia, and a rather confused search for meaning. I'm faced with the usual questions for this middle stage: What was this about? Why did I need to go through this? What did I learn? What can I bring back to my life and my community? I'm definitely in the perseverance stage where "all my old ways don't work." And since I'm not a very patient person, I also wonder why it's taking me so long to get to the third stage, which looks like a lot more fun.

I can almost hear one of the elder guides saying to me, "Just stay with it...."

Recognizing Initiation

On one of my visits with Arielle, we were walking through a beautiful forest of Douglas fir trees and ferns as she described a camping trip in the Wasatch Mountains in 1979. "It was fall, a cold night, just before the snows hit the mountains. I was sleeping outside —"

I interrupted her immediately. "Alone? No tent?"

"Yes, alone and no tent," she replied with no clue why I would be so incredulous. Alone on a mountain, not even inside a tent — not something I would do for love or money. I didn't know where she was going with this story, but fear was already rising from deep within me.

"Right before dawn, I was awakened by pressure on my blanket," she said. "I was aware of an 'unseen presence' I had never felt before. I was immobilized, yet totally alert. I had an overwhelming sense of primal fear. I didn't know whether I should try to move to see what it was or remain completely still. I turned my head just enough to see a huge cat, a jaguar. Time stopped. Inside, I expanded my presence while remaining totally still. The cat scratched my right thigh, through my jeans, from hip to knee. One long scratch and two smaller ones."

I was holding my breath.

Arielle continued, "Days later I asked the spirit of the jaguar, *Why did you do this?* The answer I received was, *So you would know it was real, it really happened.*"

Even after thirty-five years of doing therapy, I'd never heard anything like this. At least I could recognize that this was a mythic story. Yes, it really took place, but the meaning of the experience seemed to originate from a world beyond this one. And only someone who has traveled through expanded states of consciousness, like Arielle, would know enough to ask the jaguar why and get an answer.

But Arielle continued to be in mystery about this experience until thirty-five years later when she went on a vision quest. Another participant was supposed to bring her a gift when she met Arielle at one of the checkpoints. This participant happened to be an ordained minister in her eighties. She told Arielle, "I prayed about what to bring you and was told to give you this specific gift, but I've had it for twenty-one years and didn't really want to give it away so I left it in the glove compartment of my car."

Together they hiked to her car, and the woman handed Arielle a small leather pouch. Inside was a carving of an obsidian jaguar. Arielle held it in her hand for the remaining days of the vision quest. She said she "cascaded back to the cat I'd met before," feeling that these events were connected. Arielle sensed the jaguar entity was with her as she filled a notebook with the insights and teachings she received on the vision quest and connected them to other jaguar visions and symbols from decades of traveling in expanded states of consciousness.

We were standing, having stopped walking in the forest, and I told her with certainty, "This was an initiation."

This kind of story should not be interpreted psychologically. It should be heard in a whole different way and held by the listener as a numinous event. These things happen and they need to be received, recognized, and protected. The psychedelic therapist has to have enough experience in unseen realms to be able to recognize when a real-life event also lives and has an impact in spiritual dimensions. Living in more than one reality is part of the meaning behind the phrase "swimming in the sacred," as the elder guides do.

At long last, Arielle felt she understood the message. She happens to be one of those people who, unlike me, doesn't have fear — hence her sleeping outside on the side of a mountain.

Arielle said, "This was about knowing *fear*, experiencing my edge of fear. I've never felt the paralysis of fear again. This was an important teaching. I remain unflappable when supporting others in ceremony to let go of their fear."

Some processes take a very long time.

Distinguishing Wisdom from Ego

When I said to Arielle, "This is an initiation," I recognized this statement as coming through me, not from me. I hear this every once in a while in my voice — it's a voice with more certainty, one that's authoritative and wise. Personally, I'm more agnostic; I tend to question and am well known for being outspoken, meaning I have a tendency to put my foot in my mouth. I recognize the difference, though, even if I don't know whether the authoritative voice that sometimes comes through me is inspired by an outside source or by my inner wisdom, my higher self. Differentiating between inner and outer wisdom at this level is a philosophical dilemma and may not be important anyway. What's important is that I listen to myself when I hear this quality in my voice, and other people seem to respond similarly.

However, separate from this wise voice, I also had my own egotistical, more foot-in-mouth response to Arielle's story. I said, "I don't think we have jaguars in North America." Need I mention that I know nothing about big-cat wildlife on any continent? I don't even know the differences between jaguars, pumas, and mountain lions (a confusion shared by many, as I discovered when I later researched the question on Wikipedia). Who cares? Clarifying animal species is totally irrelevant for Arielle's amazing story, and the good news is that, in the moment, I didn't pursue this line of questioning, which would've totally distracted Arielle from her experience. I caught myself and didn't indulge my ego. I wish I could say I do that all the time, but...

A numinous experience should be left untouched, honored and respected from afar. It has its own way of working through a person, healing and changing them as the experience deepens and moves through their inner life. This is why a psychedelic guide or therapist has to have their own experiences in these other realms, inner and outer, to know when to sit in silence and "just" be present to the whole, mysterious unfolding.

Fearlessness in the Face of Danger

Like Arielle, most of the women elder guides are remarkably fearless in pursuit of their own healing, their apprenticeships, and their work with others. Personally, I'm racked with fear, and this alone is probably the greatest difference between the guides and me. Accordingly, I've been fascinated by fearlessness. In a *New Yorker* magazine profile of two famous rock climbers, they both agreed that they "don't have an emotional reaction to danger."[23] The risk of injury and death doesn't seem to frighten them. They see it, calculate it into their plans, but don't have the baggage of an emotional reaction. Neither do the women elders.

I think of the underground guides as spiritual warriors in the tradition of Tibetan Buddhism. This doesn't mean they're all enlightened or even psychologically sophisticated, but they are remarkably one-pointed in their life's work with entheogens. Fear does not stop them.

On a Sunday afternoon in Brooklyn, I was swapping stories with J.P. Harpignies, who seems to have been everywhere in the psychedelic world for the last half century. We landed on the one person we know in common, one of the elders I interviewed, Radha. J.P. had met her in the jungle when she was studying with a powerful Peruvian shaman. He said, "She's a warrior."

"Yes, yes," I agreed overenthusiastically. I'd not heard anyone else describe one of these women elders in the same way I thought of them.

"She's got nerves of steel, that one," he went on.

I added to the picture. "When she heard that the shaman she was studying with was abusing women in ceremony, she confronted him immediately. And when he didn't stop, she left him cold."

Our conversation paused as we sat in reverence of Radha, fearless, ethical, and unstoppable.

The Ability to Be Present

In practice, most of the time the guide's job is to be present, to hold a safe container for the journey. Jamie Beachy, director of the Center for Contemplative Chaplaincy at Naropa University, does the best job describing being present: "Presence, for me, [is] about being connected to something that is broader than myself.... So when I bring my presence, I'm also mediating something greater than myself."[24]

The guide's commitment is to be in the service of the journeyer. This means paying attention with an open, receptive focus. I have heard of guides, sitting nearby, available and yet immersed in a book. I don't think this qualifies as the kind of presence I'm suggesting. Some guides write down whatever the client says or does during the journey, and those notes can be powerful clues for the integration process.

The guide needs to be grounded in her own body in order to focus on the person in front of her. She has to sift through what she's picking up directly in her felt bodily sense and differentiate what belongs to her client and what's hers. She has to recognize and manage her own projections so the client has a free, open psychic space without interference.

The guide can then work with a dual awareness of the journeyer: She senses into their experience even with minimal clues and, at the same time, attends to her own bodily felt sense of being in the moment. Both aspects of this dual awareness are nonverbal. If the guide has her own inner chatter going on, that will interfere with her awareness both inner and outer.

The concept of presence also arises in anthropology when

Westerners encounter indigenous elders who demand more of them than they're normally called upon to find within themselves. In 1992, Petra Rethmann lived with a reindeer-herding brigade in the northern tundra of the Kamchatka Peninsula, and she studied with Shura Shishkin, a woman she called grandmother. This indigenous elder was not impressed with an anthropological study and demanded more of Rethmann. "Now, in hindsight, I think that all Shura Shishkin was asking of me was to be present. And to do that, I had to let go. Let go of the anxiety and desperation. Of my discomfiture. Of my shame. Of the stories I was telling myself about myself. This was what it meant to be in the present."[25]

Being present requires an inner quiet and spaciousness in order to be receptive to any signals, intuitions, or guidance from unseen sources. Experience with one's own interiority in a range of expanded states allows the guide to feel into the client's journey. The more experienced the guide is with the entheogenic landscape, the more likely she'll recognize where her client is in their journey. As the guide attunes to the person in front of her, she can match what she's perceiving with her own inner experiences. This enables the guide to speak and act with the authority of someone who's "been there," especially when "there" is an exotic psychic locale.

It's been reported that some shamans can see into the ayahuasca-fueled visions of their patients and even enter into these visions.[26] Westerners trained by indigenous shamans report seeing dragons, snakes, and other mythic creatures in their client's bodies. One shaman told me after a ceremony that my head was clear but my torso was dark, and that was well before my abdominal surgery and year of dismemberment. For Western guides, it seems that cultivating a dual awareness is a more realistic goal than seeing such creatures.

The guide has to intuitively know when to say or do something and when to remain attentive and receptive. It can be challenging to resist the urge to "help" in some way when what's called for is nondoing, "just" being present. Harder still is knowing when action is appropriate and not for the sake of making the guide less anxious. The guide needs to know how to be centered and grounded, how to manage her own thoughts and feelings so she doesn't project them onto the client. Asking "What's happening now?" too often can interfere with the journeyer's experience. No client wants to pause an ecstatic moment to try to find the words to reassure an inexperienced guide.

Most of the women guides I interviewed are quite confident while still being aware of the realistic risks involved in their work. However, one guide talked about her lack of confidence, and she has done the least amount of underground work. She even mused about how less-experienced guides are forging ahead while she remains hesitant, but she seems to accept that anxiety is part of her healing process. Another guide described an emergency midjourney that necessitated taking her client to the hospital. This story was enough to terrify me, but the elder described it with great equanimity and an ethical commitment to do what was best for the client. The ER doctor turned out to be very discrete as he grasped the full extent of the situation. From my anxious point of view, they were very, very lucky. Just another way I wouldn't qualify to do this kind of work.

On the other hand, I've talked with self-appointed guides who are way too overconfident, and they scare me even more. One said, "I've done a lot of tripping and I'm sure I can handle anything that comes up." This is not the same as the storied confidence the elders have deep in their bones.

Carl Jung's Guide

When Carl Jung dove deeply into the unconscious, he had a woman guide, Toni Wolff, who, like the psychedelic women elders, has too often been overlooked. In fact, Jung's family insisted that Wolff's name and contribution be edited out of his memoir, *Memories, Dreams, Reflections*.[27] Although Jung never gave Wolff the public credit she deserved, he did write a private dedication in her copy of *Psychological Types*: "This book, as you know, has come to me from that world which you have brought to me. Only you know out of which misery it was born and in which spirit it was written. I put it in your hands as a sign of gratitude, which I cannot express through words."[28] For the psychedelic women elders, working for decades in silence, not much has changed.

Jung's descent was not a psychedelic journey but a spontaneous process that went on for years and served as the foundation for the development of Jungian psychotherapy. Toni Wolff was with him every step of the way with her highly developed gifts of intuition and acceptance and her implacable faith in the process. As Nan Healy described in *Toni Wolff & Carl Jung*: "Wolff knew her way into the darkness and she knew how to return. She could bring others into the unconscious and bring them back safely again."[29] Wolff was totally accepting of whatever strange experiences Jung reported, and evidently she had no fear, again, like the psychedelic women elders. Healy wrote, "It was her confidence, during this period, that helped stabilize Jung. Her confidence steadied him as he encountered his visions." She "possessed the fortitude and the courage necessary to stand up to intense unconscious contents." Wolff guided Jung through these years, which he recorded in *The Red Book*.[30]

Jung described the same kind of permeability between the unconscious of the psychedelic guide and the journeyer when explaining the process with Wolff: "T.W. [Toni Wolff] was experiencing a similar stream of images. I had evidently infected her, or was the déclencheur [trigger] that stirred up her imagination. My phantasies and hers were in a participation mystique. It was like a common stream, and a common task!"[31] Sonu Shamdasani, Jung's translator for *The Red Book*, wrote that some of Jung's entries in *The Black Books* "indicate a liminal, imaginal permeability in which [Wolff] would interact with some of Jung's figures."

This is the participation mystique that is also required of the psychedelic guides. And how does one teach this subtle capacity to open at unconscious depths? Only through years of thinning the veil and osmosing knowledge and wisdom into visionary realms via years of apprenticeship.

During this time of descent, Jung and Wolff together developed the technique of active imagination, in which the patient is encouraged to engage in dialogue with images from dreams or visions.[32] This is precisely what Arielle did when she asked the spirit of the jaguar, *Why did you do this?* The jaguar was real in flesh and blood during the encounter on the mountain, but days later, it was the spirit of the jaguar that Arielle engaged with using active imagination. At this level of depth, spiritual work, perceptions, and images can move seamlessly between our inner and outer worlds.

I have to confess that I continue fruitlessly to ask the wrong question again and again: "Is this voice I hear real in the outer world or a projection from within me?" It was with great relief that I discovered that Saint Augustine expressed the same bewilderment in 387 CE in his *Soliloquies* in a dialogue with "Reason." He wrote: "When I had been pondering many different thoughts to myself for a long time, and had for many days been seeking my own self and what my own good was, and what evil was to be avoided, there suddenly spoke to me — what was it? I myself or someone else, inside or outside me?"[33]

This is the very thing I would love to know but don't.

Chapter Four

GUIDANCE FROM UNSEEN OTHERS

All of the women underground guides reported receiving guidance from unseen sources — plant teachers, ancestors, angels, and unknown entities that were experienced as autonomous, intelligent, and intentional. Some of the elders referred to their intuition or inner healing intelligences, but there was little distinction between an inner source of guidance and an outer source or entity. It is more like their inner intuition enables them to receive information from an outer, unseen source.

The psychedelic elders talked about this guidance in different ways, but the message is consistent. They receive help, information, downloads, instructions from an unseen source. Cedar explained, "I receive direction from the spirits. The spirits told me to give my people grounding food after the ceremony — nuts, cheese, dark chocolate, fresh or dry fruit, or warm soup. To welcome them home."

In my interview with Janet, we spent over an hour talking about her psychotherapy and psychedelic training. She had traveled to the Netherlands for a legal immersion experience with psilocybin truffles. She said she was in a small group with other therapists in what she described as an ideal situation. This was a very interesting story, but she told it without the passion and commitment I'd heard from other elders. I was polite and slightly bored. Then Janet said that the psychedelic therapist training she's had in the States "doesn't prepare you to hold space no matter what," the way her years of specialized trauma therapist training and practice have. From there she somehow segued into "I grow San Pedro here where I live." The San Pedro cactus contains mescaline, like peyote, and my notes have a line drawn across the page at this point, indicating that everything shifted. Janet came alive with the depth of her love for this plant, and I heard all the passion and commitment I was used to hearing in the other elders. Evidently, the cactus is Janet's medicine, though I found out later that she also has a close relationship with mushrooms. At this point in the interview, we were talking on a whole different level about San Pedro. She said, "We all have spirit helpers whether we're aware of them or not."

Medridth described a slightly different perspective: "I work intuitively. I just know. And the knowing is very playful — we're all in the garden together." Medridth has the kind of joy that comes from a secure childhood filled with love. She didn't have childhood spiritual experiences to report when I asked about her early years, but she described a neighborhood where no one locked their doors and she could ask anyone on the street if she needed help. As a therapist, I couldn't help but wonder if this was complete denial or partial whitewashing. Medridth grew up in a large, metropolitan area, though it was quite a while ago. She was remembering a childhood in the thirties.

With my usual therapeutic pessimism, I listened for inconsistencies in her story. But there were none. She said, "On my first trip with ibogaine, I saw fifteen to twenty of my ancestors, some clearly visible and some in shadows. They continue to support me. I can call on them for support." On another trip with the same medicine, Medridth asked, "How did I get here, working with the plants?" On that journey she described watching the film of her life: "I saw a tall woman, my maternal great-grandmother, who was a witch." This woman is also part of Medridth's ancestral support team. It's more than age that makes Medridth the eldest of the elders. She has a wisdom that has grown from this safe, loving childhood, embedded in an extended family and community.

I couldn't help but think of an experience I had with a gifted therapist who worked with me almost like a psychic medium in family constellation therapy.[1] He asked me something I had never learned to ask clients in graduate school: "How many generations do you have to go back in your family to find a healthy maternal figure?" I scanned desperately and came up blank. I only know two generations back, and they were surely no help. After an uncomfortable silence, I gave a wild guess, "Seven generations...maybe." That would have meant I had an ancestor who was a healthy maternal figure from the 1800s in Eastern Europe, which isn't likely. Whenever I read stories about dead relatives greeting someone as they're dying, I think, *Oh no, I hope it's not grandma...again.*

A few of the underground guides studied in the Arica spiritual school, where archangels are part of their training, and they call on one from the Kabbalah for protection. Medridth described her process: "I work with archangels. I project them from inside me. Their energy is present whether I call them or name them or not. I assign authorship when I call energy inside me — call it energy of the universe. I ask for protection. I can see the archangels; I don't hear them. I thank them individually. I invite participants to call on their own spirits for protection. We all create a safe container."

This is an amazing statement describing movement of an inner image, the archangel, from Medridth's inner world into the outer world, where she asks for help from what she now perceives as an autonomous source of power and protection. In reciprocity, she thanks the archangel, treating the spirit as real. This time, to address the most obvious question — Is the archangel real in either Medridth's inner or outer world? — I will turn to Jungian James Hillman.

During a lecture on Henry Corbin, who had died the year before, Hillman opened by calling on the spirit of Corbin: "The presence of a person does not depend only on his visibility, the invisible Henry Corbin is among us."[2] In my imaginal realm, Medridth and Hillman would recognize each other as kindred spirits. Hillman continued:

> We misunderstand the mode of being of these images, the figures in our dreams or the persons of our imaginings. We believe these figures are subjectively real when we mean imaginally real: the illusion that we made them up, own them, that they are part of us, phantasms. Or, we believe these figures are externally real when we mean essentially real — the illusions of parapsychology and hallucinations. We confuse imaginal with subjective and internal and we mistake essential for external and objective.

This might sound like the Mad Hatter at Alice's tea party, but it's Hillman's way of pointing to "the interpenetration of consciousness and world." Elsewhere, Hillman attempted to describe this permeable boundary between inner and outer world in a different way: "We can never be certain whether we imagine them [figures] or they imagine us. All we know is that we cannot imagine without them, they are preconditions of our imagination. If we invent them, then we invent them according to patterns they lay down."[3]

Medridth, with total acceptance and no doubts, moves seamlessly with her archangels through this interpenetration. Jung did the same inner-outer dance during his years of descent: "There are things in the psyche which I do not produce, but which produce themselves and have their own life."[4] Or as Jung's editor, Sonu Shamdasani, described it: "Jung was both a participant in and scribe of his interior imaginal dramas, bearing witness to what he encountered."[5] And I might add that this ongoing relationship is therapeutic, a concept we will explore later.

Yes, but Are Imagined Beings Real?

Most psychologists elegantly sidestep the question of what is and is not real, but at least one British parapsychology researcher, David Luke, has valiantly waded into the ontology question raised by discarnate or disembodied entities. He focuses mostly on smoked DMT (dimethyltryptamine), which hurls the journeyer into unknown realms within seconds. Encounters with unknown entities are common. In *Otherworlds*, Luke wrote, "It's the seeming reality of the experience at the time, and the similarity of such encounters with those of others, that have led many to seriously ponder the ontology of these beings."[6]

Luke reported that after about fifty journeys smoking DMT, he began to get "the feeling I was intruding upon a cosmic gathering I wasn't invited to." He felt he was trespassing and that he surprised an entity he described as an "ominous luminous voluminous numinous...[who] proceeded to let me know that I should not be there and that I should certainly not be peering into the hallowed space beyond it, which it clearly guarded." Luke was sufficiently frightened to stop smoking DMT for fourteen years, and he only tried it again recently as a volunteer in a brain-imaging study.

It's fascinating to me that Arielle, one of the psychedelic elders, described a similar trespassing experience when she was a child. No medicines were involved, and she called this a lucid dream that she could reenter at will when awake. "I was in a maze with doors, hallways, stairs, different rooms. I went through a door and encountered and surprised an entity, a very old, ancestral being. The entity admonished me, 'You're not supposed to be here.' The entity put on a cloak of skin with lots of wrinkles to look like an old being."

Arielle asked the entity, "Why are you putting this on?"

"To make it okay to talk," the entity replied. "So that you will be able to understand me and not be frightened."

"You don't need to do that for me," Arielle told the entity.

Arielle must have been about eight years old, which would be in the late 1950s, or long before *Harry Potter*.

Luke and Arielle tell a similar story but with completely different emotional tones. The child Arielle was unfazed — she actually reassured the entity about its appearance. Luke, on the other hand, was cosmically terrified and eventually coined the phrase "ominous luminous voluminous numinous" to convey his experience of *mysterium tremendum*.

In one study, psychiatrist Rick Strassman delivered intramuscular DMT to his research subjects, who reported seeing a range of entities they described as beings, aliens, guides, helpers, clowns, reptiles, mantises, bees, spiders, cacti, and stick figures.[7] His subjects clung to the feeling that these entities were real even though Strassman tried to assure them they were not. It should be noted that Strassman discontinued this study due to these strange entity encounters, which were upsetting or even threatening and seemed to have no therapeutic value. The reports of encounters puzzled Strassman so much that he turned to the Old Testament to find comparisons between the DMT experiences and those of the ancient prophets.[8]

Strassman's reports are in direct contrast to that of religious studies scholar Anna Lutkajtis. The difference in findings could be a reflection of their academic specialties, or it could be that injecting subjects with DMT, as Strassman did, does not lead to the therapeutic entity encounters so often reported in ceremonial rituals. Lutkajtis summarized findings that indicated entities often provided biographical information that led to psychological insight. They also provided cosmic insights into the nature of the universe. Such personal and transpersonal revelations may mediate the therapeutic effects of psychedelics.[9]

Whether or not entities become helpful or therapeutic can depend upon their being asked by the journeyer or guide: *Are you a helping spirit? What can you teach me? Do you have a message for me?* We can pass right by spiritual teachers in the other realm if we don't remember to ask, or if we assume, often based on their form or other preconceptions, that they are not likely to be helpful.

Similar benefits were also reported by people in a New York University study using psilocybin-assisted psychotherapy for terminal cancer patients.[10] In the long-term follow-up, seven of thirteen participants reported encounters with spirit guides who were "recognizable familial figures," some of whom had already passed. These guiding spirits, in the form of a vision or a voice, helped the person navigate the psilocybin experience and provided reassurance. And they did more: They apologized, and they expressed their love for the traveler as part of their guidance. Unfortunately, participants were not asked about any ongoing relationships with these spirit guides or how these encounters changed the way these relationships were held by the participant after the ceremony.

Surveys of Unseen Others

Separately, a team at Johns Hopkins has conducted two recent, large online surveys asking about encounters with unseen others and compared the groups using no drugs, psilocybin, LSD, and ayahuasca DMT (omehod). The first study looked at encounters with "the God of your understanding, Higher Power, Ultimate Reality, or angels." The second study focused on people who had inhaled DMT and encountered an autonomous being or entity.[11]

The results from these two studies were similar in that respondents perceived the entities to be independent, autonomous, conscious, benevolent, intelligent, sacred, eternal, and all-knowing. Their experience was realer than real, and they believed the entities continued to exist after their encounter. Many of the people reported that these encounters were spiritually significant and that their lives became more satisfying and meaningful after the experience. Many reported changes in their worldview, with atheists no longer identifying as atheists.

Roland Griffiths, the lead author, described these two studies in a talk at the Harvard Divinity School. He seemed to be most interested in the finding that "the majority of atheists in both groups no longer identified as atheist....[This] suggests that these experiences were conversion experiences for the majority of atheists who participated."[12] Griffiths comes close here to realizing that such a radical change in worldview might be crucial to the psychedelic process and therapeutic outcome. But he doesn't have the whole picture because that requires a leap in understanding the centrality of relationships with unseen others.

Unfortunately, Griffiths did not ask the most important question: *Do you have an ongoing relationship with a spirit, ancestor, plant teacher, or unseen other?* This would be the question that more accurately reflects the lived experience of the elder guides. I only knew to ask this question in my 2012 "Study of Ayahuasca Use in North America" because I received advice from one of these women elders. This group of women has more experience with the process of working with entheogens than any of the academic research teams, and yet they are rarely, if ever, consulted.

In my study, 75 percent of the subjects (fifty-four out of eighty-one) reported that they had an ongoing relationship with the spirit of ayahuasca, connecting through thoughts, feelings, or visions in a psychic or intuitive manner. Thirty-five of the fifty-four said they called upon the spirit of ayahuasca for help, support, guidance, and love. As a result of this relationship, subjects said that they felt loved and lovable, connected to the Great Mystery, and able to forgive themselves. One said, "I glow light." When asked how this relationship was unfolding, twelve said slowly, six said as a result of the ceremonies, and two said in mystery.

Plant Teachers

The relationship with plant teachers is at the core of entheogenic shamanic practice. Anthropologist Luis Eduardo Luna summarized the situation:

> Within the context of indigenous spirituality,…the worldview [is that] there is an underlying spiritual aspect to everything that exists, an intimate relationship and even dependency between the seen and the unseen.…The preservation of the individual and the community…depends upon finding the proper balance in this complex reality. Sacred plants, such as ayahuasca, facilitate the perception of such complexity. Gifted individuals may establish alliances with spiritual forces and interact for the benefit of others."[13]

Or as ethnobotanist Kathleen Harrison explained at a lecture in the Botanical Garden at UC Berkeley, "The plants know the world is in trouble. They have to go where the trouble is."[14]

I heard the same message on a Zoom call with a Shipibo

shaman in Peru. He told me, "We are here to help you." He meant that with his connection to the plants and healing spirits, he was dedicated to helping us in the West.[15] I have to admit I was both reassured and amused by his statement. *After all, who has the flush toilet?* I thought. But then his words soaked in and I realized, *Yes, thank you. We are in trouble. We need your help.* The same message is repeated in Stephen Beyer's article entitled, "What Do the Spirits Want from Us?" And my interaction perfectly encapsulates Beyer's own answer: "Above all else, they want us to be grateful and humble."[16] I'm learning.

In the book *Plant Teachers*, Jeremy Narby adds precision to the concept of plant spirits, saying that the use of the word *spirit* projects "an opposition between the material and non-material onto them that doesn't exist." The concept does contain a dichotomy, but it's "between the visible and the invisible rather than between the material and the nonmaterial."[17] This differentiation is a far more subtle and refined approach to unseen others than the question "Are they real?"

One-third of the women elders were trained primarily by indigenous shamans. This doesn't mean that they only use ayahuasca in their work — they use a variety of entheogens, except for the two Native American women, one of whom uses peyote and the other primarily uses prayer and ritual. The cosmology surrounding the use of plant medicines is centered around the independent existence of plant teachers or doctors. The plants are sentient.

Klara, who apprenticed with an indigenous Shipibo shaman, told me that after five years of working with ayahuasca, she tried LSD. She was disappointed that there was no one "there" to talk to, no one to guide her. Alyana, one of the Native American women, was told by her clan mother to "pray from your heart, sit by the fire, just you and Sacred Mother Peyote." And so the relationship began.

Jeremy Narby's coauthor of *Plant Teachers* is Rafael Chanchari Pizuri, an indigenous vegetalista or plant specialist. Narby writes that Chanchari "refers to the 'mothers,' or 'owners,' of plants — invisible entities specific to each species that are like a personality."[18] Noting the conflicting cosmologies between scientists and *curanderos*, Narby sarcastically predicted that "a scientific perspective on the 'mother of tobacco' will probably not be available anytime soon."

In fact, Narby objected to my referring to "Grandmother Ayahuasca" in my book *Listening to Ayahuasca*, since he feels many indigenous tribes consider the plant teacher to be male.[19] Needless to say, this is a gender disagreement over an invisible entity. The spirit of the plant is most often referred to as "grandmother" in North American circles, which are developing their own belief system, possibly based on misappropriation. In *Plant Teachers*, Narby is adamant, "Ayahuasca...has no fixed persona."[20]

The apprenticeship training with an ayahuasca shaman means years of dieting with different plants. A *dieta* involves a long list of restrictions: no salt, sugar, fats, meat, liquor, spices, or sex, and sometimes no socializing with anyone who is sexually active. A *dieta* usually lasts at least six months.[21] The purpose is to eliminate all distractions so the apprentice can form a relationship with the plant, taking it inside their body, attuning to the spirit of the plant, listening and learning the secrets of the plant. An intimate relationship develops, built on mutual trust and love. In this way an unseen other is perceived as real in the outer world and brought inside the body to create an ongoing bond and connection for information.

When she apprenticed in Peru, Connie Grauds remembers, she was sequestered in the jungle like a monk during her *dietas*. She learned to be "quiet, calm in my body, mind and spirit. [To be] pure to be able to talk to spirit doctors, to call refined spirit doctors reliably — they give the diagnosis and treatment. *We do the healing*, they said. *You do not*. After five years of this, the spirit doctors talked to me about reciprocity — *You've never asked what you can do for us. We will heal your patients but you have to serve us.* The relationship with spirits is reciprocal." Connie's assignment was "to bring people into nature and get out of their way," meaning for her personal ego to take a back seat. Connie has lived up to this assignment.

As I've mentioned, I interviewed three women whom I don't consider underground elders, mainly because they've only been working ten years, but also because their training is different. Klara and Carmen are trained primarily with ayahuasca, having apprenticed with a Shipibo shaman, while Sarah is self-trained with mushrooms. However, they are immersed in the process of learning from the plants. They're dedicated and enamored of the spirits, and they can give us a glimpse into the lived experience of developing a relationship with the plants.

"My knowledge is directly from the plants under Maestro's guidance," Carmen described. She says her position is as both an independent learner and an apprentice. It's very important that she's continuing her education with the plants *under* the guidance of a shaman.

Carmen detailed how her relationship with the spirit of ayahuasca is unfolding over time: "I had to learn. I would get angry at her [ayahuasca] — she taught me how to appreciate her. I had to learn to be in collaboration with her. I was trying to put myself above her — I had to surrender to her, to be guided by her." In a soft, gentle voice, Carmen described how she hadn't had any ayahuasca for the past three months, and she's finding a new way of relating to the medicine. "I sing to myself when I go to bed and I have dreams. It feels more profound and deep — I feel guided and protected. [The spirit of

ayahuasca] is waiting for me to reach out and open my heart."
Carmen is a young shaman, and she's able to describe her process of developing her relationship with a plant spirit as she's
living it with great intimacy and humility.

Klara told me how she first met the spirit of ayahuasca in
her very first ceremony. She heard *I found you* and entered into
a relationship with the plant spirit from the very beginning,
just five minutes into ceremony, hardly enough time for the
biochemicals to be working. Ayahuasca said, *We're going to do
deep work together*.

Later on, Klara spent three months isolated in a tambo
in the jungle on a *dieta*. She didn't speak to one person. Klara
said, "This is the way you learn to support healing. You learn
to connect to the plant and the plant moves through you in a
dieta." Klara described how intense feelings of anger and jeal-
ousy moved through her during this time of isolation. She was
alone in the jungle, eating very little, and with no distractions.
Klara explained, "The laws of the spirit world don't allow you
in until you earn your way in." This is not an easy path.

Radha explained, "The plants are the primary teachers.
Don't mistake the practitioner for the plants." I heard this said
another way from a Shipibo shaman when people expressed
their great gratitude after a ceremony: "Don't thank me. Thank
the plants."[22] This is not said with false humility but is, rather,
a simple statement of how things work. Radha described her
experience of an ongoing relationship with a plant: "Ayahuasca is my constant companion in so many ways, a part of
me." Again we hear the merging of outer and inner, plant and
human.

Radha also described how the plants can show up and look
completely different even after years of connection. I asked
her, "How do you know then if it's the same plant spirit?"
She thought about this and said, "There's a fit I recognize."

Evidently, somehow they're familiar. "I know it's the plant because I've called it," she explained, but that seemed to be circular reasoning and neither of us was satisfied with that answer. Then Radha simply said, "I know in my heart." And that was that.

Cedar, an academic expert on shamanism with forty years of practitioner experience, corrected me about this issue of circular reasoning. I let all the women I interviewed read the finished manuscript to be sure I got things right. Cedar told me that Radha's explanation "was a shamanic understanding, that in shamanic traditions, you specify the Spirits you are calling upon, so then you can trust who shows up — whatever form they take. If they shift forms, you might assume there is a reason and ask about it."

I hope the contrast between my interpretation of Radha's statement and Cedar's explanation shows the difference between the author who is slightly experienced and Cedar who is deeply knowledgeable and experienced. It might be a subtle clarification, but it's everything in terms of working with unseen others in visionary realms.

Consulting Colleagues

Just as therapists receive supervision from more experienced therapists or colleagues, so do shamans. Even experienced shamans compare what they've seen in a patient and what it means, and then they strategize their treatment approach.

I know this because I've recently been attending ayahuasca ceremonies via Zoom with a family of Shipibo shamans, a younger brother and an older brother and his wife.[23] They drink the medicine in Peru and we, the patients, don't. These ceremonies have been helpful to me especially following my year of dismemberment, and so I've referred friends to this shamanic family. I hear about the ceremonies from both sides — my friends tell me about their experience, and the shaman's apprentice, who's acting as the translator, tells me what he experiences. One of the friends I've referred is a difficult case, and he wasn't sure the ceremonies were helping him. His wife and I encouraged him to continue. Then, after his latest session, he said the three shamans "each sang to me first and it was like a blast of energy, like they were coming after me." Yes, they were. The translator told me afterward that the shamans had met beforehand and agreed to sing to my difficult friend first, to focus on him. They were successful. My friend had his heart opened in a way that sixty-some years of spiritual study, body work, and therapy had not managed to accomplish. He has been dedicated to personal growth and evolution, but as I say, a tough case.

Two weeks after that Zoom ceremony, I asked my friend, "How have you changed since that ceremony?"

"I've given up on trying to fix my grown children," he said.

Mind you, the kids are in their sixties, and I've been telling him to give up on them for years, albeit ineffectively. He feels relieved about this new perspective. How did he move from his nonverbal experience of tears running down his face while the shamans directed their *icaros* his way to being able to accept his children as they are and letting go of trying to save them? No medicine in him and via Zoom. That's the mystery.

In contrast with Carmen's ayahuasca apprenticeship, Sarah has been working for ten years with mushrooms, but with no guiding shaman. She says she was "called by the mushroom spirits," and she doesn't use any other medicines in her work. Describing her relationship with the mushrooms, Sarah says, "We're partners, a team." She has high ethical standards and lives somewhat like a nun in a remote area where people come to her for retreats. Sarah has studied with a number of spiritual teachers, and her intuition expands into psychic ability and mediumship. But since she is not under the guidance of a shaman or psychedelic elder, she has no one to ask, "Did you see that? How did it change? What does it mean?" These are important questions apprentices ask as they learn and develop. Anthropologist Evgenia Fotiou comments on this same issue: "My research with Western apprentices of shamans shows that part of the shamanic training might be not learning to 'see,' as I originally thought but, rather, learning to interpret what one sees, manipulate it, and navigate through it."[24] As Sarah has no bounds to her imagination, no one to consult with regarding these kinds of questions, she lives in her own magical world.

Carmen, Klara, and Radha are part of a community of people who sit in ceremonies with the same maestro in Peru — Carmen and Klara are students while Radha is a colleague of this maestro. Klara described how they learn from each other: "What's the story here? What did you see? We try to find the story [of the patient] together, cross-referencing."

I've now met everyone in this small group of dedicated shamans and am awed by the love they share and how they support each other. They've been in ceremonies together for years, have sung to each other forever to crack through the layers, to get to the root of the trauma. They've also held each other in their arms to ground the healing in the body. I've also been around for their disagreements, which feel like family arguments, and I marvel at how they have learned to work around their egos and remain in love with each other.

This working around their egos — perhaps dancing around their egos is a more elegant description — is significant in understanding how entheogens heal. This is a good example of the kind of flexibility, hard-won through many years of entheogenic journeys, that's necessary to get "over yourself." We first have to have an observant inner witness to recognize when we're caught in our egos — thinking, *I'm right. You shouldn't have....* Then we have to disidentify with our position and find a way to reach across the chasm our reactivity has created. Quite a bit of emotional intelligence is needed, which, unfortunately, often eludes me.

My Ongoing Existential Crisis

When I listen to Klara, the spirit of ayahuasca comes alive for me even without any medicine. It's as if there's a residue of the medicine inside me that resonates with her story. She told me, "The spirits are so real — I see them in my dreams," and I have no doubts. It all seems self-evident. However, I can't help but think: *Does seeing spirits in dreams mean they're real?* I have to laugh at myself. When will I stop asking this wrong question?

As always, I can't answer this question. My truth is, I'll probably never be sure if plant spirits are real, much to the chagrin of my dear friend Joe Tafur, author of *The Fellowship of the River.*[25] He doesn't suffer with not knowing — he grew up with a mother who's a Catholic mystic, and so he had a familial foundation for communing with the Holy Spirit. I grew up with a foundation of secular Jewish agnosticism, and my questioning is deeply entrenched. Joe has hopes for me, though. He said, with that big smile of his, that this book would break me out of my existential dilemma. I can shyly admit that I'm partially out, sort of like a baby bird breaking through an eggshell, not quite clear what's on the other side.

What has pushed me farther out is my experience over Zoom with the three Shipibo shamans. Still stuck in my Western perspective, I think it's crazy that plant spirits can work over the internet, and yet I feel the ceremonies have helped me. Perhaps right there is the split between my head and my heart. How can this possibly work? Can the *icaros* carry healing energy over such distances and via Zoom? Can they transcend space and time? From a shamanic perspective, yes, of course they can.

I started doing monthly ceremonies with the three Peruvian shamans when I was right in the middle of my dismemberment year. When the elder shaman sang, I felt like his *icaros* unzipped me from stem to stern so he could sing directly into my body. The healing energy of the *icaros* permeated my body especially in the area of my major surgery. His singing seemed to align something in me like a magnet under a paper aligns iron filings. I attended monthly ceremonies, and whenever the woman shaman sang to me, a lighthearted joy lifted my heart. Joy is not big in my emotional repertoire, but I smiled from the moment she turned her attention to me. My experience is that the healing energy of the plants came through, and I have absolutely no way to explain this in Western logic.

A few anthropologists have written about personal experiences with spirits that have moved them from participant observation to "radical participation," as Bonnie Glass-Coffin phrased it in a 2010 issue of *Anthropology and Humanism.*[26] In the same journal, Edith Turner stated, "It is all becoming clear. There are spirits." And David Hufford wrote, "The experience of spirit encounters turns out to be very common in the modern world as elsewhere. What is less common — although this is changing — has been the willingness to talk about such things."

An increasing number of people are willing to talk about such things. In 1979, anthropologist Michael Harner created the Foundation for Shamanic Studies to teach shamanic understandings to Westerners based on his experiences with ayahuasca doing fieldwork in the fifties.[27] However, it was only toward the end of his life, in 2012, that Harner wrote *Cave and Cosmos*, which fully described his transformed worldview and detailed his experiences working with spirits.[28]

Ethnobotanist Kat Harrison generously shared her experience of meeting the spirit of *Salvia divinorum*. In ceremony, she wrote, "suddenly there was a shimmering, the *curandero* blew the candles out for total darkness, and within seconds I was completely in another realm, astonished....I was in the presence of a great female being, a woman, twenty feet high and semitransparent....There were butterflies and hummingbirds flying around and through her. Her great translucent face, the intensity of rainbows, leaned toward me and away....I felt a great longing for her to move toward me, to touch me."[29]

One research scientist, Monica Gagliano, also shared her experience and encountered significant pushback to her career even though her research findings are remarkable. On a *dieta* with ayahuma (a tree that grows in the Amazon jungle) under the guidance of a Peruvian shaman, Gagliano received specific instructions for studying Pavlovian learning in plants. Gagliano said, "I transcribed as she [the spirit of ayahuma] dictated."[30] Gagliano also drew diagrams she received from ayahuma showing how to set up her experiment once she returned to Australia. She has since published broadly in the new disciplines of plant communication and plant cognition. Perhaps our Western worldview is changing, albeit slowly.

Yet questions remain. Robin Carhart-Harris reviewed the research on increased suggestibility under the influence of LSD with its heightened neural plasticity, cognitive flexibility, and lowered reality testing.[31] He raised the delicate issue of setting and how it influences the interpretation or framing of an experience. There's concern that the artwork in the room, music, and even the Mystical Experience Questionnaire could prime subjects to view their experience within a certain religious frame. For instance, the musical playlist suggested by Johns Hopkins psychedelic researcher Bill Richards is primarily Western classical with a number of pieces from the Christian tradition. It should be noted that, traditionally, no psychedelic substance is taken devoid of a cultural set and setting. The issue is the level of consciousness we bring to the cultural setting of the entheogenic experience.

At the Harvard Divinity School, a panel of chaplains emphasized how their interfaith training made them more aware of how to work with psychedelics within an interreligious context, something the medical and therapeutic team may not know how to do.[32] Matthew Johnson from the Johns Hopkins team agreed with the chaplains, writing that the "danger is that scientists and clinicians will be imposing their personal religious or spiritual beliefs on the practice of psychedelic medicine."[33]

When I planned my ketamine experience, I had long discussions with the therapist who made the playlist — the music was very important to me. I asked for specific pieces, and the therapist reserved the right to add his own as well. I agreed. When one of his selected electronic pieces came up in the journey, I quickly requested the therapist skip it. But then his selection of the St. Petersburg Chamber Choir's "Alleluia, Behold the Bridegroom" came on, and I was immediately enthralled.[34] I asked for it to be repeated — I don't know how many times. As I was coming out of the journey, beginning to sit up, my first words were, "Does this mean I now have to convert to Christianity?" I thought, as a lifelong agnostic, I was being hilariously funny. My two therapists hesitated and then caught on to my joke, and we all had a good laugh. I think they were relieved, though, that they didn't have to answer my question regarding conversion. This example illustrates the potential power of religious elements in the setting and the need for therapists to learn how to explore this delicate area.

Anthropologist Tanya Luhrmann, in her exploration of spiritual experience, avoids any questions about ontology.

Rather than asking "Is God real?" she asks how people develop and cultivate a relationship with an invisible other. She theorizes that people use their imaginations to create small experiences of feeling the presence of an invisible other, or in the case of Christian evangelicals, Jesus. She posits that some people have a gift for being able to do this. One of the elder psychedelic guides, Arielle, also refers to this gift, saying, "We all have thin veils." Luhrmann said some people are better at blurring "the boundary between the inner world and the outer world, which makes it easier for people to turn to a faith frame to make sense of the world and to experience invisible others as present in a way they feel with their senses."[35]

Psychologists have tried to measure this gift of permeable boundaries or having thin veils, as the psychedelic elder described. The leading contender is the concept of absorption, which is usually measured using the Tellegen Absorption Scale and was first studied as it relates to responsiveness to hypnosis. Two examples from the scale are "fantasy absorption" — "I am sometimes able to forget about my present self and get absorbed in a fantasy that I am someone else" — and "openness to experience": "I enjoy — or would enjoy — getting beyond the world of logic and reason to experience something new and different."[36]

The higher a person scores on a measure of absorption, the more likely they will be to respond to hypnosis as well as to guided imagery and relaxation cues. And the more likely they will experience synesthesia, empathy, creativity, flow, and self-transcendence. The concept of absorption encompasses qualities that will be familiar to everyone experienced with psychedelic journeys — there's a receptive immersion in the experience, the inner world responds, and internalized associations and elaborations of meaning occur, along with a surrendering of control.[37] So it comes as no surprise that two studies found that the trait of absorption predicted responses to psychedelic medicines, including mystical experience and visual effects.[38]

The ability to be absorbed by the imagination, to experience the world differently, is at the heart of spiritual experience. Psychologists Michael Thalbourne and Peter Delin developed the concept of transliminality, meaning "ease in crossing the threshold."[39] This is another way of describing a thin veil. They found that transliminality related to dream recall and interpretation, religiosity, and mystical experience.

A variety of faith traditions refer to traits of absorption and transliminality in amazingly similar ways, and I might add, so does Jung's active imagination. For example, Ignatius de Loyola suggested a colloquy "by speaking exactly as one friend speaks to another....Imagine that Christ our Lord is present before you upon the cross, and begin to speak with him."[40] Brother Lawrence echoes this advice in his classic book *The Practice of the Presence of God*: "That we should establish ourselves in a sense of God's Presence, by continually conversing with Him."[41]

The Islamic scholar Henry Corbin described a process of cultivating the experience of God. First, he wrote, "the faithful must place himself in the company of his God and 'converse' with Him. [Then] imagine his God as present...facing him. [And finally,] contemplate his God in the *subtle* center which is the *heart*."[42] In this progression, the imaginal God is first projected into the outer world from within and then made real in conversation and visual encounter, and finally brought back into the body, into the heart, which is both a physical organ and an energetic mystical center. This is an intentional blurring of the inner and outer worlds as well as of the physical and energetic subtle body.

When a Sufi teacher came to visit me years ago, he announced he had a new teacher. Since lineage is so important in Sufism, I was shocked. He went on to say his new teacher was Sufi poet Farid ud-Din Attar from the twelfth century, and he then presented me with one of his books, *The Conference of the Birds*, as if it were hot off the press. From the introduction: "The parables in this book trigger memories deep within us all. The stories inhabit the imagination, and slowly over time, their wisdom trickles down into the heart. The process of absorption is unique to every individual, as is each person's journey."[43] In this modern description of an ancient book, we encounter the very same process of blurring the inner and outer worlds.

Absorption and Dosage

I think we have to consider that people who score high on absorption or transliminality might do better with a lower dose of psychedelic medicine when they journey. Or, another way to phrase this is that these people are likely to be over-dosed. They tend to enter into expanded states more easily and so require less intensity for liftoff. When I asked Arielle, who had referred to "thin veils," if this was true for her, she agreed, but then added, "I still like the high doses. I like to fly. I'm going home."

Cedar, however, said, "I have been overwhelmed by the physiological effects of high doses — what might even be considered 'normal' by some. I've learned from such experiences that low doses allow me to fly just as deep and for at least as long as others." Two other very experienced voices from the sixties agree. Mountain Girl, or Carolyn Adams Garcia, who traveled with both the Merry Pranksters and the Grateful Dead, said, "The egotistical lunge toward high doses is not a good idea....More is not better. It really isn't. That's my biggest message."[44]

Myron Stolaroff, who interviewed Leo Zeff for *The Secret*

Chief, also wrote in praise of lower doses. He said they allowed him to "resolve a lot of interior debris…and the after-effects of the experience stayed with me in a rewarding way for a much longer period of time.…Since I had learned to deal with my feelings, I became much more adept at handling them as they came up in daily situations."[45] Stolaroff's personal description regarding dose is central to the process of integration: How do we apply what we've learned in ceremony to our daily lives?

Jung's Active Imagination

"If we look inward, the 'other' looks at us too."[46]

This is Marie-Louise von Franz's commentary on the process of diving deep into the unconscious, as Jung did during his descent. With psychedelic medicines, it's difficult to know whether we're looking inward or outward into another world. But this might not be the right question to ask, similar to my question, Are they real? James Hillman said that Jung "doesn't go into the reality of the figures. In other words, how can you believe these figures are independent: How do I know they're not just part of me? How do I know they're not complexes or projections of my various opinions? He doesn't deal with all that psychologizing of what comes to him. He takes it as it comes."[47] I'm slow, but with Jung as a model as well as the psychedelic elders, I think I'm making progress on this issue of compulsive psychologizing.

Jung explained to Barbara Hannah why he referred to his confrontation with the unconscious as a "dangerous enterprise." Hannah wrote, "Jung once told me that the unconscious itself was not dangerous. There was only one real danger, he said, but that was a very serious one: *panic!* The fear that grips a person when something very unexpected confronts him, or when he begins to be afraid of losing his footing in the conscious world."[48]

I daresay every psychedelic elder has experienced this panic, either in themselves or in their clients. There comes a moment in the journey when the challenge is to let go, surrender, and trust the medicine and the guide. Often this is the moment right before ego dissolution. At this moment, the guide has to hold steady, rooted in her own experience.

The best advice for this moment that I've seen comes from a seemingly unrelated opinion piece in the *New York Times*, "The Bat Mitzvah Question I Wasn't Expecting: 'Are We Safe at Synagogue?'" But here is wise advice for this challenging psychedelic moment. The author quotes from the card her grandfather gave her on the occasion of her bat mitzvah: "*hazak v'ematz* which means have strength and be courageous: The expression is not an endpoint, but a beginning."[49]

Jung's best-known unseen other was Philomen. Sonu Shamdasani wrote that this figure "represented superior insight and was like a guru to him. [Jung] would converse with him in the garden."[50] Such seemingly casual conversations are the essence of relationship, not just a random appearance of a spirit, but an ongoing, deeply involved, and unfolding relationship. Jung's unseen others, like the psychedelic elders' unseen others, are taken as independent, sentient, and helpful. Hillman goes further: "Jung says…that we think the figures we uncover in our dreams or in active imagination are the result of us, but he says we are the result of them. Our life should be derived from them."[51] After all, where would Jung's whole theoretical edifice be without Philomen?

On the other hand, if one's unseen other is not helpful, but instead harmful, then that's an entirely different situation. A relationship with an unseen other that leaves someone overwhelmed, distressed, or struggling to cope may require professional intervention.[52] It's the impact on the person that is the dividing line between a spiritual relationship with an unseen other and a pathological process.

Psychologist Jeffrey Raff provided more details about how this kind of relationship unfolds: "Imaginal perception is not only an act by which we see an object, it is also an act that transforms both the seer and the seen."[53] Shamdasani captures the same phenomenon about relationships with unseen others: "A double movement is taking place. While [Jung is] working on this, the figures are working on him." And: "Jung allows the figure to work on him. It's not he who works on the figures. He lets them instruct him."[54]

The psychedelic women elders deeply understand that their work is all about their ongoing relationships with unseen others. It's the relationship, not the drug. I do understand why the academic research teams can't talk about guidance from unseen others. However, these ongoing relationships are central to healing and to the spiritual nature of these medicines. The medicalization of psychedelics is losing this spiritual core.

The Process of Discernment

Revelations from personal history to insights about the nature of reality have a noetic quality to them in the midst of an entheogenic journey, and this imbues them with a sense of being "realer than real." Adding confirmation to this style of intuitive knowing is the belief that there exists an inner intelligence that can and should be trusted.[55] However, we all know examples of heartfelt messages that led to inflation, personal disasters, and heartbreak.

With their decades of experience, the elders don't just follow the guidance of their unseen others without reflection. They listen, consider, hold their understanding in their hearts, and engage in a process of discernment.

When I complained to Maureen about people who tell me, "I dreamed Grandmother Ayahuasca told me to lead ceremonies," she explained to me that this is *not* authorization. It means "go study." It's an invitation to drink, maybe to train, a process that takes about a decade of devoted study. Not quite what people have in mind after such a dream when they leap into leading ceremonies with a muddy mixture of medicine and recorded music.

This raises the whole question of how we interpret what we experience with these medicines, what we think we're told by spirits or plant teachers. What's the concrete practical message and what's the existential meaning? How does the message influence or totally change our lives? And how do we know? Is this message from a reliable, wise source? Can I trust the source or the message itself?

In *Plant Teachers*, Jeremy Narby confronts these questions in a straightforward way in conversation with his coauthor, Rafael Chanchari Pizuri, an indigenous healer. Rafael, who goes by Chanchari, gives an answer to the question of discernment that is worthy of a professional diplomat, leaving us in the ambiguous, shamanic dark. But Narby persists and they finally arrive at the real problem — our egos.

Narby: So it seems to me that one needs to learn the difference between seeing things that are true and seeing things that are not. Does that seem right to you?...So that means that ayahuasca misleads people, doesn't it?

Chanchari: It's not that ayahuasca lies, but rather that lies and truth exist in the world, and ayahuasca allows you to see this....I make a distinction between hallucinations and visions....Sometimes you have what seems like an intuition and you think "maybe that's how things are happening," and this is not true.

Narby: And how do you learn to tell the difference?

Chanchari: You need human values to be able to make the

distinction. And this takes practice and experience, not just one or two days, but over a long period.

Narby: So the problem is that one contributes to the process by making projections?

Chanchari: Yes, that's right. That's where the lie is: You have what feels like an intuition, you are imagining things, and then you affirm them, but they are not true.[56]

The process of discernment is most often clouded by our egotistical strivings or our unconscious. One of the early guides from the fifties recognized this temptation in the first sweep of psychedelic optimism. Admitting his inflation, Myron Stolaroff wrote, "I am more convinced than ever that my interest in saving the world is an escape from my own personal growth. It is most important to develop oneself and one's family and home."[57] Tend your own garden, in other words. Still good advice for those currently enamored with these medicines and their role in "saving the world."

Religion professor Bill Barnard, in *Liquid Light*, his memoir about Santo Daime, wrote, "Developing the ability to discern the difference between genuine Knowing and our own egoic desires doesn't come automatically or easily."[58] He then goes on to quote the pertinent warning from Roshi Bernie Glassman, "I could be wrong." So could we all.

Anthropologist Luis Eduardo Luna is most direct. Although not a therapist, he stated the issue clearly, "The real problem has to do with ego inflation."[59] In other words, the shaman or guide is meeting their own needs rather than serving the needs of the patient. This is what leads to abuse of vulnerable people seeking healing. This is why we need colleagues who can help us see what we're missing in our own healing process, our learning to work with the medicines, and our understanding of our position in all of this. We need beloved, fellow travelers to remind us to be humble.

Medicine hunter Chris Kilham also warned about visions that can go wrong. While "some are, in fact, prescient, insightful, revelatory, and wise, other visions are mere head salad. If you are going to journey with the aid of psychoactive substances, you must learn to discern the difference between manna from the gods and mental coleslaw. The former may set you on a new, luminous life path. The latter may send you down a rabbit hole."[60]

When talking about discernment, most of the women guides reference their own intuition, which they feel has been sharpened by years of working with entheogens. They also refer to trusting a deep sense in their bodies, a sort of visceral process of discernment. Maureen explained that when she hears a voice, she takes the words into her body to notice how it feels. She said, "Working in the subtle realms with these medicines requires a body wisdom, an inner knowing. Where in my body do I have unshakable trust? Once I locate that place, then I can practice being there." Maureen credits one of her teachers, Angeles Arrien, with this practical wisdom. When you're in that place in your body, there's no push or pull in either direction. You're in a neutral place, and from there, you can move forward.

Maureen then came to the same conclusion that Rafael Chanchari Pizuri reached with Jeremy Narby. You need, Chanchari said, to "grasp the difference between ayahuasca visions and your own projections, and to learn self-control."[61] Discern what's yours and what's not yours, and then manage it with discipline and ethical behavior. This is learned through the apprentice relationship over a long period of time via very small, subtle corrections.

Rose said she hears from the spirit of ayahuasca if her ego comes up during ceremony. She'll hear, *That's your ego. Feel it in your body.* Rose explained that "the ego wants control, doesn't want to surrender even though that's what's called for. The sense of self doesn't want to give way, it's resistant."

Radha described how she differentiates between her ego and the plant medicines. "I know when I'm clicked into the channel that opens, when I'm tuned in to the station that's always present. It's like I'm tuned in to a wavelength of the plant as a source of information. A file is shared, not transmitted, shared. Now I'm in sync — I am it." And then she prays, "Let me balance confidence and humility."

What each of these women refers to is a bodily felt sense of recognition in contrast to an ungrounded intuition or inspiration. The venerable Tenzin Priyadarshi refers again and again to a similar somatic sense that guided his journey into Tibetan Buddhism. In his memoir, *Running toward Mystery*, he refers to a "sound [that] vibrated through my bones," to "ancient stories [that] are still alive in my bones," and to a "voice resonating inside my bones."[62] His bodily felt sense, in his bones, confirms his intuition that he's on the right path, finding his way without fully comprehending how his childhood journey will impact the rest of his life.

Quakers talk about the process of discernment as central to their spiritual practice. With a soft and open heart, they take the time to become quiet and turn inward to their deepest knowing through solitude and silence. They withdraw from the noise and distraction of the everyday world as well as from their inner, compulsive voices that often loop with negative messages. The prayer is for indifference or an interior freedom in which they are free from undue attachment to any particular outcome.[63] The attitude is one of equanimity, with no investment in the answer that arises from within. This is not an easy psychic state to maintain, but it is key to being able to differentiate between the ego and that still small voice.

Lest this appear too simple, I have to add that others, far wiser than I, have acknowledged that there is no clear-cut formula for discerning between divine inspiration and ego inflation. Janet Adler, teacher of Authentic Movement, which is a therapeutic process almost totally based on subtlety close to a mystical awareness, stated, "Intuitive knowing can, in fact, be projection."[64] And if that warning isn't enough, Llewellyn Vaughan-Lee, a Jungian psychologist and teacher of Sufism, cautioned, "There are no rules for this work of discrimination except the simple practice of sincerity and self-awareness."[65]

At the end of every talk I give, my final slide is a photo of the ocean, overwritten with my best advice regarding discernment:

> Listen to the Message
> that Leads to the Love
> that Permeates the Universe.

Chapter Five

VISIONARY REALMS

I was sitting with Alyana, a woman guide from the Diné (Navajo) tribe, as she recounted a very traumatic childhood filled with sexual abuse from multiple male relatives. Despite her harrowing story, or perhaps as a result of her harrowing story, Alyana has warrior energy with clear intention and discipline for medicine diet. She prepared three months for her first ayahuasca ceremony, followed a traditional diet, took ten days off all electronic screens, had a massage, did sweat lodges and enemas, and finally a two-to-three-day fast. Even after all that preparation, she said the ceremony was frightening: "I didn't know if I'd come back out of it."

Alyana said she was trying to control what was happening in the ceremony, and "all of a sudden a door opened. I talked to my grandfather who appeared in the fireplace. I watched my childhood traumas replay like a movie in the dark. I purged and purged, pushing out memories from within my body, stored like pockets. I peed myself during the uncomfortable purging episodes. I shriveled and rocked myself, stared into the fire. Took a little water to purge whatever remained within, and after the last purge, I knew I was done and felt awake."

This was quite a journey — Alyana traveled in time and space, met people who were both dead and alive, saw her young self being abused. She said, "I took three doses, did the trauma work for all the women, generations before and after me. The shaman sang to me as I gave birth to my daughters all over again."

In the visionary realms, time, space, and causality no longer exist. Healing can happen beyond the present moment, reaching farther than the person in ceremony. We have no way of explaining this even with our sophisticated brain studies. Entheogens open us to visionary realms, and when we return to consensus reality, we are forever changed, just as Aldous Huxley described in *The Doors of Perception*: "[the person] who comes back through the Door in the Wall will never be quite the same as [the person] who went out."[1]

I've asked a lot of experienced travelers, "Where do you go when you journey?" No one knows but the best answer was, "There's no there, there." Yes, it's a mystery, but these are the visionary realms. They are ever-present and timeless; they interpenetrate with consensus reality. In the same way that fish don't realize they live in water, we don't realize we live *in* visionary realms. It's not that we travel *to* these realms; we wake up *in* these realms. And the psychedelic elders, with their thinner veils, swim in these waters.

Darlene, an underground guide from the lineages of the Diné (Navajo) and the Ash:wii (Zuni), described several incidents in her life that reflect the permeability between our consensus reality and the mysterious visionary realms. Darlene attended a conference in Oregon where a petite, Native American woman sat down next to her. "We had telepathic conversations. She said, *Granddaughter, you'll be given instruments of healing and you may not know what to do with them. Hang on to them and the teachers will appear.* I mentally asked, *Real? Guardian angels, ancestors,* the woman answered silently."

The story becomes a little vague here, as these kinds of stories do. It's hard to pin down concrete details when the story comes from a visionary realm. At a later time, in Arizona, Darlene exited a post office and got into her car in the parking lot. She said, "I noticed an old, '67 Chevy with a stepside parked next to me. An elderly Native American man gets out of the Chevy and comes over to my car and taps on my window. 'I have a gift I was told to give to you,' he says, and hands me long stems of white cedar wrapped in a bundle. 'Place them in a sacred space and keep them.'"

Then, the story continued.... At another time, Darlene visited a bookstore in Sedona, Arizona. A woman was working as a psychic at the bookstore, and she invited Darlene into the back room for a reading. She said, "As we sat, the psychic said, 'Someone wants to be with you. You have two questions you can ask.' The psychic closed her eyes and started to move her shoulders and her facial expression began to change." The petite Native American woman Darlene had met at the Oregon conference began to speak to her. Darlene recognized the laughter coming from this woman. "I asked, 'Are you the elder that I met in Oregon many years ago?'"

"You remember me?" the woman chuckled.

"What's your name?" Darlene asked.

The elder replied, "My name is Ma'a."

I've been to lots of conferences; I've even been to Sedona bookstores. Nothing like this has ever happened to me. Darlene's story reminds me of Baba Hari Dass's autobiography *Path Unfolds,* which contains story after story of his wandering around India dressed in a loincloth and meeting monks at every turn — crazy, enlightened, or all of the above. Both their stories are filled with serendipity, miracles, and unexpected help. Linear chronology, planning, and control have no place in how their stories unfold. In fact, Hari Dass's teacher told him, "One thing leads to another and the path unfolds by every event in life. Life is for learning."[2]

Radha described how she moves elegantly from one realm to another: "All of my dreams are ceremonies." She sees different plants in her dreams, hears new melodies for *icaros* (healing songs), and gets help with diagnoses for specific people coming to her for healing. In turn, she asks her apprentices, "What's happening to you in your dreams? What information is coming?" When a friend was dying in Mexico, Radha said, "I'll sing to her spirit." Here again, time and space are transcended. The visionary realm is not limited in those ways. We are all present; we are all together.

Klara started to see visions of a very old Shipibo woman with a pipe. In a dream, a ceremony, at the grocery store. Again, it's hard to pin down details in these stories. The women themselves don't really differentiate between the worlds. "She's with me always, not just in ceremony," Klara explained. "I can't separate myself from this woman." Klara asked her, "Who are you and what is this connection?"

Klara continued, "The spirits are so real for me. I see them in my dreams. They give me melodies." In ceremony, Father Tobacco is her ally for seeing with her eyes closed. Klara described one incident: "I had a quick vision of a man in the group as a five-year-old boy, and after the ceremony, I had a vision of him falling as a child. The man was about fifty years old. He called his mom to ask her about a fall.

"His mom said, 'When you were five years old, we went to a park with your uncle, and you fell off the monkey bars and you were in a concussion for days.' The senior shaman worked with this man, and he cried for the first time in his adult life."

Klara has been working for about a decade. Maureen, who has been working for decades, said, "This is how you learn to have more trust in nonordinary clues. It develops with practice." Maureen also talked about nuance in the visionary realms, how you can be expansive in these unseen worlds: "You can create space with your breath in yourself and in the other person." Now that's quite a statement. It goes beyond even time and space and envisions visionary realms as both inner and outer, between and within both people.

The Imaginal Realm

Henry Corbin, a scholar of Islamic mysticism, used the terms *mundus imaginalis* or *the imaginal* to describe this mysterious reality. As psychologist Mary Watkins wrote, "By using the term, 'imaginal,' Corbin hoped to undercut the real-unreal distinction, and to propose instead that the imaginal not be assessed in terms of a narrow conception of 'reality,' but a broader one which gives credence to the reality of the imaginal."[3]

Unfortunately, the word *imaginal* is so close to the word *imaginary* that people confuse the two. Corbin tried to avoid exactly this confusion, writing: "I had to find a new expression to avoid misleading the Western reader, who, on the contrary, has to be roused from his old engrained way of thinking in order to awaken him to another order of things."[4] This was not quite a new enough expression for us sleepy Western readers, as Corbin came to realize. He said, "If this term [imaginal] is used to apply to anything other than the *mundus imaginalis* and the Forms as they are located in the schema of the worlds which necessitate them and legitimize them, there is a great danger that the terms will be degraded and its meaning be lost."[5]

For example, it's way too tempting to equate the imaginal realm with Jung's collective unconscious, as some do in an attempt to simplify.[6] We have access to the collective unconscious every night when we dream or when we enter into fairy tales or myths. We don't have to be transformed to enter into that world, nor do we mistake the collective unconscious for being more real than our daily life.

In contrast, the visionary or imaginal realm is, as Corbin wrote, "a very precise order of reality, which corresponds to a precise mode of perception."[7] It lies invisible between "the empirical world of the senses [and] the abstract world of the intellect....It's a real world which is neither the sensible world nor the world of abstract concepts." Corbin said it's a world that is ontologically as real as the world of the senses and of the intellect. Episcopal priest Cynthia Bourgeault described the imaginal realm as "invisible but always interpenetrating."[8]

The precise mode of perception is the imaginative power, which is "a purely spiritual faculty independent of the physical organism and consequently surviving it," Corbin wrote.[9] This faculty is a function of the spiritual heart, not the anatomical heart or even the emotional or sentimental heart. This heart is capable of seeing through the veil. Psychologist James Hillman wrote, "The heart's way of perceiving is both a sensing and an imagining: to sense penetratingly we must imagine, and to imagine accurately we must sense."[10]

Sufi poet Rumi wrote, "Everyone sees the unseen in proportion to the clarity of his heart, and that depends upon how much he has polished it. Whoever has polished it more sees more — more unseen forms become manifest to him."[11] However we polish our heart is the way we can perceive and enter into visionary realms. Of course, psychedelics help — they open portals.

Professors Angela Voss and William Rowlandson warned

that "the rational mind simply cannot grasp the totality of such gnostic insight and if it tries to do so will inevitably reduce it to its own parameters of vision, often with a lofty disparagement of its validity."[12] Corbin had his own concerns in this department: "We must make a real effort to overcome what one might call Western man's 'agnostic reflex,' since it is responsible for the divorce between thinking and being."[13]

I must admit to my own agnostic reflex. It's my first reaction, entrenched from my childhood family, honed by Western education, and topped off by thirty-five years of private psychotherapy practice — we are who we are because of previous experience and trauma, not to mention our genetic loading. Clearly a causative approach, drenched in linear time, and partial to blaming others. But things happen in these invisible realms that go beyond these limits, as Alyana described when she felt her ceremony healed the generations before and after her. Most psychotherapists don't think like that. The closest they might approach this possibility is via family systems theory, in which if one person changes, then that changes the whole system and allows others to change. But that's not quite what Alyana is saying. This is precisely how we can water down what happens in the visionary realm so that it fits into our preconceived notions. She says the generations before and after her were healed in the ceremony *as* she was healed. This kind of healing occurs in visionary realms and then manifests in consensus reality.

Tenzin Priyadarshi wrote about a visionary realm experience he had while staying in the monastery with one of his teachers, Sasaki. In the middle of the night, he went to Sasaki's room and was startled to see that "the whole room was flooded with a blinding light....Sasaki was lit by the firelight and yet at the same time silhouetted, his profile stark against a blazing circle of light, edged in tongues of flame." The next day, his teacher told him, "What you saw last night was for you only.... There are other ways of knowing and engaging with the world that are also valid.... The reality we encounter in our day-to-day lives is less solid than it appears.[14]

Becoming Well Traveled

The underground guides I interviewed are exceedingly well-traveled in these imaginal realms. To be more concrete, they have taken most every psychedelic in most every dose. They are enthusiastic explorers.

In contrast, I felt I had an obligation to experience ketamine for the first time while writing about these visionary realms, even though it's not technically a psychedelic but a dissociative. Personally, I was wary of ketamine. When I was living at Esalen in the late sixties, I witnessed the esteemed scientist John Lilly become a shadow of his former self when he was clearly in the throes of an addiction to this drug. To be clear: I had my ketamine experience at an aboveground clinic with a medical doctor and therapist present for the entire five hours. And I traveled.

It's perhaps this ketamine experience, even more than my varied underground experiences, that has broken through my agnostic reflex. My personal self was missing during most of the journey, so all that was present were these amazing landscapes of light as if the world had turned into a translucent ice palace, almost like a stereotypical heavenly realm. And then another world opened up from the earth below with primordial caves and unexplored depths. Whenever I remembered myself, I was in awe. The two women sitters took turns holding my hand even though I had told them I didn't need it. Surely that's a lesson for all sitters — often clients don't know what they need or they have trouble asking for or accepting help. I was all of the above and immensely grateful for their hand-holding, since I felt like they were grounding the string of a balloon that could easily float away.

Most of the current generation of psychedelic therapists do not have the extensive personal experience that the underground elders do. They do not have years of ecstatic and challenging journeys and all the in-between ones. They simply haven't had and don't have the time to explore. The current batch of psychedelic therapists are needed immediately as these medicines become available to a general public awash in depression and anxiety.

There's even some current professional discussion about whether or not psychedelic therapists need to have their own journeys. This would certainly seem nonsensical to the underground elders, as part of their code of ethics is never to serve a medicine they haven't personally experienced. In fact, as I was finishing an interview with Rose, she was just starting to drink the ayahuasca concoction she was planning to serve the next night. "I have to try it myself first," she told me.

It's important to admit, though, that something is lost in the current professional haste. It might be in the preparatory session discussions about navigation in visionary realms. There could be a depth of confidence missing during challenging moments in session. Or an inability to follow a client into realms not yet experienced. Afterward, there just might be a lack of recognition as the traveler unspools the journey for self-reflection and integration. The women elders have been changed, each in her own way, by years of journeying. Their veils are thinner, they transition between worlds with greater ease, they have faced death and returned. Without these years of experience, a mysterious element is missing. It's better to acknowledge that something has been lost; that way, the new batch of psychedelic therapists will be alert to their own limits and able to learn from them.

Other Ways of Knowing

In a 2010 interview, Stan Grof mentioned the value of a "heuristic perspective" for psychedelic journeys.[15] I had to look up the word: *heuristic* means to discover or learn something for oneself, as in experiential learning. What better description could there be for what happens during and after a psychedelic journey? So much emphasis has been placed recently on ego dissolution, complete mystical experience, and emotional breakthrough that we're overlooking an essential process.

Although it's impossible to clarify exactly what the psychedelic elders have learned, it's clear that they live in a different world than the rest of us. They tend to be quite private. Many work through the night in totally discrete ceremonies. The women are open to receiving messages from the natural world in the form of symbolic events, whether a bird call, wild animal sighting, or wind shift. These events seem meaningless or, at best, obtuse to most of us, but such signs can be important signals for people trained in the sensitive art of tracking. So what are the women elders tracking?

I think the women are tracking nuances at the interface of the material world and the visionary realm. I think they're tracking subtle shifts in their own state of consciousness as they receive knowledge or intuitions. They're building trust in their subtle perceptions, which accrues over years of practice with medicine journeys. This approach to learning is an example of gnosis, which religious scholar Egil Asprem calls "an approach to knowledge that is unmediated, direct, transcendent, ineffable knowledge."[16]

In the introduction to *Transpersonal Knowing*, the authors identify themes involved in this kind of learning: "authenticity — that this is one's own knowing; immediacy — there is little or no conceptual mediation; connectedness — the boundaries that separate and create the sense of an isolated self seem to dissolve; and transformative capacity — the knower is changed by the knowing and, at the same time, openness to change in one's sense of identity opens one to the knowing."[17]

This last statement is the best description of lifelong learning with entheogens. The learning is not about content; it's about transformation. Entering imaginal realms again and again, the underground elders are changed by these experiences. Unseen others in the visionary realms continue to work on them long after the ceremony. The women develop a strong faith based on experience that goes beyond belief and rests securely in certainty. After spending hours with them, I get a sense that their physical bodies are less solid than the rest of us. They've thinned, not only the veil separating worlds, but the corporality of material existence.

I'm not saying these women are enlightened, awakened, or perfect. I'm not idolizing the psychedelic guides, but they do have some of the most extensive entheogenic experience in our culture, and they have been changed by these experiences. It's the inner transformation that opens the portals to the visionary realms. As Corbin expert Tom Cheetham described, "Entry into the imaginal signals not a change of place, but a change in your mode of being....It involves a kind of opening. And mystics tell us, the openings go on forever."[18]

As I try to pin down this ineffable process of learning through years of journeys, I keep returning to Maureen's statement: "You can create space with your breath in yourself and in the other person." I even called her to ask her what she meant by this or what more she could say about it. It's a statement that only makes sense in the crack between worlds. I understand it to mean that, as Maureen opens up her inner space with a breath, her client receives the benefit of an expanded inner space. Of course, she couldn't explain how this works, but she had the best retort, "What don't you understand about it?" We both broke up in laughter. Then she went on to say this can only happen in the moment, when she's totally present, in the ineffable now.

Making a Lifelong Commitment

The women psychedelic elders have been engaged in a gnostic approach to learning for decades. They started with their own healing and continued by deepening their relationships with the medicines. And then, of course, they began to work underground with clients. Each of these stages is distinct even though they overlap and continue into the present. The elder guides are still working on their own healing and deepening their connection to the medicines. This is their commitment to themselves, to the medicines, and to their clients. How many of the newly hatched psychedelic psychotherapists have this kind of dedication? What are we losing?

I have to admit that I was at first taken aback when I heard Medridth, the eldest of the elders at eighty-seven years old, enthusiastically say she "wanted to do another ketamine journey." But now I've heard similar statements from many others. Kendra Smith, who describes her history-making trip at Timothy Leary's house in chapter 1, said recently that she'd like another journey — at ninety-eight years old. Albert Hofmann, the chemist who discovered LSD, took one last trip at age ninety-seven.[19] And there is the famous story of Aldous Huxley going out with a final injection of LSD. His wife Laura described this last trip in a letter to family: "Aldous' asking for moksha medicine while dying is a confirmation of his work, and as such, is of importance not only to us, but to the world."[20]

Rather than being a treatment for specific symptoms, the medicines are a part of life, used in many ways throughout a life span, reminiscent of the way the Eleusinian Mysteries were embedded in the ancient culture. People would return to Eleusis at least once a year for the sacred ceremonies to connect to the divine and to learn about the afterlife as a preparation for death. Many of the women talked about how their medicine journeys are an integral part of their lives. Cedar said, "I say no to people who want to [journey] regularly…even though I do journey yearly." Debbie, one of the elders, expressed the central importance of the medicines in her world by saying, "I have my life in psychedelics." She added, "The more you work [with the medicines], the more your heart opens." Maureen explained, "Medicine journeys are a lifelong path," and then she reflected, "I hope the hard stuff's over with." The women elders are in agreement that entheogens are part of their life's work on themselves and in the world.

Medridth described her approach as being a "more spiritual way of working with the medicines," in contrast to what the research protocols prescribe. "What we do is more esoteric, still hidden, more internal, intuitive. We would need to be underground even if they [the medicines] become legal as a medical treatment."

Medridth continued: "I follow an intuitive process. I just know. I have a deep relationship with each medicine. There's one source inside me, a mystical place. All learned via medicines."

Medridth specializes in working with women, helping them to realize their potential, helping them "clear out stuff they don't need like competition, putting self or other women down." She sees her role as a good sister. Medridth is actually being humble here, as she's also a spiritual teacher to many of her beloved sisters.

A Larger Perspective

Here's my story about learning from Medridth, which has nothing to do with the medicines and of course everything to do with the medicines. However, neither of us was in an expanded state. I had already interviewed Medridth twice, a few hours each visit. But I had one more burning question that I thought I could ask in a phone call, since I didn't want to intrude on her for yet another meeting. I was visiting the Conservatory of Flowers in Golden Gate Park, and at the appointed time, I walked out of the humid world of great, green-growing plants and called Medridth.

"I have one quick question," I said. "Is the bottom line all about taking responsibility for ourselves, our lives? Is this what it's all about?"

Without hesitation, Medridth said yes. Then she explained, "We are responsible for our intentions and our choices. Responsible to ourselves and to humanity."

For me, this message was both enlightening and personally helpful. When I lived at Esalen in the late sixties, Fritz Perls, the founder of Gestalt therapy, was at his peak. He preached an extreme version of self-responsibility, but unfortunately, his message was riddled with his typical misanthropic attitude that basically came out as a "fuck you" to others and the world. I was in my early twenties, trying to figure out how to be a grown-up. While I learned a lot from Fritz about freedom from other people's expectations, I couldn't filter out the "fuck you" from his message of self-responsibility.

Medridth also studied with Fritz Perls, but her message of self-responsibility is infused with love and compassion, both for self and others. She goes beyond self-responsibility to our responsibility to humanity, which is a far broader perspective and identity. She avoids blaming anyone else for anything in any circumstance, which is the same sentiment expressed in the poem "Invictus": "I am the master of my fate / I am the captain of my soul."[21] These words helped Nelson Mandela survive intact through twenty-seven years of imprisonment in

South Africa, so that when he returned to the world, he was able to help heal it.

The same message is inherent in logotherapy, which was founded by psychiatrist Viktor Frankl and based on his experiences in a concentration camp during World War II. Frankl wrote, "Fundamentally, therefore, any man can, even under such circumstances, decide what shall become of him — mentally and spiritually."[22] His concept of self-responsibility was to develop the inner freedom to choose one's attitude, independent of external reality. Bishop Desmond Tutu presented another version of this theme in a film celebrating his friendship with the Dalai Lama: "You can overcome the most horrendous circumstances and emerge on the other side not broken."[23]

This level of self-responsibility lifts us out of the usual psychotherapeutic approach to understanding and possibly blaming parents, external conditions, and ex-spouses for our current woes. After all, we can work on our personal history the whole rest of our lives and never change. There comes an existential point when we have to get over ourselves and over our stories about ourselves.

As a psychotherapist, however, I have to add that this level of responsibility builds on a foundation of therapeutic work regarding parents, external conditions, and exes where we learn to recognize our defensive patterns, emotional constrictions, and rigidities. This is ongoing work as our self-awareness and objectivity develop. We cannot skip this foundational level of work via spiritual bypassing. This is the most common mistake in working therapeutically with entheogens. Spiritual experiences don't necessarily lead to ethical behavior, and if we don't clean up our personal history, we are likely to act out old issues in ways that are harmful to others as well as ourselves.

One of the women elders, Charlotte, was clear that she

didn't want to do this kind of foundational work with entheogens Instead, she specializes in working with high-functioning clients for, she said, the "wellness of well people…who have the capability, resources, and inclination to act for the betterment of the world." These people "already have a therapeutic process," from either previous or concurrent therapy. Her preference reminds me of the stance Carl Jung took later in his life — he only wanted to work with people who had already completed Jungian analysis. As Hillman and Shamdasani wrote, he "recommended that people had psychotherapy *before* they came to him, and that they needed a preparation that should be gotten elsewhere."[24] This "preparation" is the personal history work, the foundational therapy working on parents, childhood circumstances, and relationship trauma. Jung wanted to focus on visionary realms with patients, using active imagination to encounter figures and allowing the presence of these unseen others to unfold in the patients' lives.

Accordingly, Charlotte doesn't want to see the psychedelic medicines limited by the medical model, which requires a diagnosis to qualify for therapy. She maintains that the medicines have a "bigger message, larger than individual psychological healing." She believes the medicines "want us to wake up to our inherent connection as part of nature, to stop destruction threatening our own extinction." She said the "medicines propel people into a greater place of empathy and compassion and focus on how to make the world-at-large a better place." Accordingly, she wants to see her clients take action in the outer world and not just be "hooked on experience."

"A ceremonial ritual speaks deeply to the psyche," explained Charlotte. She's interested in how psychedelics create bonding among participants, leading to a sense of tribal community. Journeyers learn how to use the symbolic world, to receive guidance and information that leads to creative breakthroughs.

Charlotte said, "I know I'm a heretic on this, but..." She hesitated before describing a small network of trusted friends who have been journeying together for decades and "not always with a guide."

Not always journeying with a guide is, yes, heretical. But the truth is that it's not unusual for very, very experienced people to gather in small, trusted groups to journey together. This doesn't mean any of them would recommend this practice to others. There's a basic rule that one person should always be straight, in consensus reality. I think Charlotte was brave to share with me this aspect of her life, and I think it reflects another way that entheogens can be a spiritual practice for a lifetime.

Practice for Death and Dying

Psychedelic elder Ann Shulgin wrote, "The death door is an actual experience which most explorers in the world of the human psyche will eventually encounter. It takes many forms, most of them gently welcoming, and its message is, 'Here is the way back home, when you decide to return.' It does not seduce or entice; it's just there."[25]

The death door was such a common experience that Ann included a rule about dying as part of the four agreements she insisted upon for a guided MDMA journey: "If you (the patient) should see the friendly death door and know that, by stepping through it, you can be done with this life, you will NOT do so during this session. You will not end your life in such a way, when you are here with me, because such an act would cause me great injury, and you will not injure me, as I will not injure you."

Ann acknowledged that "this rule may sound cold and uncaring," but it was intended to shock the client into realizing that they are entering into a life-and-death situation. She explained that a few deeply depressed patients have been tempted to go through the door but were sent back. However, she did hear of one person's death, and she said there might be more who stayed on the other side of the death door. "The therapist in such a case faces not only her patient's death, but the inevitable legal and professional disaster that results from it." This example provides a clue to the kinds of risks that the underground elders accept as part of their calling.

I know of a suicide attempt unrelated to psychedelic journeys in which the woman went through a tunnel to arrive at a door, and the door wouldn't open. She said she sat in the tunnel a long time in front of this locked door. Then she came back. She survived the suicide attempt and never tried again. "It was too frustrating, just being stuck there, at the door."

Even more common than the death-door experience is a life review, which might include a remembering, a vivid viewing like a movie, or an actual reliving of scenes from the past — traumatic events, significant milestones, joyous occasions. When this happens during an entheogenic journey, time is compressed, and the voyager often feels as though they've been gone a long time or everything happens in a flash.

The concept of a life review, sans psychedelics, was first described by Robert Butler, the founding director of the National Institute on Aging, who said the life review was a naturally occurring and universal reflective process, a normal developmental task of old age or when facing one's mortality. This was not a simple process of reminiscence, but an active reconsideration of life experiences that, at best, leads to a reorganization of personality, providing new and significant meaning and, at the same time, preparation for death.[26]

In addition to whatever neurological explanation exists for psychedelic life reviews, it could also happen because we think

or fear we're going to die as in a near-death experience (NDE).
Besides the common refrain after an ayahuasca ceremony, "I'm
never doing this again," a frequent response to psychedelics is,
"I thought I wasn't coming back. I thought I was going to die."
At the moment of letting go, just as the ego melts, there can
arise a fear of dying. This confrontation with our own mortality
might be part of what sparks a life-review process even if we're
not in the latter part of life.

There's an intuitive connection between ego dissolution
during entheogenic journeys and near-death experiences. Both
lead to a more-spiritual, less-materialistic approach to life
with an emphasis on personal relationships, nature connectedness, greater well-being, and most importantly here, a marked
decrease in the fear of death. Two studies indicated a similarity between near-death experiences and ketamine or injected
DMT.[27] A third study, comparing psychedelic ego dissolution
and NDEs, "hypothesized that neurophysiological mechanisms underlying NDEs could be activated spontaneously or
in non-life-threatening situations where the physical threat is
only perceived and not necessarily actual," as in a psychedelic
journey.[28]

Stan Grof said entheogenic journeys offer "real experiential training for dying [via] compelling encounters with death,
so profound and shattering as to be indistinguishable from
actual biological annihilation."[29] He quoted a patient who had
an LSD session and then had an NDE: "Without the [LSD]
session, I would have been scared by what was happening [in
the NDE], but knowing these states, I was not afraid at all."[30]

Since an entheogenic journey often includes a confrontation with mortality, it makes sense that it could also stimulate
a life review. The best outcome of a near-death experience, a
life-shattering psychedelic journey, and a life review is that all
lead to a reorganization of personality with a greater level of
peaceful acceptance of one's own mortality.

This level of acceptance is not typical in our Western culture — we prefer to ignore the fact of death while modern medicine inanely tries to prevent it at all costs. However, there are exceptions. As Shamdasani wrote, Jung argued that "death should be seen as a goal rather than an end, and he designated the latter part of life as 'life toward death.'"[31]

I'm in the latter part of my life, and dear friends are dropping like flies all around me. It's disconcerting to say the least. I feel like I've entered the death zone on Mt. Everest where the brightly colored, high-tech tents cling to the rocky terrain while the wind tries to blow them off. On Mt. Everest, 14 percent of climbers die. In life, 100 percent of us die no matter how desperately we cling to this world. To raise our awareness of living toward death, as Jung suggested, we can sign up for the app WeCroak, which is inspired by a Bhutanese folk saying: To be a happy person, one must contemplate death five times a day.[32]

Other cultures have more traditional rituals that embrace the reality of death and impermanence, like meditating on charnel grounds. Arielle told me the story of her visit to Tibet with a group of friends, including Stan Grof. It just so happened that the 9/11 terrorist attacks occurred on the same day they were overlooking the Sky Burial site where bodies are prepared by monks and set out on the plateau to be devoured by vultures. Stan gave these words of advice: "This is a sacred ceremony. I suggest you open yourself to this experience and be fully present. How you respond to this ceremony will tell you about your relationship with death." Arielle described how she stood silently in the thin air, with reverence, witnessing the vultures land and tear.

Psychedelic guides sit with people as they encounter death in their journey. The guide's relationship to death will inevitably be present in the setting. Difficult moments will erupt. The wife of Aldous Huxley, Laura Huxley, framed the challenge like this: "The most difficult thing for you as a guide is to not have an opinion, to let the person [get] whatever he feels, whatever he sees."[33] Guides must do this even in the most difficult of moments. This is a position of dispassionate nonattachment.

I've only seen this kind of dispassionate position a few times in my life. Once was an interview at the Rubin Museum of Art where a Tibetan monk told the story of his capture and torture by a Chinese army captain…for years. When the monk was finally freed, an opportunity arose for him to meet this army officer. The monk was neither angry nor vengeful. He was simply himself, open and cheery. The Chinese captain fell at his feet. I listened spellbound, seeing no signs of trauma or resentment as the Tibetan monk shared his story.

The other example is quite recent. A sixty-seven-year-old friend of mine is dying of glioblastoma, an inoperable brain tumor. All his adult life he's been a serious spiritual student. About his inevitable demise, he wrote in an email to me, "I have no attachment and no aversion to what happens."

Medridth maintains this position of dispassion as she works with people. She said that she's "able to see a person's potential. I connect with it to help you strengthen and manifest your potential. I hold space for it. I can recognize it because I'm already connected. In life, all petty tyrants are our teachers. I use this in ceremony." This keeps Medridth from getting attached or "feeling that I have to change you or have an agenda for you. I'm very clear about keeping out of it. I'm not responsible for your evolution process."

Medridth's position is that a person can "let go of stuff they don't need — stuff from childhood, trauma, personal history, past lives, karma. They can become less of a victim unless they want to continue for a payoff. It's their choice."

These are strong statements, especially when working with

people who are close to death, when they are in the process of life review, reflecting upon the meaning in their life and whether they have lived up to their potential and their destiny, whether they did their spiritual job, as I call it. Or whether they even identified their spiritual job.

Whether months, weeks, or days, the time before death is ripe with opportunity to resolve unfinished business that becomes salient during a life review. The dying person has the chance to heal relationships, accept personal failures, and face themselves in a far more honest and conscious way. The dying person can rise above their personal identity, forgive themselves from a larger perspective, and share love with their family and friends. It's their choice, as Medridth would say, according to their conviction for self-responsibility.

A teacher of "orphan wisdom," Stephen Jenkinson wrote in *Die Wise*, "Dying changes what life means if you are willing....You can change how you understand your life....I've taught for years that dying must be allowed to change everything. You might think it inevitable that dying has that power, but a couple of decades in the death trade persuaded me without doubt that there is nothing inevitable about it. It is enormously hard work, to get your dying to tell your life's story."[34]

This opportunity to expand even as death approaches was recognized in the first round of psychedelic research during the fifties and sixties. One of the earliest studies gave a shot of 100 micrograms of LSD to eighty terminal cancer patients in hopes of reducing the anguish and stress of dying. The research findings showed that "the patients gained a special type of insight from this experience...making them more responsive to their environment and family," along with a greater "acceptance and surrender to the inevitable loss of control."[35]

In a 1970 article, psychiatrist Walter Pahnke reported that terminal patients had a more positive mood and less anxiety after LSD sessions. Their increased openness and honesty allowed for greater resolution in their interpersonal relationships, and they were more willing and able "to live each moment fully for the here and now."[36]

These historical findings set the stage for psychedelic compassionate care for the dying. A New York University psilocybin study for terminal cancer patients focused on the degree of demoralization, which it described as "a measurable form of existential distress characterized by poor coping and a sense of helplessness, and a loss of meaning and purpose in life."[37] Demoralization is associated with higher levels of discomfort and pain, anxiety, depression, and suicidal thoughts. The psilocybin journeys were seen as a spiritual intervention to ease demoralization as death approached. The study authors wrote: "Access to the transpersonal realm has the potential to alter a terminal cancer patient's perspective to their existential suffering."

Psychologist Tony Bossis, one of the study's authors, emphasized the importance of the therapeutic relationship surrounding the psilocybin experience and the support that relationship provides to encourage the patient to turn toward their feelings around dying. He wrote, "While difficult, by turning toward suffering, [the patients] spoke about experiencing a greater acceptance and openness to the mystery of death."[38]

The best example of the importance of an experienced guide who understands both the possibility of terror and the need for surrender is from one of the terminal patients in the study: "It really hit me strong. And it was terrifying....Absolutely nothing, nothing to anchor myself to, nothing, no point of reference, nothing, just lost in space, just crazy, and I was so scared. And then I remembered that Tony and Michelle were right there and suddenly realized why it was so important that

I get to know them, and they get to know me....I think it was Tony who took my hand and said, 'It's all right. Just go with it. Go with it.' And I did."[39]

That's the point of surrender, which can go either way — toward resistance and a terribly challenging experience or toward ego dissolution and an ecstatic unity with all things. It's at this point in the journey that the presence of the guide is critical. Tony's words were simple but no doubt spoken from his depth of understanding and experience. And the patient trusted him.

For most of us, it's not an instinctual response to move toward what looks like more suffering. Learning to do so is a navigational skill practiced in journeys. This capacity to trust the medicine, trust the guide, and surrender is an essential skill when facing our own physical demise. It constitutes a different relationship to death.

With their history of psychedelic experiences, the baby boom generation faces death with precisely this skill — letting go into dissolution and the unknown. When one of my friends met with his doctor to receive the news that he was terminal, he responded, "I've done a lot of acid in my life. I'm ready." He had traveled with the Grateful Dead in his youth and he was true to his word. He spent his last year designing and building a base for a dining table, lovingly working the wood into a smooth shine — part of his legacy. When we have dinner around this table, we think of him.

As we witness how our loved ones die, we learn about how to die — perhaps like them, perhaps not at all like them. We see a range of how to approach what one friend of mine calls "the final exam." With my recent spate of dear friends dying, I've come to the conclusion that one of the final challenges is to accept that one is loved and to allow that love to really permeate our being, to enter into our heart. Finally. To let go of all the defenses that we think are protecting us but are also defending us against the vulnerability of feeling loved.

The overwhelming experience of feeling loved during an entheogenic journey is both healing and preparation for dying. This is a numinous experience that reaches the heights described by Sufi teacher Hazrat Inayat Khan: "She [Love] took me gently by my arms and lifted me above the earth, and spoke softly in my ear, 'My dear one, thou thyself art love, art lover, and thyself art the beloved whom thou hast adored.'"[40]

This ecstatic psychedelic experience makes real the lines from "Desiderata" by Max Ehrmann: "Be gentle with yourself. You are a child of the universe no less than the trees and the stars; you have a right to be here."[41] Even atheists report feeling rocked in the arms of God at this point in the entheogenic journey. Experienced guides recognize when this happens during a journey and know to remain silent, sharing in the sacred moment.

There is another way the medicines prepare us for death — they help us shift from a materialistic worldview to one that knows we're more than our bodies.[42] This has been a particularly difficult shift for me to make and sustain even after many journeys — even after I sense a connection to an essence that's beyond my physical reality and beyond my personal identity, something that transcends the "me" I live with. The journeys have brought me to this eternal thread from before birth to after death, throughout this lifetime. Something I've always known and forgotten many times. The medicines remind us of this other reality.

I've traveled to visionary realms and held long conversations with loved ones who died years ago. I've risen out of my body to be greeted by voices who reassure me, *You won't be alone.* I think the elder psychedelic guides sense that I've been there, and this is part of the reason they've confided in me, shared their secret lives with me. Journeying into visionary realms is an initiation that prepares us for the final journey. And it's good to have a guide on both sides of the veil.

Chapter Six

SOMATIC SENSING

It was Freud who said, "The ego is first, and foremost, a body ego."[1] We become who we are in the first few years of life as we learn to live in this body, in this world — learning to breathe air for starters, learning to survive in the family we've chosen or landed in depending on our belief system. The ego emerges gradually as our neurons connect and we find ways to move in our newborn body and discover we have personal agency. We learn we can make things happen, even if it's just rolling over at a few months of age. Such agency "is the technical term for the feeling of being in charge of your life," as Bessel van der Kolk wrote.[2] Of course, no baby is in charge, but figuring out how to make something happen, even just turning over, leads to a feeling of personal agency. This is the very beginning of a sense of what's me and what's not-me; some things I can make happen and some things happen from outside of me.

It used to be thought that this distinction between me and not-me developed over months, but recent studies have shown that "infants discriminate between perceptual events that are either self- or not self-produced."[3] In other words, we are born with some level of awareness of a boundary between inner and outer. French psychoanalyst Didier Anzieu called this boundary between mother and infant the "skin-ego" and emphasized "the importance of the body in the process of becoming 'myself.'"[4]

Mothers intuitively know how important and sensitive a newborn's skin is and select the softest of soft receiving blankets to welcome their baby. Numerous studies have found that preterm infants who receive massage therapy, which reinforces the skin-ego, gain weight faster than those who don't receive massage.[5] Psychiatrist Daniel Stern's careful, fraction-of-a-second, frame-by-frame observations of the mother-infant dyad have emphasized touch as well as attunement in facial expressions. This has led to the therapeutic realization that the relationship is the focus, not two separate individuals.[6] Given the recent emphasis on the dyadic dance between mother and infant, Freud's concept of the body ego may be reformulated "as a body-in-relation ego."[7]

What does all this have to do with entheogenic journeys? Think of ego dissolution. What's dissolved? By definition, the ego, which is first and foremost a body ego. Our skin-ego melts away. We are no longer our bodies, as we are no longer ourselves. The boundary between inner and outer disappears, and we enter into the unity mystical experience.

In the research studies that have initiated the current psychedelic renaissance, great emphasis has been placed on the unity-type mystical experience, and perhaps this is as it should be given the impressive therapeutic results.[8] The Mystical Experience Questionnaire currently used at Johns Hopkins includes the following factors: mystical/unitive, positive mood, transcendence of time and space, and ineffability.[9] The unitive component is the dissolution of an inner/outer boundary.

The underground psychedelic elders work with these

medicines in a very different way. In contrast with the research studies, which use a cost-effective treatment approach to a psychiatric diagnosis, the women guides work with the medicines as part of the sacred journey of life. In fact, I've heard a few of them complain about people coming to them specifically to have a mystical experience. For example, Janet explained, "Since Michael Pollan's book came out, I get calls from people looking for a mushroom sitter. Just reading the research results from Johns Hopkins and elsewhere, it's easy to have unrealistic expectations." Nothing, of course, is guaranteed.

There are a plethora of other experiences that can arise during an entheogenic journey that have been overlooked. In this chapter, I'm interested in experiences that have to do with the skin-ego or the boundary between inner and outer.

One example is Beth, a forty-year-old professor, who attended her first ayahuasca ceremony. Beth told me how she experienced the presence of her dead father. She was glad to connect with him. Then she felt him move into her body. In other words, Beth's skin-ego, her boundary between inner and outer, was porous. She didn't choose to let him in; it just happened. And Beth was uncomfortable — she didn't want her father's presence to cross her personal boundary into her body, and she didn't know how to extricate him. I didn't know Beth's personal history regarding any previous boundary violations with her father from her childhood or with anyone later in life. Had we been in a therapeutic context, that would have surely been my next question.

I could tell, however, that Beth would score very high on the Tellegen Absorption Scale (see page 109). She was creative and open with a very thin veil. Before the ayahuasca ceremony, she'd had spontaneous experiences in expanded states of consciousness. Beth's absorption personality trait also made her very susceptible to anything said to her during or around the time of the ceremony, even more so than the usual suggestibility typical of a psychedelic experience.

The next morning Beth told the woman coleading the ceremony about her experience and her discomfort. This woman has about two decades of experience (meaning, for me, she would've qualified as an underground guide in this book), and she said something to Beth like, "You should have been grateful to have your father visit you during the ceremony."

Beth felt shamed. She didn't mean to be ungrateful, but she knew she was disturbed by her experience.

I can't keep track of the number of unhelpful comments from so-called guides or shamans that people have reported to me about their psychedelic experiences. This is usually when my conversation with the person turns therapeutic.

"I'm sorry she said that to you. She didn't really understand what happened," I told Beth.

Beth was immediately relieved. She was a mature woman who knew herself, but she was more vulnerable because of her porous skin-ego, the recent ceremony, and the leader's position of power. Bottom line, Beth was gaslighted, told her feelings were invalid. She was shamed by the leader. This was precisely the wrong thing to happen to her at this susceptible time and after feeling her personal boundary had been crossed.

I don't expect every guide or ceremony leader to be a psychotherapist, but I think they do have to be very careful what they say to people immediately after the experience. They have to know how vulnerable and suggestible people are at that time. It would be helpful for all guides to understand how people who score higher on the absorption trait have a more porous skin-ego and may be more open to unwanted experiences during ceremony. In fact, these same people may also need lower doses of the medicine as they shift states of consciousness more easily.

Awareness: Inner and Outer

Western culture, with its emphasis on appearance, highlights the musculoskeletal body, which provides proprioceptive information or awareness of the position and movement of the body. Think sports, modeling, dance. Exteroception is the perception of the outside world via all of our senses. In contrast, interoception is the felt sense of the internal state of the body, both conscious and unconscious.[10] It's a neglected sense in our culture, but over the last decade, as one commentator wrote, "there has been a six-fold increase in [scientific] publications on interoception."[11]

This attention has been cross-disciplinary from philosophy to neuroscience, often with an emphasis on how interoception leads to a felt sense of self. Psychiatrist Bessel van der Kolk has built on neurologist Antonio Damasio's work[12] to conclude that "the core of our self-awareness rests on the physical sensations that convey the inner states of the body."[13] At this point, we are back to Freud and the body ego.

Psychologist Wolf Mehling developed a method for measuring different aspects of interoceptive awareness. Examples of items in the scale include: "When I am tense I notice where the tension is located in my body. I notice changes in my breathing, such as whether it slows down or speeds up. I can refocus my attention from thinking to sensing my body. I notice how my body changes when I am angry."[14] As with other psychological measures, there's a range of variability in levels of sensitivity and vigilance relative to the awareness of internal workings of the body.[15] This capacity for inner awareness can also be trained via mindfulness meditation, for instance, or a variety of body/mind approaches or athletics. My daughter is an opera singer, and her decades of voice lessons focused mainly on interoceptive awareness from breath training to voice placement — all internal and taught largely by metaphor and listening. In martial arts, the teacher asks for more centeredness in a movement or for energy that extends from within to beyond the physical body.

One of the most fascinating examples of interoception is described in Matthew Sanford's memoir *Waking*. Matthew became a paraplegic at age thirteen after a catastrophic car accident. The medical assessment was that he would have no feeling whatsoever in his lower body. However, he found his own path of recovery — not through movement but by developing presence throughout his entire body. He wrote, "I must reach intuitively into what may feel like darkness," and "It is simply a matter of learning to listen to a different level of presence, to realizing that the silence within my paralysis is not loss. In fact, it is both awake and alive."[16] There are levels in somatic awareness, some as fine as gossamer threads, almost imperceptible, but when embodied, they can mean everything.

Psychedelic experience also provides an expansive array of interoceptive experiences, from the traditional ayahuasca purges to energetic streaming through chakras. And interoceptive awareness plays a key role in integration following entheogenic experience. As the journeyer becomes more sensitive to internal bodily states, they can notice the initial stirrings of emotional reactions in their daily lives. By catching these interoceptive signals early, they create a chance to decide how to manage the arising emotions. This is that very brief bit of space before we react, and it embodies the everyday wisdom to count to ten before we say anything in anger we might regret. This is something I still struggle with, most recently at an ayahuasca church meeting. Ironic, I know.

Physician Drew Leder added an important consideration that "interoceptive experience is never 'pure sensation' but always shaped by interpretation," our cultural milieu.[17] In 1968, when I arrived at the Esalen residential program directly out of college, I realized immediately that I had entered a totally different cultural milieu. The program focused on meditation and body work, both of which value interoception, and I had a knack for it. I would've scored high on the above scale.

Developmentally, I was twenty-one and still trying to "find myself," and at Esalen, I had the opportunity to experience the major body/mind approaches of that time. My burgeoning sense of self became rooted in these experiences. After the six-month residential program, I joined the massage crew at Esalen, which was strongly influenced by Charlotte Selver's meditative approach to Sensory Awareness. This was before the onslaught of more physical techniques like Rolfing, shiatsu, and myriad others. Charlotte Selver influenced us to cultivate an interiority, to trust one's inner sense, to silence the mind enough to enter into the interior.[18]

Stephen Batchelor wrote about solitude as a way of entering into this same sense of the interior. In an NPR interview with Krista Tippett, he described how, in a meditative practice, "we actually start sculpting, refining, shaping the contours of our inwardness, the contours of our interiority."[19] He also talked about the "extent we can somehow open up a nonreactive space within us. So solitude, the practice of solitude, is the practice of creating an inward autonomy within ourselves, an inward freedom from the power of these overwhelming thoughts and emotions."

My approach to massage at Esalen was that the sense of self develops from inside and then, with permission and freedom, permeates the entire body and energy field. I wanted to give my massage clients a sense of their whole body, their personal wholeness, permission to fully embody themselves. As I worked, I would think to myself, as if granting permission to the client, *This is you; this is all of you.* I was, of course, personally working on this sense of embodied wholeness as part of "finding myself," so I was teaching through massage what I needed to learn.

When the women underground elders talk about being grounded, it's this inner sense of embodiment that they mean. Maureen said, "Only fly as high as you can ground deep. The guide is like a kite string. Anyone can get someone high. Takes skill to bring them back." Most of the research protocols suggest hand-holding or other touch as a way to help ground the participant, which includes asking permission to touch in these ways during the preparatory meetings. How the elders talk about grounding is quite different. Their rule that you only take someone where you've been yourself opens a different quality to their grounding — a meeting in a familiar space so the journeyer knows they are not alone. They have a guide who knows how to keep them safe because she's been there.

The elders' intuition is rooted in their somatic sensing — they just know; they feel it in their bones. They receive messages from plant teachers, spirits. Yes, they pause to cognitively reflect on their intuition, deciding whether to go with it, to wait, or to ignore it. All are good possibilities and an example of integration of different states of knowing. But the source arises from within. For example, as I mentioned earlier, Rose said, "In ceremony, if my ego comes up, the medicine will say, *That's your ego. Feel it in your body.*" That's a sense of somatic discernment.

Each elder in her own way talked about an inner certainty she felt from within, an inner intelligence. Medridth explained, "The answer is inside and will emerge....Medicine journey of the soul, the core of who we are. Everyone has that soul — a mystical experience helps them discover that part. Medicines help open you up to remember. All that information is inside you."

Cedar has experience with Sensory Awareness and Continuum, both deep trainings in sensing the interior of the body, and she explained that, for her, somatics are part of the work. It's interesting to note that she doesn't mean as part of a psychotherapeutic integration stage, since she doesn't do that. She uses smudging, Tibetan bells, and relationship with spirits for the integration ritual. This is a very different model from the research protocol. She said, "Healing unfolds differently for different people." There's no script.

For London's Imperial College in 2021, psychologist Rosalind Watts developed "Psilocybin for Depression: The ACE (Accept/Connect/Embody) Model Manual." This takes a similar approach to somatic experiencing that psychologist Eugene Gendlin described in his 1978 book *Focusing*. However, Watts differs from Gendlin in a subtle but important way. The Imperial College manual instructs: "Where do you feel it in your body? Can you find a label for it?"[20] Gendlin tells his readers: "Be silent just to yourself....I would like you to pay attention inwardly, in your body....Now see what comes there....Sense within your body. Let the answers come slowly from this sensing."[21]

This may seem like a small linguistic difference, but when working with the subtle sensing of our interior being, it's a wholly different process. Watts's instructions evoke a cognitive response in terms of location and label. This is not the same as shepherding the person into their interoceptive mode, which is what Gendlin's inviting vagueness does.

Further along the focusing process, Gendlin described ways to deepen the experience. He suggested asking, "What does the felt sense need?" This question encourages a dialogue with the body; unlike Watts, it is not just a concrete check-in about location. Gendlin also stated, "Focusing is not a mere body sensation....It is a physical sense of meaning." Working with this felt sense allows the meaning to develop and emerge into a shift in perspective. That's what leads to insight.

These contrasting approaches to embodiment are emblematic of the difference between following a script (Watts) and working from within (Gendlin). The therapist or guide has to have significant personal experience with focusing to really understand the process.

Somatic Empathy

When I did my guided MDMA session with one of the psychedelic elders, I was on the floor on a mattress covered, as usual, with a blanket, and I wore earphones and eyeshades. I imagine my guide could hardly see me, but she sensed me, called it "tracking," throughout my journey. This capacity to enter into the somatic experience of the voyager is crucial for guiding. But it is difficult to teach, especially when it's rarely even described or emphasized.

From an entirely different field of study, cognitive scientist Anil Seth wrote that empathy was one of the first things he studied in his neuroscience career. "Vicariously catching someone's feelings — known as 'emotional empathy' — and thinking about what they feel — 'cognitive empathy' — might seem like two sides of the same coin, but they activate almost entirely different brain systems, suggesting that these 'pieces' of empathy are independent."[22] I don't know what parts of the brain light up during the kind of embodied empathy my elder guide used to track my journey, but this question is worth exploring.

The capacity to track with small clues that may not be noticed by the untrained eye is very similar to wilderness tracking. I've walked next to naturalists in the forest and realized they see a totally different trail than I see. I never noticed the small mushrooms sprouting or the scat in the undergrowth. But walking next to someone who "sees," staying by their elbow like the apprentices from chapter 3, I gradually learned to see more and more. This is how learning to be a guide works as well.

Neuroscientist Antonio Damasio described a slightly different perspective: "Because we can depict our own body states, we can more easily simulate the equivalent body state of others."[23] As we understand the significance of our own body states, we can then begin to understand the body states of others. I think this is at least part of how tracking works during guiding.

Peter Levine, founder of Somatic Experiencing (SE), described this same capacity when asked what special skills an SE therapist needs: "You need to learn to pay close attention to the sensations in your own body. You need to learn to listen to your clients in a different way, so that when a shift happens in a session, you can notice it in their body as well as in your own."[24]

Psychologist Sharon Stanley has written: "The intersubjective joining of two embodied people creates a new synthesis of inner subjective realities, a somatic interpersonal knowing that can be perceived by each."[25] There's a deep physiological connection between two people, whether they are college roommates whose menstrual cycles coordinate or long-married couples who begin to look alike. This connection, or lack of it, shows up in the video studies of mothers and infants as they learn how to "dance" with each other in rhythm and timing.

We all tune in to each other whether we want to or not, and sometimes it's difficult to distinguish between what's me and what's not-me. Author Marion Woodman described this dilemma: "I am teaching myself to listen to the sensations resonating in my flesh and to differentiate between sensations originating without and sensations originating from within. As I allow others to affect me, I have to hold more firmly onto my own center of awareness."[26]

Woodman is describing an embodied process of discernment that is essential for both guides and therapists. We have to know what is ours versus what belongs to the other person and how to catch our projections onto the other. It would not be helpful to me if my guide during an MDMA session had her own issues around death and then became frightened for me as I entered into my encounter with dying. In that state, I could osmose her fear even though I am hidden under a blanket and paraphernalia. As we've seen, our boundaries become very porous when we're under the influence — another good reason for being very careful about choosing a guide or shaman.

I don't know any better way for teaching and training the capacity of somatic empathy to either psychedelic therapists or guides than for them to have their own experience receiving it. And I mean being tracked while journeying. The more experience, the better, and that takes years. Or as Radianthawk, trained by indigenous shamans, said, "If I wasn't initiated, I couldn't do this healing."

I asked her, "How many years?"

"At least seven, eight years. Never done."

Energetic Clearing or Cleaning

I think there's a special case to be made for the somatic experience of ayahuasca, but it's possible that others have had similar experiences with a wide range of medicines, especially mushrooms. Here, however, I'll take the liberty to report personally on ayahuasca.

The first issue is the purge, the black sludge that erupts from either end of the alimentary tract. This is the most obvious topic, and as in most of my ceremonial experiences, I don't want to linger here. But it's important to mention it, as these are the classic methods of cleaning out during an ayahuasca ceremony. Toxins and other "stuff" need to be cleared out before healing energy can be brought in via the *icaros*.

I'm not alone in feeling that ayahuasca has a permanent place in my interiority. In fact, I've had to make an effort not to focus primarily on that medicine while writing this book, since the psychedelic elders use the full panoply of entheogens. Psychologist Alex Gearin described how the ayahuasca experience includes "codes, designs, and aesthetically rich visual inscriptions that permeate the body and surroundings — bridging 'inner' and 'outer' worlds....It is not simply an enhancement but is the site of radical alterity, a change in the experience of corporeality....Some drinkers described how the spirits(s) of ayahuasca have become embedded in their bodies to heal them and to teach them esoteric wisdom."[27]

I'm most interested in the energetic entrance of the plant medicine as it sweeps through me, scanning my body almost like a machine. In fact, the CT scans I've endured recently feel quite similar to my ceremonial experiences, and I've found this to be quite comforting. The ayahuasca scans are far more comprehensive though, moving throughout my entire body, head to toe, and infiltrating my inner space with great refinement. This happens usually toward the beginning of the ceremony, almost like a diagnostic test to see how I'm doing. I also hear a mechanical hum as this process begins, and I'm prone to thinking, *Uh oh, here it comes.*

At that point, there's a surrender. It's not that "I" surrender. Rather, I am surrendered. I've entered into a process where I don't have control, and there's no choice not to surrender. This is not the big surrender where "I," my sense of self, no longer exists, but one of the many small surrenders where I have to find the psychological and somatic flexibility to willingly go along; in other words, to not resist. I willingly allow my boundary to evaporate. I trust the medicine.

Psychologist Rosalind Watts captures this moment of surrender in her description of the preparation for psilocybin patients in the Imperial College studies. As part of intention setting, she includes some practice "in letting go of mental control and surrendering to felt experience in the moment."[28] This is an important skill to practice, as it's not usually encouraged in Western culture.

At some point the diagnostic scan turns into treatment, which is mostly about cleaning with some kind of high-powered, penetrating pulsations, not unlike something my dental hygienist uses to clean my teeth. At this point I lose my body boundary; there is no longer a me and not-me. My boundary is not only porous, it's nonexistent. There's no difference between my inner and outer. I am vibration and the vibrations are cleaning me.

Then there are the *icaros*, which also enter directly into my body. In a recent Zoom ceremony with the Shipibo shamans, I experienced the *icaros* permeating my lower abdomen inside my pelvic girdle, precisely where the surgery from my year of dismemberment occurred. It was almost as if the song's vibrations were cleaning off the interior side of my pelvic girdle. I thought to myself as this was happening, *I can imagine how someone could misinterpret this as sexual*, knowing with certainty that it was not. It was cleaning.

After the ceremony, I told Maestro Nelson that "this was a very strong ceremony."

He just smiled and said, "We've been working on you for a while now so we can go deeper."

There are layers and levels to the opening and the cleaning. The best description I've found of the Shipibo *icaros* is in the YouTube video "Explicación de Los Cantos Medicinales Ikaros" by Pedro Favaron, a Western-educated literary scholar who married into a Shipibo tribe.[29] Anyone considering attending an ayahuasca ceremony should understand that the *icaros* are essential to the healing process and arise out of the relationship the shaman has with the plant or tree. The *icaros* *are* the medicine. Favaron explains, "The healer sings to the Ishpingo [tree], asks for his energy, and with that force coming from the Ishpingo, the medicinal plant enters the patient's body and it cleans inside the body."

Favaron continues, "Since the rising of New Age use of ayahuasca, the sense of its chants has been distorted a bit.... Ikaros chants are not pretty songs born from an inspiration after having taken ayahuasca and that speak from the heart and about grandparents. That has nothing to do with medicinal chants. The medicinal chant responds and tells about the patient's disease to cure it. Chants are a response to what the doctor is seeing: the diagnosis."

The diagnosis is often made symbolically. Radianthawk explained, "I need to clear any dark energy blocking their life force."

Klara, after ten years in practice with ayahuasca, has a more complex view, influenced from a growing focus on body-oriented trauma work. "I don't slay dragons [that she sees in the body]. I go to the child who experienced the trauma. Then the dragons don't get angry." She explained that she "doesn't do more until I know the story." This allows for more subtle, specific work.

Radha also talked about cleaning out trauma but slightly differently: "Trauma is a spiritual attack on the soul. That energy sticks. We clean that energy."

I asked her, "What is that energy?"

She explained, "We envision a symbol, could be a dragon

somewhere in the body. It's energy left in the energy body of the person. That's what we clean."

In terms of seeing into the body for diagnosis and more, Klara told me that when she met a very experienced *curandera*, the woman said, "I see you've dieted two plants." This was true. Klara said to me, "The ethereal world is very real." This kind of confirmation is an important part of training and one of the many reasons for learning from elders.

Some of the women elders have energy training from other-than-medicine sources. Three of the women were trained in Native American rituals. About half the women elders talked about clearing and cleaning, and the three Native Americans actually worked on me to clear my energy. They all used ritual objects and worked far longer than is usually done by unapprenticed Westerners. When my MDMA journey was coming to an end, the underground elder worked on clearing me for at least an hour. Radha was most succinct: "It's all about the cleaning."

Opening the Heart

When I'm able to navigate during an entheogenic journey, and this is certainly not always the case, I focus my awareness on breathing through my heart. This may not be anatomically accurate, but it is esoterically correct. Note the shift from the physical to the metaphysical. I feel my ribs move, I feel the spaces between my ribs open, I feel subtle movement throughout my sternum and up under my clavicles. I imagine my breath circulating around my heart so that it reaches into the space in back of my heart and in front of my spine. My heart space becomes more three-dimensional. The breath lifts toxic energy, burdens, and even scars from the heart center, allowing this energetic refuse to be exhaled into the farthest reaches of the solar system.

According to Mohammed Rustom, the Sufis describe the same cleansing: "The mirror of the heart must be polished from the rust that tarnishes it."[30] I would like to describe this as subtle energy cleansing, but in all honesty, sometimes it feels like I'm shoveling shit. Life happens and residue gathers around the heart center and accumulates unless we have a way to clear it, to purify the heart.

This purification allows the eye of the heart to open and function as an organ of perception with refined, subtle faculties that, Kabir Helminski writes, "open us to the imaginal world, a dimension in which meanings are embedded as images."[31] The heart carries us between our material "reality" and the unseen world — it's neither this nor that. As Rustom says, "The mirror of the heart, when purified, acts as a type of intermediary which reflects the beauty of the unseen onto phenomenal existence."[32] Through the heart we bring the lessons of the entheogenic journey into our everyday world.

A number of the elder guides talked about the importance of the heart. Debbie said simply, "The more you work, the more your heart opens." She didn't say, "The more journeys you take." The heart opening is not about the number of journeys you take, the dosages used, or the range of medicines ingested. The heart opening is all about the work, which is in part a Western version of purification, and the work happens mostly after the ceremony, as the next chapter explores.

The movement from head to heart is exemplified in the indigenous story of the eagle and the condor. As John Perkins writes in *Touching the Jaguar*, this story describes how the people of North America follow the "path of the mind, of science, technology, and industry while the people of Latin America follow the path of the heart, of passion, intuition, and spiritual connections with nature."[33] Now is the time for the eagle and condor to fly together as the Westerners open their hearts and the indigenous peoples share their traditional ways. One example is the interest in Native American ways of managing forests to prevent devastating forest fires.[34]

Two of the women shared personal stories of heart openings. Carmen told me how a butterfly landed on her heart during a ceremony and said to her in an internal voice, *Open your heart for your own life, for what you have right now, your life now.* Mary, an elder with a strong Catholic background, was working with mushrooms when her heart opened on fire. She saw flames in her heart, and that was all she needed to know. Mary recognized immediately the Sacred Heart of Christ, flaming and shining with divine light.

Creating Interior Spaciousness

The practice of clearing and cleaning creates more interior space. Mary referenced the need for even more spaciousness, saying, "My intuition is very powerful — I need more space for it." This was not said in an egotistical way. It was a very down-to-earth, practical assessment, like, "I just got a bigger sofa and I need to make room for it."

I asked a very experienced meditator about his somatic experience during meditation. He happens to be a physical therapist and a lifelong yoga student, so I thought he'd be very aware of his felt experience. He was very thoughtful and said, "I open up space inside, and when it gets big enough, it blends into the space outside." Here, again, we encounter the surrender, the intentional letting go of the ego-defining boundary.

Use of the smoke of Amazonian jungle tobacco, or *mapacho*, is fascinating in this regard, as it travels through the inside space of the body into the outer world and back again. Anthropologist Dena Sharrock studied how Shipibo shamans use *mapacho* smoke for healing. She wrote, "Intention [mind] merged with the smoke [physical/body], which is infused with the plant's *ibo* [spirit], comingling as they emanate from the *Onanya* (Shaman) and pervade the body and Self of the patient. All participants, then, are rendered existentially transformed as they emerge through the shamanic practices, entwined with each-Other."[35] Her article is appropriately titled, "Smoky Boundaries; Permeable Selves."

Even more specific to the merging of inner and outer space, Sharrock explained, the shaman used "smoke to connect the realms of the interior to the unbounded realms of the spiritual world. Rather than rendering these realms separate, however, this act simultaneously stimulates an embodied experience of the unbounded spiritual realms accessible within the Self while enabling a perceptual experience of the Self as expanding beyond previously recognized boundaries of ordinary consciousness, ultimately revealing each as part of the other."

This brings me back to Maureen's statement: "You can create space with your breath in yourself and in the other person." The way she described it, "you can match your breath with theirs, match rhythms. It's not invasive. It's like putting a blanket around them." The breath is unique in that it moves regularly from our interior space to the outside world, and it's under our conscious control, at least to a certain extent. Thus, as Maureen expands her inner space, the somatic connection or empathy between her and her journeyer creates more space, more allowing, more surrender for the person under the blanket. There's a magic quality to this somatic connection that British professor Lynne Hume has studied. Hume wrote, "One of the keys in magical work is...that by changing consciousness it is possible to act directly upon the inner worlds and thus, ultimately, upon the objective world."[36]

Encountering Archetypal Figures

The inner world is not a still space; there's continuous movement throughout via the breath and visceral digestion. In addition, there's the inner impulse to move, which is, at first, unconscious and then gradually emerges into conscious awareness as the movement is initiated. The time between the brain's initial decision to move and the generation of physical movement has been found to be a fraction of a second or up to five or ten seconds, given more sophisticated brain imagery technology.[37] We move unconsciously before we realize what we're doing. Toni Wolff, Jung's guide throughout his descent, had the intuitive insight to recognize the presence of the unconscious in movement while seeing Tina Keller-Jenny in analysis. In their work together, they used movement as another form of active imagination.[38]

This movement approach to active imagination was further developed in Los Angeles by Mary Whitehouse, who said, "Following the inner sensation, allowing the impulse to take the form of physical action is active imagination in movement."[39] Janet Adler, who studied with Mary Whitehouse, wrote that she "differentiates between movement patterns [in active imagination] that can be traced to personal history and those that seem to come from a transpersonal source," or the collective unconscious.[40] Figures come alive within the somatic experience the same way Philomen came alive to Jung. Emilie Conrad, the founder of Continuum, described her "internal landscape, feeling the visions living in me."[41] This is where entheogens enter the somatic experience — as a way to access archetypes.

Psychedelic psychologist Bill Richards defined an archetypal experience as "a state of mind in which the ego encounters, and sometimes approaches and identifies itself with, one or more visionary figures."[42] Unfortunately, this definition doesn't encompass the somatic experience of such visionary figures.

Movement therapist and Jungian analyst Joan Chodorow quoted Jung, who predicted that if the archetypal figure is numinous, it will lead to consequences. Thus the archetypal figure leaps from the inner realm of somatic experience into the outer, so-called real world.[43]

In a therapy session with my Jungian analyst, I recounted an experience from an entheogenic journey in which I was being hunted by dangerous men on Jet Skis. We were about to take a break in our sessions due to a holiday, and she cautioned me not to allow these archetypal figures to move from my inner world into my outer world. At the time, I didn't know how that could happen nor did I know how to prevent it. But forewarned is forearmed, and I managed not to encounter any men dressed all in black with dark sunglasses on Jet Skis.

Learning how to "see" into the body, to perceive subtle movements, and to feel energy surrounding the body are all nuanced skills essential to psychedelic guides, shamans, and somatic therapists. These capacities are not taught in graduate schools and cannot be taught via Zoom classes. The refining of the senses needed to see at this subtle level can only be learned at the elbow of a mentor, who says to the apprentice, "Did you see that?" The apprentice says no for a very long time until they eventually learn to see and can finally say, "Yes, I saw that."

A good example of how an inner archetype can become "real" is dramatized, albeit fictionally, in the film *Joker*, starring Joaquin Phoenix, who won an Academy Award for his performance. Over the arc of the movie, his character transforms from a disturbed and dysfunctional loser into an archetype of malevolence, Joker. And the transformation is embodied in his dancing, most of which was choreographed, but not all. Phoenix is not a trained dancer, so his movements have an authenticity. Gia Kourias, the *New York Times* dance critic, described the somatic transformation: "The Joker takes control with strutting, confident steps — his ultra-erect posture makes it seem as if he's looking down on the rest of the world."[44] The damaged young man overidentifies with the archetype of the Joker and emerges in the final scene with terrifying power — just as the movement therapists, not to mention Jung, predicted.

Traveling through entheogenic worlds, it's possible to encounter a wide range of archetypal figures who have varying degrees of benevolence. We are more open during these travels than in our day-to-day lives. Our somatic boundaries are more permeable. It's the guides' responsibility to create a safe space and to clear our energy fields, both inner and outer.

Chapter Seven

WHAT THE HELL IS INTEGRATION, ANYWAY?

Integration is a big topic of conversation in the psychedelic renaissance. The term *psychedelic integration* can mean any sessions or activities following the journey. It's touted as part of a sales pitch for psychedelic therapy trainings, which are attempting to cash in on the current media excitement. Psychedelic integration is advertised by both licensed and unlicensed therapists, with little psychedelic experience themselves. And there's a gray, ambiguous territory between offering therapy sessions following a psychedelic journey and actually guiding such an experience.

If, by trying to strike a cautionary note, I sound somewhat cynical, that's because I am. I have grave concerns about the monetizing of the psychedelic journey, which for some is more of a gold rush than a renaissance.

We don't have a place in our Western culture for mystical experiences that are occasioned by entheogenic journeys. So far, we are medicalizing these experiences. At the same time, some propose that it's the spiritual experience that leads to the therapeutic outcome, something Al Hubbard realized in the 1950s.

In fact, Hubbard developed one of the earliest approaches to integration by introducing religious symbols toward the end of the psychedelic journey. His intention was "to assist the patient in forming a new and healthier frame of reference that would carry over after the drug wore off."[1]

In the psychedelic-assisted studies, integration is supposed to happen in the time-limited therapy sessions following the journey. Evidently, the sooner the better, as there might be a critical period in the weeks following the journey when the brain has increased neural plasticity and may be more open for rewiring.[2]

However, integration doesn't always work in predictable ways, especially when entheogens are used periodically over a lifetime for psychospiritual development, the way the women elders use them. The process is different for each person and for each medicine at each dose. The integration of a numinous experience can take a lifetime to flower, as exemplified by Arielle in her encounters with a live jaguar (see page 80) and, twenty-five years later, an obsidian one. Her jaguar journey continues to this day, as full of mystery as ever.

The hope or hype is that psychedelic integration will heal our old traumas, but that's not the same as erasing childhood wounds. We encounter our lifetime scars again and again no matter how many journeys or how much psychotherapy we do. The intention should be to learn to recognize our patterns so they don't dominate our lives and, hopefully, invite them in for tea, as Ram Dass so famously recommended. We can develop compassion for our brokenness and carry those exiled pieces of ourselves in our hearts, where they can crack us open to a larger love. In this way our childhood wounds become our teachers.

Here is the full quote from Ram Dass: "What has changed is that before [my neuroses] were these huge, big things that were very frightening, and they took me over....And now they're sort of like little Shmoos. They're little, friendly beings, and I invite them in for tea."[3]

Jungian Barbara Hannah said the same thing in a different way: "Every widening of consciousness is indeed the greatest gain we can make. Almost all of our difficulties in life come from having too narrow a consciousness to meet and understand them."[4] A shift happens that changes the balance between our "little Shmoos" and our capacity to hold them without identifying with them.

This shift in perspective is the core of integration. As our inner space expands, we open up to new ways of being. Perhaps we can embrace our polarities with more grace and less projection of blame. Or become kinder and more forgiving about our own frailties and failures. I'd rather not talk about integration as a term but, instead, consider lifelong learning about how to be human, how to inhabit our bodies, how to realize our interconnectedness.

The elder psychedelic guides know that these medicines are for more than psychiatric symptom relief; they are for sacred journeys. The guides have had to practice underground at great personal risk because our culture doesn't have a sacred container for these medicines to be used in such ways. And our modern Western culture doesn't have a good track record when we do encounter sacred ceremonial use. Consider the Western treatment of indigenous tribes whose use of entheogenic plants is well integrated into their culture via traditional ceremonies and initiations. To this day we are stealing land and resources from the very people who carry the most sophisticated knowledge of healing plants in the Amazonian jungles.

Or consider the tragic outcome when we have encountered sacred medicines. In 1957, R. Gordon Wasson wrote a *Life* magazine article about the Mazatec *curandera* María

Sabina and the "little saints" or magic mushrooms that she introduced him to.⁵ This story inspired a flood of Western psychedelic tourists to find her, which eventually forced Sabina to move from her home to get away from them, since they "didn't respect our customs." She said, "From the moment the foreigners arrived to search for God, the saint children lost their purity. They lost their force; the foreigners spoiled them. From now on they won't be any good. There's no remedy for it."⁶

Currently, the psychedelic renaissance exists within the medical and legal institutions of our modern world — not exactly our most spiritual contexts. As we say about so many things, we have to do better. Our Western culture has to learn a variety of ways to work with these sacred medicines for healing and for spiritual insight, and maybe for creative purposes, initiation ceremonies, and preparation for death. The women elders know that these medicines are a way of life, that they open us to larger worlds, that integration is a lifelong process, that we are never done.

Psychedelic Therapists Need Psychedelic Experience

When I was in private psychotherapy practice, every once in a while I would get a phone call from a prospective client asking me if I practiced a particular approach to therapy, often one that was au courant. Even if I had training in whatever approach the person was seeking, I would never admit it. I always said, "I'm eclectic. I use whatever approach seems best for that particular person at that particular time. Anyway, the most important thing is the therapeutic relationship." I must admit, none of these inquiries ever resulted in a new client.

I resisted my impulse to tell them they were asking me the wrong question. Instead, they should have asked me: Do you sometimes laugh or cry during a therapy session? How many years have you been in private practice? Have you had therapy yourself? How many times? How long? Was it successful? Are you in therapy now? Do you have supervision or consultation with other therapists? Do you sometimes share something about yourself in a therapy session that's relevant, but without sharing too much? And perhaps most importantly: Do you love your clients in a way that serves their best interests?

You can ask similar questions of psychedelic integration therapists or coaches: How many years have you yourself been working with these medicines? How many journeys have you taken? With which medicines? Under what circumstances? How long have you been doing psychedelic integration work with others?

I understand that these are challenging questions given the illegal status of these medicines, but a therapist can answer without stating where the experiences took place. And these questions will weed out therapists who are jumping on the integration bandwagon, perhaps with a sincere interest, but with little actual experience. For instance, I know one competent licensed therapist who is on a few integration lists and has attended more than one training in psychedelic integration therapy, but he has little personal journey experience. I refer people to him for regular therapy but not for psychedelic integration therapy, which requires a whole different learning curve.

In 2017 I attended a daylong conference workshop on psychedelic integration therapy. I struggled to be open and accepting, but by 11 a.m., I walked out, something I rarely if ever do. Not one of the four presenters had enough clinical experience, much less psychedelic integration experience. There has been such a need to understand how best to make use of these amazing journeys that we have professionally barged ahead with little experience. I feel we should just admit that we don't know if there even is a best way to do psychedelic integration therapy.[7] A study team at Yale didn't mince words: "While psychedelic integration is widely discussed as part of psychedelic therapy, it remains vaguely conceived, undertheorized, and may lack an operational relationship to the problem being treated."[8] We are only just beginning to describe a few different approaches.[9]

However, we do know one thing from the underground elders, even though they don't do "psychedelic therapy." They all started with their own healing. Not one of them said, "I was called to do this work and launched into guiding others." They all said in one way or another, "I was on the path of my own healing." And each of them has continued along that path, working with the medicines throughout their lives. As they say, "This is a way of life," one that is "never done."

As I've mentioned, many of them had childhood spiritual experiences that inspired them to search for expanded states of consciousness — author Joe Tafur recently told me that the Shipibo shamans describe such children as the "curious ones." The women guides in this book were primed and able to recognize the sacred healing power of their medicine experiences. Somehow, the territory felt familiar. And they have persisted, working on themselves for years without any intention of stopping. Working with the medicines and their own healing is the central theme of their lives.

I suggested to Maureen that she have two dates in mind when asked about her experience: What year did you first take a medicine journey? And what year did you first guide someone on a journey? "It was so long ago," she said. "I have to think about it." A few days later she told me, "My first experience was sometime in the sixties, and it was five years before I sat for anyone." Anchoring her experience in this way says everything about her training and her life, and it also distinguishes her from a raft of inexperienced, so-called psychedelic therapists.

As of today, this elder guide has been working with the medicines on herself and with others for decades. Doing so, she said, "We encounter our core wound — *oh, this again.*" With a shamanic perspective, Radha agreed, "We can't get away from our family-of-origin work. Early trauma is a spiritual attack like soul loss. That energy sticks and needs to be cleaned in ceremony." Medridth said, "We can do deep work on family healing," and she often does ceremonies with entire families present. Other elders mentioned family-of-origin and early-life wounding and how these healing themes resurface over time, even after decades of journeys.

Theirs is an important, long-term perspective when we consider psychedelic integration. It's too simplistic to assume we integrate an experience and the core issue is resolved. Or if the core issue is not resolved, that we haven't integrated our experience. Psychedelic integration covers a far more complex process of healing and unfolding throughout life.

Levels of Integration

In this section I propose several levels of psychedelic integration, but I write it as a psychotherapist — it's not based on my interviews. The elder guides are very clear about their boundaries, and they don't offer psychotherapy as part of their journey work. They are guides, not therapists. Some are willing to do follow-up sessions, but when more is needed, they refer people to a therapist who is a kindred spirit or they suggest another ceremony. I, however, have spent my adult life either in therapy or practicing therapy, and I think that psychedelic integration, however we describe it, is a vital part of any journey.

The most basic level of psychedelic integration, or the simplest approach, especially in a group ceremony, is a sharing circle the morning after where each person describes an aspect of their experience, usually by holding a talking stick and taking turns. Depending upon the size of the group, each person might have an informal time limit of five to ten minutes. The leader or another participant might be allowed to add a comment, but there's a very limited exchange — the goal is usually reverent listening to the story each person selects to tell from their all-night experience.

The next level, which I refer to with a slight snarky intonation, is what I call spa integration. Rest, walk in nature, write in your journal, get a massage, attend a yoga class. These are all good things to do, but they miss the opportunity to sift through an experience, to do the inner work necessary to reflect and mull over any personal messages and meanings that can emerge from a journey. Such insights or teachings need to be attended to in some way that preserves them for future reflection. If these thoughts are not recorded, they are like dreams that disappear by lunchtime, like gossamer threads that float away in the breeze. What was hard-won overnight can quickly become unavailable to conscious memory no matter how relaxed the person is.

On the other hand, if the person does none of the spa integration suggestions and dives right back into their daily life, they can also lose contact with their ceremony experience and miss any teachings that might arise. In fact, there's a rebound effect that some guides and therapists have begun to notice. Especially when working with ketamine, some people shut down immediately once the drug effect wears off. No matter how open and receptive they might have been during the journey, they revert right back to their defensive structure afterward. This is very frustrating for the therapists, who thought they were making "amazing progress" only to see the issues buried as deeply as before, with defenses hardened.

In the next day or so, some people choose to reenter an

expanded state through meditation, dreams, or listening to the same music from the journey. These are ways to travel back into the ceremony but in a state of consciousness that's in between the psychedelic experience and consensus reality. This consolidates the experience and keeps it vitally alive for postceremony reflection.

In the psychedelic-assisted research studies, there are at least three ninety-minute therapy sessions devoted to integration. According to "A Manual for MDMA-Assisted Psychotherapy," these sessions generally include a "discussion of the meaning of memories, thoughts, feelings, and insights experienced during the sessions and how these new meanings will be manifested in daily living."[10] The therapist will have notes from anything the person said during the session, which can help bring elements of the experience into the light of day and consensus reality. Also, the therapist knows the person's history and can bridge meaning and teachings from the journey into their understanding of the past as they move into the future.

The therapeutic relationship is the container for the journey and should be considered a critical aspect of the setting.[11] The continuity between the preparatory sessions, the ceremony, and the follow-up sessions is crucial — it establishes the relationship between guide and patient and encourages the connection from intention to insight to actions. The trust and support during the ceremony help the journeyer to let go during that crucial moment of surrender, and this can make the difference between a traumatizing journey and a mystical one.[12] NYU psychologist Tony Bossis emphasized this in an interview: "The therapeutic rapport and trust between the participant and the therapists...significantly helps in mitigating anxiety during the psilocybin session."[13]

It should be noted that the significance of the therapeutic alliance in traditional psychotherapy is well established from both a clinical and a research perspective.[14] However, when I discussed the importance I was placing on the therapist-patient relationship, Amy Jones, an experienced psychedelic therapist, warned me, "I wonder if seeing the relationship as the healing mechanism might fuel a grandiosity in some that exacerbates the risk of falling out of balance." This is a very important warning. When a therapist becomes inflated, unethical behavior can follow; too often that means crossing boundaries or inappropriate sexual behavior. Jones suggested that peer supervision, consultation, or just good friends could keep the psychedelic therapist "grounded and in moral alignment."

Her comment reminds me of the collegial group of shamans I mentioned earlier who, even after years of study and practice, continue to consult with each other and sing to each other in ceremony (see page 104). The Shipibo family of shamans I work with over Zoom also discusses their work both before and after the Zoom ceremonies, coordinating their intentions and treatments. I have no idea what they talk about, but I imagine it might be like a clinical case conference, yet quite different of course.

Preserving Numinous Experiences

Creative expression via art, poetry, movement, or music is one of the best ways to preserve a journey experience. In the creative process, there's an inner movement from the imaginal realm of the ceremony into a more concrete form in the outer world. Then that image can be perceived consciously and allowed to reenter the psyche. Something from the journey is captured in this way and moved through different states of consciousness. Jung's paintings in the Red Book are the best examples of images moved from the inner world into the outer world.[15] His paintings are archetypal and speak to many people in psychic resonance.

However, not all of us have talent for creative expression. I must admit I have written a few journey-inspired poems, but my attempts at art or even traditional mandala drawings with easy-to-use oil pastels are ho-hum. But I'm good at Google searching. After my ketamine journey, I searched for an image that matched my experience of the ground opening up and earth beings arising out of the depths to sing to me. Not an easy vision to find on the internet, but photos of Fingal's Cave on the Isle of Staffa off the coast of Scotland were close enough.[16] The photos do not exactly match my ketamine vision, but the structure of the cave has the same feeling of the earth opening up, and the photos bring me back to that exalted state of the journey.

Integration means exactly this — to bring an expanded state of consciousness into consensus reality so the feeling, meaning, significance, teaching can transfer from the imaginal realm of the journey into daily life. So what's the meaning of my earth-opening experience? I can't put it into words, but I've spent a good part of my life living on the dramatic edges of continents similar to the landscape surrounding Fingal's Cave. From my first arrival in Big Sur at age twenty to the island off the coast of Maine where I now live, my physical environment matches this imaginal landscape. These extreme coastal cliffs open my heart with a primal sense of belonging. Numinous experiences must be recognized, valued, and allowed to continue in the psyche free of psychological interpretation. With luck and intention, these images will manifest in unexpected ways as life unfolds.

Integrating Numinous Experiences

The only way I know for therapists to be able to recognize when an image is numinous is from their own in-depth experiences in expanded states of consciousness. This is the critical difference between therapists who have minimal entheogenic experience and those who are well-traveled. Psychologist Elizabeth Nielson raised the legal problem with providing entheogenic journeys as part of the training for psychedelic therapists.[7] Current training programs might offer a breath workshop or travel out of the country to retreat centers where a medicine journey is legal. This approach is better than no opportunity, but it provides very limited experience, especially when compared with what the underground elders have done.

The therapist needs to develop an inner map based on their own experiences with numinous images, childhood history, past lives, personal or collective trauma, ancestral history, and current life issues. Traveling through these states of consciousness, personal and transpersonal, will yield a familiarity with a wide-ranging psychic landscape. The therapist learns how to move from these inner spaces to the outer world and back again in their own lives. By doing their own work, they develop a kind of psychic fluidity across states of consciousness that enables them to recognize the level of material the client is reporting.

Years ago, I had a therapy client who was also attending breath workshops. I never knew which way our sessions would go. She could work on childhood issues with a neglectful, critical mother or she could describe her travels into other realms of cosmic energy. I had to be able to match her state of consciousness, often shifting multiple times throughout one session. I felt more focused, with an almost surgical intensity, when she described scenes from her childhood. And when she launched into her breathwork journeys, I could travel with her, feeling more porous, almost out of my body. Her issues with her mother never disappeared, but as her spiritual awareness expanded, her childhood history shrank and became less relevant. Her numinous experiences were integrated into and inspired her current life choices.

If the therapist has not done enough inner exploration, they won't have the fluidity or experience to recognize the psychic source of the client's material. The therapist might misinterpret a transpersonal experience as a personal one. This is one of the most common mistakes a therapist can make in psychedelic integration — such a misinterpretation can disrupt a therapeutic alliance at a deep level. The patient is sharing a very private experience, one they might have never told anyone for fear of being demeaned, misunderstood, or called crazy. The person feels as though they are placing their very soul in the hands of the therapist. If the therapist misinterprets this moment, the person will likely cut off such sharing and terminate therapy. That's how strongly people feel about such misinterpretations.

For example, Arielle herself described one of her childhood spiritual experiences to me as a "dream" (see page 42). However, later, she seriously objected to this phrasing and wrote: "I cannot accept labeling these childhood memories as dreams. I still have vivid memories of these early, very real luminous experiences. Now I realize these naturally induced visions were from realms in expanded states of consciousness." These are sacred images, real and alive as ever in her psyche.

As I've mentioned, I maintain that the psychedelic therapist's personal variables make an important difference in the therapeutic alliance — how much entheogenic experience they have, how much personal therapy they've done, and how skillful they are about their use of self.[18] The therapist's ability to differentiate between personal history, archetypal material, and numinous experience and respond accordingly is central.

I recently told a dream to a Jungian analyst friend of mine. It was a lucid dream about being in meditation and waking up, still in the dream, to realize that my mind was silent for the last ten minutes of the meditation. I assure you that such silence has never happened to me in my waking-life attempts at meditation. My friend's response? He listened carefully and simply said, "That's a big dream."

Jung wrote that "big dreams" often "prove to be the richest jewel in the treasure-house of psychic experience." These "dreams have to do with the realization of a part of the personality which has not yet come into existence but is still in the process of becoming."[19] My friend was able to recognize my dream as a big dream because he himself has had such dreams and had them recognized by other Jungian analysts. This example highlights the importance I've placed on both personal experience and professional mentorship.

Not much needs to be said in response to a numinous experience. In fact, the less said the better. My dream, and the memory of it, continues to work inside me — it's as alive today as it was when I had it, and how this dream unfolds within me is as ineffable as an entheogenic journey, shrouded in mystery.

In psychedelic integration work, the therapist must be able to not only recognize numinous moments in dreams or journeys but be willing to be personally expanded by the client's sharing of the experience, the energy coming through. The therapist has to be fluid and permeable to shift states of consciousness in response to the client, to receive the numinous story with an open heart and hold such experiences with reverence and awe.

Ann Shulgin: Working with the Soul and the Shadow

I met with Ann in her comfy kitchen at her ranch in the San Francisco Bay Area. Spry and alert, in her late eighties, Ann was kind enough to take time from working on her own book to speak with me — a conversation I now treasure even more, since Ann sadly died in 2022.

Ann started off our conversation by saying, "Therapists must have done work on their own shadow. You have to know the territory. If not, you can do damage. The person must trust you one hundred percent, which only happens if you come from a place of knowledge and experience. If the person is somewhere you haven't been, it becomes obvious that the therapist doesn't really understand. You can't fool around with this. *It's the work of the soul.*" The emphasis was Ann's.

Ann knew what she wanted to say, and I scribbled notes as quickly as she talked. "How people change is very individual, different for each person. A good therapeutic sign is when the person can hear the therapist. Borderlines don't — they just want company, they have no intention of getting well. And people with strong religious beliefs don't listen either." Then she gave a warning, "Don't engage defense mechanisms people have or they will withdraw. If the person is resistant, you'll have less effect, so talk about the resistance."

Ann continued, "This is deep work with people. You have to be able to feel love and care for them. If they make you uncomfortable, ask yourself why."

I felt like Ann was distilling decades of practice into the most essential teachings while still being very practical. She said, "Drink lots of water. It's not a matter of dose. Drugs are each totally different — 2C-B [similar to mescaline] will take you out into the universe. People can still talk after the first twenty minutes. They will eventually share."

Then, almost as if we were on a journey together, Ann went to a whole deeper level. "Everyone has a deep, unconscious fear of being worthless from early trauma. This is a big issue you have to confront: You're a worthless piece of shit."

Ann surprised me with her bluntness. She looked like a sweet grandmotherly type but her words cut through that image. Ann stated the core issue so elegantly. "The shadow work is about removing this fear of being worthless." She saw this process as central to healing, and she was well known for her work with the shadow, what she called "the dark side...for self-protection and survival." These are the "repressed, closed off, long-denied aspects of his nature; all the unacceptable, shameful, dirty, monstrous parts as taught by his parents.... The person doesn't want to be this way consciously and is terrified that this is who I am unconsciously."[20] This is the fear of being a "worthless piece of shit."

Jungian analyst Murray Stein added color to the description of the shadow: "Generally the shadow has an immoral or at least a disreputable quality, containing features of a person's nature that are contrary to the customs and moral conventions of society."[21]

Ann saw the confrontation with the shadow as a central healing mechanism of the entheogenic journey, emphasizing "a great deal of discussion — before any drug ingestion — not only about the nature and function of the Shadow, but also of the need to feel compassion for the innocent child he had been, and to understand why and how the child developed certain habits of behavior and emotional response."[22]

Ann was clearly different from the other elder guides in that she prepared the client for shadow work, she engaged in a "therapeutic dialogue" throughout the journey, and then she looked for certain changes or indications of healing after the session. Her approach is important to this topic because of her historical role in the development of the therapeutic use of entheogens and also because she so carefully cultivated the integration process before, during, and after the journey.

Talking with me, Ann explained, "The shadow usually presents as an animal, a beast. The most terrifying work is to face that monster in the basement [the unconscious]. Step into and see through the eyes of the monster."

This was quite a dramatic moment in our conversation, but I intentionally interrupted the flow to clarify. "Is this your original technique? To step into the beast and look through the eyes?" I asked, admittedly being a stickler for appropriate credit.

"Yes," Ann said.

I went back to writing down every word. She said, "Once you step into the beast, you have total lack of fear and a tremendous surge of power. The beast is eventually tamed, incorporated, owned, appreciated, brought home, and becomes the prince. You learn to love that side of yourself, and that's the transformation."

"The shadow is a part of yourself, an ally, a fearless friend," Ann continued, "but it never develops good table manners."

At that point we laughed — we were sitting at the kitchen table.

How Does Psychedelic Healing Happen?

The longest standing and most prevalent theory is that it's the unity mystical experience that leads to therapeutic change.[23] How this works — how an experience of oneness or ego dissolution leads to improved psychological outcomes for a variety of psychiatric symptoms — well, this we don't know. And we don't know whether the correlation between mystical experience and therapeutic outcome is causative. Psychologist Leor Roseman and others from Imperial College warned, "We must exercise caution about ascribing too much to this relationship. It remains possible that as yet unmeasured and therefore unaccounted for components of psychedelic therapy play important roles in mediating long-term outcomes."[24] There's growing interest in the importance of emotional breakthrough, psychological insight, and neurological plasticity. When it comes to understanding the healing mechanisms of psychedelic therapy, it's almost as if the more we know, the less we understand.

Also the unity mystical experience is only one type of spiritual experience. We don't know much about experiences of cosmic darkness or the void. Or why some of those experiences lead to chronic depersonalization in some and to a peaceful acceptance of death in others.[25]

For instance, I was talking with the indigenously trained shaman I work with and he mentioned singing *icaros* to ferry someone across the dark night sky, sailing across realms in a dugout canoe, helping them transition at the end of life.

"I know that sky! I've been there," I exclaimed as if I were recognizing a restaurant in Paris where I'd had a great meal. I'd encountered that spacious void with twinkling stars in the vastness when my father died and then, again, in my first ayahuasca ceremony that took me back to the experience of my father dying (which I describe in *Listening to Ayahuasca*). This is familiar terrain. I can see the dark emptiness from my island home on cloudless nights. I look up at the sky with my feet on the ground and I know where I'm going when I die and it's surprisingly reassuring.

How do I integrate this experience from almost two decades ago? Not exactly in a therapeutic context — instead, it lives on inside of me. I can visualize the dark spaciousness, see the beauty, and float into emptiness. My hope is this experience will prepare me for my own death.

There could also be different healing mechanisms with different medicines — different mechanisms of healing across different levels of consciousness. In other words, one experience might help me heal from feeling like "a worthless piece of shit" while another entheogenic experience might help me accept death with equanimity. Or an addiction might be healed when a plant spirit admonishes, *Stop drinking*. Healing works in mysterious ways and we might be limiting our understanding by trying to fit the process into a cause-and-effect paradigm — this leads to that — especially when we don't really know how it works.

I did a recent presentation on psychedelic integration, and after every few slides I had one that said, "What are we integrating into what?" The first "what" refers to the priority focus: What was the original intention? What does the person choose to recount from all that happened in the journey? What does the therapist choose to focus on? "What are we integrating into what?" is even more important and more difficult to consider. Are we pouring new wine into old bottles? Are we entering new data into an old program? As I said earlier, I'd rather not talk about integration. I'd rather talk about transformation. How can the psychedelic therapist support and nurture the transformation of the whole person, what I call the psychic architecture, the way the personality is organized? The experience should not be co-opted by the same personality structure to inflate the ego with yet another great story or accomplishment, as in the consumerism approach to sacred journeys: "Yes, I've been to…and this is what I experienced. …."

Signs of Transformation

For Ann, transformation was when the person realized the shadow was "only part of the self," not the whole self and not "bad." As the person becomes conscious of what was previously unconscious, the shadow is transformed into an inner resource. Ann called upon this resource when she was playing a challenging game of chess or walking down a dark street: "Be in your beast side. Step in and step out consciously. Make decisions with your conscious self." As she wrote elsewhere, "Ultimately, the Shadow will take its place as a devoted ally and protector, available when needed to the whole self, respected and validated by the conscious mind."[26] Ann's perspective was Jungian, so this work with the shadow was her outcome measure, not easily quantified. In general, the current psychedelic research uses psychological scales to measure diagnostic symptoms as well as physiological measures to confirm self-reports on smoking or drinking. NYU has used video interviews to document clinical transformations in terminal patients.[27] The way we conceptualize and measure the outcome of an entheogenic journey will influence how we focus the process of integration.

The underground elders each have their own way of describing transformation, but some themes emerged. First, they described warning signs if there was not enough progress. Maureen said, "If we don't listen to what the medicines say to us, their wisdom will go away." Rose surprised me with her strength to set limits: "If there's no change, then there are no more ceremonies." This reminds me of the *Seinfeld* character the Soup Nazi, who so famously said, "No soup for you." Moreover, Rose warned that the spirits will scold you if there's no action, or they'll purposely confuse you if you're not listening. Cedar, equally soft-spoken, also set strong boundaries: "I say no to people who want ceremonies too often."

Radianthawk said the medicines want to know "whether we're active partners, cultivating our relationship with them." A number of women echoed this process of developing personal relationships with the medicine. Medridth explained, "I can feel the plants are a part of me, inside my body." Alyana said, "You become the medicine — you walk it, you pray it." Rose explained that it's "my relationship with the plant spirits that protects me. They help me power up to protect myself."

Radha, with her indigenous training, shared her experience of dieting with a plant: "I become infused with the awareness of the master plant I'm dieting. I notice how I receive information from that plant and how that changes over time. My channel opens and I tune in to the station for that particular plant. This connection remains available and then opens more fully when needed. It's always present. If I've dieted well and maintained a good practice, I fall into sync with the plant. I become it. Ayahuasca, the mainstay of my practice — ayahuasca is my constant companion."

A number of the elders mentioned the heart. Mary talked about "bringing the teaching into the heart," and she shared how her work with journeying gave her permission to love and noted that "my heart flowered." Debbie also described how her heart opened as a result of her personal medicine work: "I have faith in the process, not a belief, a knowing." Heartfelt knowledge. She sees "life as therapy," which was something I used to look for in my psychotherapy clients to indicate they were ready to terminate treatment. Their lives were unfolding in a way that enabled them to grow and learn on their own. Life with a capital L is the real therapist.

None of the elders referenced psychological symptoms related to psychiatric diagnoses, which is what the current research protocols emphasize. The women guides were more philosophical, having the perspective that working with the medicines is a way of being in the world, a way of life, a lifelong path. People become happier, more creative, and more resilient.

A number of women talked about a deepening of the way people experience their bodies as a sign of transformation. They say that people become more at home in their bodies, learn how to clean their energetic bodies, let go of stuff they no longer need to carry psychically. There is a sense of living in two worlds, being grounded in the physical body and more aware of the subtle body. Jessica, an elder with a private psychotherapy practice, cited Angeles Arrien, who taught how to walk a mystical path with practical feet. Cedar, from a shamanic point of view, described how to be present in your feet. Mary, who works with mythopoetic realities, said, "There are dozens of mythologies," indicating a rich source of archetypes and ancestral support. "There's always something to learn — you can embody mythological symbols or visions," leading to an expanded array of inner resources for support and teachings.

The guides also looked for psychological changes as part of the process of working with the medicines. Janet, the guide who is also a therapist, said, "The more medicine work you do, the more other parts of the personality emerge. You become more multidimensional." Cedar looked for a deepening "growth in wisdom and compassion."

Medridth said, "As you use the medicines over time, the process becomes more refined. You get more specific help."

This process of refinement leads to a more sensitive perception, an opening to expansive subtle realms, trusting nonordinary clues from the natural world. Radianthawk described this process as learning how to be truly present to spirit. She teaches how to move energy, how to transform the heavy energy of the physical body into the lighter energy of vibration.

The Inevitability of Suffering

Radianthawk also asked a very important question for integration: "How do we work with things that are difficult?" This question opens the issue of how we relate to suffering as part of life, something the Buddha prioritized as the first of the Four Noble Truths.[28] Medridth said that suffering, learning how to be here in a physical body in this world, is the biggest teacher. Tony Bossis came to a similar conclusion based on his work with people facing death. He explained to me that psilocybin journeys "alter the patient's relationship to suffering. They learn to move into suffering, to develop a new relationship to suffering. They learn to trust and surrender."

Maureen said, rather matter-of-factly, "No one skips dismemberment" — a fact I found surprisingly comforting after my personal year of dismemberment. She continued, "I've been taught to go through to the other side, to see what's underneath, what's on the other side of the suffering." In other words, surrender to what is and be curious about what emerges next.

I have to admit I suck at this — I'd rather avoid suffering, but the problem is that resisting increases the pain. I remember hearing Ida Rolf talk about this when I was in my early twenties. I didn't really understand the full meaning of her message at the time, but I knew it was important so I remembered it. She said that the central teaching that comes through Rolfing is how to work with the pain. I've gotten Rolf work all my life and can't say that I've gotten any better about working with that or other pain. I'm still the patient who explains to the nurse drawing blood or giving an injection, "I'm no good at this. I hope you are." Then I close my eyes and turn away to emphasize my point.

I would feel worse about myself if I hadn't just read the same confession from a renowned Tibetan monk, Yongey Mingyur Rinpoche. Perhaps not exactly the same confession but close enough to be therapeutic:

> I had to make resistance itself the object of my awareness. Then I could work more directly with the sensations in the body. I do not like these sensations. I started off feeling bad. And now, added to that, I feel bad about feeling bad. Slowly I brought each sensation into the guesthouse of awareness. I let go of the resistance, let go of the negativity, and tried to just rest with feeling small, unloved, and unworthy. I brought these feelings into my mind — to the big mind of awareness,

where they became small. The guesthouse-mind of awareness encompassed the feelings, the dejection, the bleakness, and became bigger than all of them together, dwarfing their impact, changing the relationship.[29]

Yongey Mingyur Rinpoche described a shift in perspective to the big mind of awareness where the personal feelings become small. This same shift in perspective is described by Jung. As Sonu Shamdasani wrote: "What [Jung] now considered critical was not the presence of any particular content but the attitude of the individual toward it, and in particular whether an individual could accommodate such material in his or her worldview."[30]

The women elder guides point to this same shift in a variety of ways. Darlene said, "My journey is part of a larger healing." We are never in ceremony for ourselves alone. The medicine journeys "heal outside of time," Radha explained. "They cross generations and go to the origin to call in joy, fortification, and light." Maureen talked about "building inner capacity, inner space for rearrangement, to hold that change." Cedar said that her mystical experience led to a "bigger perspective." Jessica described her own shift: "You see everything connects, becomes more fluid, more creative, curious. I'm more open, filled with awe and wonder. Healing happens. I'm bigger than this." She explained that "in this process, there's less identification with the personal and you arrive at a bigger point of view." Medridth said, "You become less of a victim as you unravel the knots from your personal history."

These are the best descriptions of transformation that I've ever heard, and they have little to do with psychotherapeutic insight. The women guides are describing a shift in awareness, a shift in perspective that leads to a different way of being in the world. Connie Grauds described this same shift during her apprenticeship to become a shamana: "My personal story was transcended and then transformed. This allowed for a new perception to be possible." The mystical experience "lifted me out of my common set, my personal stories. It opened new possibilities. I didn't come back to the same constellation."

The elder guides have witnessed thousands of people transcending their personal stories and then transforming their lives. These are two separate processes and both are essential. Integration is about stabilizing and deepening the shift in perspective and then supporting how that new perspective manifests and expands into the person's daily life.

A Shower of Cosmic Love

Near-death experiences lead to this same shift in perspective, and Alcoholics Anonymous claims that hitting bottom is what leads to transformation. Sometimes it's a spontaneous mystical or quantum experience that changes everything.[31] I'm partial to Ann Shulgin's description of "being held in the loving hands of God." She called this "one of the most healing experiences a human being can have."[32] I've had this experience of cosmic love, which she considered "the greatest force in the universe," and I agree with her. The overflowing downpour of total and unconditional acceptance and love permeates the body and creates a new template in the psyche, one that heals on both psychological and spiritual levels.

This experience of being loved can heal core attachment issues, as I wrote about in *Listening to Ayahuasca*. The shower of cosmic love transforms maladaptive beliefs, such as "I'm not lovable, I'm not good enough." These old schemas or life traps form part of the personality architecture that can be dismantled or rewired during a medicine journey and then consciously restructured in integration.[33] Combining attachment theory with the REBUS (relaxed beliefs under psychedelics) model leads to a novel understanding of how healing happens. As one study said, "Psychedelics may reduce the influence of insecure, defensive Internal Working Models [schemas or life traps], opening them up to healthy revision."[34]

On a spiritual level, the overwhelming experience of "being held in the loving hands of God" can turn an atheist into a mystic. The accompanying shift in worldview opens up new beliefs about the universe, reality, the interconnectedness of all things, and life after death. The worldview is not only reorganized but transformed.

Whatever way the shift happens, the impact is the same: People become more spiritual and less materialistic, their values and priorities are less about fame and fortune and more about relationships, health, and how to contribute to the world.[35]

We do have to be realistic, however, as many people bounce in and out of AA meetings, and mystical experiences lead to inflation. We don't all transform our lives after a transcendent experience. "Choice lies at the heart of the matter," Myron Stolaroff, the author of *The Secret Chief*, wrote in his memoir. "The choice is to live out of that [mystical] state of consciousness in our ordinary moments."[36]

Maureen explained that she often witnesses an existential turning point, a choice: "I watch for a shift in how the person embraces being alive, similar to choosing to come back during a near-death experience. At that point, something shifts." She explained that "some people are pissed off to be here on this planet — they're mad at God. This work brings people to the point of choice to be here." This reminds me of Ann Shulgin's rule for a guided MDMA journey: Do *not* go through the death door. It's a choice, a choice to live this life you are given.

Radianthawk captured this existential question: "We need to learn how to live on this earth and be joyful." Darlene expressed this another way: "To say thank you for everything is a hard place to get to." Ann Shulgin agreed: "Say yes to everything that is."

As we shift consciousness to love what is, our level of responsibility expands to include a wider community, across time and the world, our planet. Our capacity for compassion expands and we find small and large ways to contribute to the greater good. Maureen described how "our goals move from head to heart, and this is how we find our purpose in the world." Medridth said the process is "learning what our spiritual job is" — what we're called to do. Mary asked, "What is our agreement with our ancestors? Why am I here? Why was I born to these people?" How can our unique constellation of gifts respond to what is needed in this world?

Chapter Eight

PSYCHEDELIC WAYS OF KNOWING

Altogether, the elders I interviewed from the psychedelic underground have thousands of hours of experience with entheogens via their own journeys and guiding others. Their role in guiding entheogenic journeys has no real counterpoint in our current Western world. They are not therapists, although they're therapeutic. Most of them don't have graduate degrees — they are neither researchers nor medical professionals. They are not ministers, as they do not belong to a religious organization. But their work is sacred.

These women have made a cultural shift to live in a sacred world, not bound by the assumptions of Western culture. It's not that they've all adopted an indigenous way of knowing or even a new age belief system. They have made a cultural shift as a result of their extensive psychedelic experience so that their relationship to time and space, causality and synchronicity is no longer Western. The women attend to signs in the natural world, shift easily between states of consciousness, and receive guidance from unseen others. They swim in the sacred.

I think they are the closest our culture has to the Eleusinian

priestesses who held the sacred container for visionary journeys in ancient Greece. That culture had healing centers and
rituals for dream incubation and nighttime journeys. As philosophy professor Mara Lynn Keller wrote, they "believed that
illness stemmed from a person not being aligned with their
divine destiny, [and] those seeking healing would prepare for
a night of dreaming by inviting a visitation of divine presence
and purpose into their lives....After a night of dreaming, initiates would tell their dream to attendants." These people were
called *therapeutes*, which is the root word for *therapist*. The initiate was "to follow the divine guidance and to perform some
action, as directed by the deity in order for healing."[1]

It's quite amazing how the current underground guides
think of their calling in a very similar way, in that they are
also interested in seeing their clients take meaningful action
following the ceremony. Charlotte, who works with well-
functioning people, wants to see how they manifest their experience: "I want to see action in [the] outer world before next
session; not just hooked on experience. [I want to see them]
clean up unfinished business in relationships. So next ceremony, they move on to next step in real-world progress in their
lives and functioning."

The elder guides follow the protocol of preparation and
setting intentions, doing the ceremony, and then integration
or follow-up to varying degrees. It's important to contrast the
role of guides with the new profession of psychedelic psychotherapy, which combines both the sitting aspect and the supportive therapy process before and after the journey. Sitting as
a guide and providing supportive psychotherapy are two different functions, requiring two different sets of skills. Expertise
in both these functions is a lot to ask as a professional require-
ment. The continuity in the therapeutic alliance from intention
to integration is valuable and distinctive from the quality of

presence and experience needed in a sitter. It might be helpful in the training of the new cohort of psychedelic therapists to clarify what's needed for each of these two different roles and functions.

The current psychedelic renaissance is exploding around the women elders who continue to work underground. A few of the guides have found discrete opportunities to train the next generation of psychedelic therapists, and some are mentoring new guides. All will continue to work underground because that is where they can practice in a sacred manner. That their work with entheogens is sacred is the central theme for all the women elders no matter what their background or training.

This is not to say that the research teams working with these medicines are irreverent. Psychologist Bill Richards, a senior member of the team at Johns Hopkins University, wrote, "If the ultimate healing force is the energy we call love that flows into time from the sacred dimensions of consciousness, the healer becomes the conduit or facilitator."[2] Despite being immersed in medical settings, the research teams make every effort to maintain a sacred container for the entheogenic journeys while, at the same time, collecting data. Not an easy balance to maintain.

The next theme in common for the women elders is they have worked on their personal healing and spiritual development for decades, most of their lives actually. Following such a psychospiritual path has been a primary motivator in their lives, opening them to therapy, spiritual trainings, mentorships, and the lifelong use of entheogenic journeys with all the medicines, at all dosage levels. These women are intrepid explorers with the required discipline and strength to stay on that steep, and sometimes treacherous, path for a lifetime.

After decades of this level of psychospiritual work, a shift happens that allows for greater freedom from personal history. It's not that the women have forgotten their old stories and traumas, but they've attained a certain objective distance that allows for greater flexibility, especially when traveling through their inner psychic space or accompanying others. Combined with awareness, this inner flexibility enables the guide to keep her own issues out of the journey space, so she can provide a clear setting for the client.

This capacity to keep their own egos in check is the most important way the guides maintain the sacred nature of entheogenic journeys. In *Listening to Ayahuasca*, I described how the Shuar shamans took all day to clear and protect the *maloca* (ceremonial pavilion) in preparation for the ayahuasca ceremony that evening. I wondered, *What have they been doing all day?* I finally decided they were protecting the energetic space from unwanted outer sources. I realize now that the ceremonial space most needs protection from the inner psychic world of the shaman or guide.

Besides the obvious, corporate financial incentives encroaching upon the psychedelic renaissance and the sacred space of entheogenic use, it's the personal failure of the guide or therapist that most threatens the sacred journey. The crossing of sexual boundaries currently at issue in the psychedelic renaissance is the behavioral manifestation of the guide not being able to protect the sacred journey space. The current psychedelic subculture entering the mainstream is like a smorgasbord of promises — it's a buyer-beware marketplace and only likely to become more complicated and difficult to navigate. In this way, it may not be so different from the array of therapists, religious leaders, athletic coaches, and doctors who also cross ethical boundaries for their own satisfaction.

Western cultures have yet to create a safe container or ritual for entheogens to be used for spiritual development in a sacred manner. Indigenous peoples have long held sacred cere-monies with elders carrying the tradition within a community setting that values each person's intention and contribution. The sacred use of entheogens in tribal communities supports the priorities of sustainability and reciprocity with the natural world. The elder women guides are carriers of these integrated ways of living with entheogens that Western cultures need to learn.

The Inner Shift from Personal to Spiritual

I was recently in a three-night ayahuasca ceremony and was surprised that I didn't have much in the way of personal issues coming up. After all, I'd spent many a previous ceremony cry-ing through the night, purging old traumas and patterns from my life history. Not this time. Besides the inevitable nausea, I spent a good bit of time focused on compassion, which seemed to be easier for me to cultivate than love. I felt compassion for pretty much anyone, including those who have harmed me, but love…that was not so easy. Still, I wondered about the shift in focus from personal issues to classic spiritual ones.

I asked Jungian analyst Jerome Braun, who's training with a Shipibo shaman, Maestro Nelson, about my recent experi-ence. Nelson taught Jerome that this shift happens as child-hood issues get cleaned out. The inner space becomes larger or the old problems become smaller; the energies are cleaned out and new energy brought in. As Gary Snyder described wil-derness quests, "Ultimately all such journeys are done for the sake of the whole, not as some private quest."[3] Charlotte said something similar: "There's a bigger message coming from the medicine — larger than individual psychological healing."

This reminds me of what Connie Grauds said to me in the kitchen (see page 5): "We don't care about the family history.

We don't even want to hear about it." After interviewing the underground guides, I understand more. It's true, they don't want to hear childhood stories, but it's not that they don't care. They might work to clean out those old stories via shamanic techniques, energetically or symbolically, but not usually in narrative form. The entheogenic path is about this shift in perspective from identification with these stories to a stance of dispassionate compassion in relation to one's own personal story. Jungian analyst Ann Ulanov described this same inner shift that "liberates us from…the complex or trauma that has captured us. The trauma is part of us; [but] we are no longer engulfed in it."[4]

We disidentify with our personal narrative — our sense of self is no longer tied up in being a victim, blaming others, mired in regrets. The Buddhist concept of attachment is helpful here. Tenzin Priyadarshi writes, "It's not about the content of any particular view [or story] so much as a way of holding the container more loosely. The mind learns to stretch to embrace ideas that may seem to be contradictory, without the stress of cognitive dissonance. It's a way of living comfortably with the mystery. And in that place of ease, where attachment to any position or view begins to relax, the grasp with which we cling to our self begins to relax too."[5]

We are no longer captives of our personal history. This doesn't mean we don't have many of the same old feelings, but we don't get caught in them. With this increased inner distance, we develop a new relationship to suffering. With a greater understanding and acceptance of the universal nature of human suffering, we learn how to navigate our times of suffering in the same way we learn to navigate challenging journey experiences. We don't resist; we trust in the process; we have guided support; we cultivate awareness. Simone Weil had the wisdom of experience to write, "We must not wish for

the disappearance of any of our troubles, but grace to transform them."[6] Like Rumi welcoming all into his guesthouse:
"Welcome and entertain them all! Even if they're a crowd of
sorrows."[7]

As our capacity for dispassionate acceptance expands,
there's a shift in balance in the psyche that opens up an inner
spaciousness, which allows for greater flexibility. This shift
sounds very similar to decentering or self-distancing, which
leads to a metacognitive awareness of inner thoughts and feelings.[8] This therapeutic technique is central to many psychological approaches, as it reduces anxiety and depression. It's
most easily summarized by my favorite bumper sticker, "Don't
believe everything you think."

This metacognitive awareness allows the guides to keep
themselves out of their client's journey. As Laura Huxley has
described, this is the most challenging aspect of guiding. The
elder has to be aware of her inner process, notice when something comes up from within, and keep her issues separate.
Guides are human — things will erupt from their psyches. To
keep the journey space safe and sacred, the guide has to manage her own energies, thoughts, and feelings.

This shift in perspective might include decentering and
the establishment of an objective witness, but it's much more
than that. The difference lies in the quality and extent of the
spaciousness that's created when we disidentify with our egos.
There's an opening of the inner space of psyche and soma that
extends beyond the boundaries of the body, out into an expansive energy field. The physical body becomes less solid and
more subtle, refined, porous. There's a permeability between
the inside space and the outside world so that no difference
remains. The inner merges into the outside and the outer
enters the inner space.

Krishnamurti described this same merging: "The outside

is the inside and the inside is the outside, and it is difficult, almost impossible to separate them."⁹ Anthropologist Lynne Hume wrote, "One becomes conscious of a transcendent reality through focusing on the interior world of the self. It is recognized that divinity is within the self and is a reflection of the divine outside the self."¹⁰

Philosopher Tom Cheetham added, "It is in the heart that the inner and outer become one."¹¹ The heart is the organ of perception of subtle, energetic worlds, usually unseen but glimpsed in entheogenic journeys and then forever sensed to be present, interpenetrating our material world. As we become more expansive, we open to the presence of other worlds through our hearts, through our breath. Psychologist James Hillman wrote, "The word for perception or sensation in Greek was *aesthesis*, which means at root a breathing in or taking in of the world."¹²

Years ago, I learned a Sufi meditation in which I breathe through my heart, lifting off subtle layers of dust and debris from everyday life. I feel my sternum float with the movement of my physical breath, and I use the subtle energy of my breath to polish the mirror of my heart, to open my heart to the world. The inner space of my heart merges with the heart of the world.

Poets describe this embodied permeability the best — such as D.H. Lawrence in "The Song of a Man Who Has Come Through." Immediately, the title foreshadows that we are dealing with transformation — "come through." The first line reads, "Not I, not I, but the wind that blows through me!"¹³ An exclamation point highlights that this is a significant transformation. The line is a perfect description of the permeable spaciousness that results when the "I" is no longer and we become permeable to the wind.

Kathleen Raine in "Unsolid Matter" captured the same

porousness as the body becomes so refined that it's no longer physical:[14]

> These bodies are of cloud so thin,
> This tenuous vesture that we wear
> Might pass through walls or worlds
> That mesh of fire, that mesh of air.

The women elders of the psychedelic underground have been cultivating this permeability all their lives. They have learned to live in this world and to travel in unseen worlds. They have learned to swim in the sacred.

Priest and scientist Pierre Teilhard de Chardin described how this very same process unfolded and directed his life. Starting with "a point that was built into me congenitally, the world gradually caught fire for me, burst into flames."[15] Yes, as chapter 2 explores, this began in childhood; at around six or seven, "I began to feel myself drawn by Matter — or, more correctly, by something which 'shone' at the heart of Matter." He wrote of his "interior development," including "the disappearance of the alleged barrier that separates the Within of things from the Without," until "Matter becomes Spirit at just the same pace as love begins to spread universally." Finally, Teilhard de Chardin distinguished his personal story from the transcendental process: "At the peak of Evolution of the Personal, the Universe was potentially becoming for me something that loved and could be loved."

One's Spiritual Job

Jungians talk about this inner shift as a movement from the ego to the Self. Jungian Sonu Shamdasani clarified Jung's position on this: "The realization was that the Self was the goal of the process of individuation. Progression was not linear but involved a circumambulation of the Self."[16] This process unfolds over a lifetime, as Teilhard de Chardin described. In his memoir, Jung stated, "In the end the only events in my life worth telling are those when the imperishable world erupted into this transitory one."[17] When the transcendent was perceived imminently.

The women elders from the psychedelic underground understand Jung's perspective. When interviewed, they recounted the spiritual unfolding that led them to their work with entheogens — from spiritual experiences in childhood to their personal healing of trauma and loss, to wise mentors, to initiations, and to their own visionary journeys. They understand their lives as a spiritual unfolding, that circumambulation of the sacred, moving closer with every turn. This is the essence of what they bring to their work guiding journeys — their presence as more experienced fellow travelers.

When we spoke, I kept telling them they were warriors, brave and strong. They don't see it that way. They are "just" following their calling. They are "just" doing what I call their spiritual job — by which I mean, the work or contribution to the community that only we can do with our unique set of gifts and experiences. Arielle used the term *soul issue* for the same concept, meaning "how to be of service." I don't know if everyone has such a calling. Some people organize their lives around accumulating wealth or fame — I don't think that qualifies as a spiritual job.

In *Listening to Ayahuasca*, I describe my rising to fulfill what I experienced as a mission from the voice of the plant spirit, what turned out to be my spiritual job. I'd been preparing for it all my life with psychedelic experiences — while living at Esalen in the late sixties, with spiritual trainings, research, and psychotherapy practice. Finally, I ended up at a retreat center without realizing that three shamanic ayahuasca

ceremonies were planned for that week. I said yes to those ceremonies before I knew what they really involved or where they
would take me.

Certainly, this description carries a whiff of inflation, but
that evaporated as I worked hard over many years to write
from a Western psychologist's perspective of healing with ayahuasca. The same spiritual job then morphed into this book,
and I have to admit that I can't really remember the birth
of this project — how did I get started? I don't have a clear
answer except to say I was in it before I realized what I was
doing. Again, I rose to the challenge even with a year's hiatus
due to my post-anesthesia-foggy and aging brain during my
year of dismemberment.

I have come through my liminal period of recovering from
major surgery, which I view now as an initiation, one that
most of us go through in one way or another in the course
of life. "No one skips dismemberment," Maureen said, and I
would add, no one evades suffering. Medridth expanded on
this theme: "Our job is learning how to be here. Suffering is
our biggest teacher." I'm on the other side now. I have "come
through," as D.H. Lawrence put it, and I'm a different person. This is what integration really means — we transcend the
smaller, constricted parts of ourselves and are transformed into
more spacious, flexible human beings.

The psychedelic elders guided me through this process, not
just in journeys, but in their presence, their stories. I dare say
I received a transmission from these women that allowed me
to move beyond my personal history. The details remain the
same — my perspective has shifted. I'm less caught in blaming others. I have more compassion. I don't know if I'm up to
knowing "how to live on this earth and be joyful," as Radianthawk described, but I'm "working" on it.

Dying Before We Die

There's something about this level of taking responsibility for my life that expands into a greater acceptance of death. Psychologist Tony Bossis said, "Death is the portal and teacher. How paradoxical? Death, the very thing that teaches us about the essence of being human and to live fully in the present, is the same thing that humans fear the most."[18] Psychedelic journeys give us the opportunity to encounter death before our time, to accept a higher level of self-responsibility.

In *The Immortality Key*, Brian Muraresku pointed out that the core of the world's religions is the mystical experience of dying before you die.[19] The Eleusinian Mysteries led to, one study said, "transformational experiences that gave initiates a new perspective on life and death."[20] Rumi had the same insight: "If you could get rid of yourself just once, the secret of secrets would open to you."[21] That's the initiation. It's captured in the psychedelic studies as ego dissolution or unity, oceanic experiences. With either term, the ego boundaries disappear and merge with the universe. "Not I, not I," as D.H. Lawrence wrote.

Ego death is part of the mystical experience, but the medicines teach us about dying before we die in many ways that do not qualify as mystical experience and are not yet being studied in academic research. Many people report communicating during journeys with loved ones who have died or traveling to realms identified as afterlife worlds. The message *You're not alone* during my MDMA journey certainly shifted my relationship to death.

The mystical experience, so valued in the medicalization of psychedelics, may not be the sole key to the therapeutic benefits of entheogens. Instead, it might be the confrontation with death that is the actual mechanism of transformation — the acceptance of our mortality along with the sense that something about us is eternal. Our belief system is changed forever. This would explain why the phenomenal outcome of the entheogenic journey is so similar to the near-death experience. The people who die before they die have a different relationship to death — they have a very vivid sense of continuation.[22] Psychological researchers may not yet know how to differentiate and then measure the confrontation with death independent of the mystical experience. Dying before you die might eventually be found to be a more specific mediator of change following either a psychedelic or a near-death experience.

In a careful study of recalled experiences of death (RED), a new term with a more specific definition than near-death experiences, the authors delineate themes that have also been highlighted by the psychedelic guides.[23] Referring to the more-than-a-life review, one subject who recalled his death said, "I was able to experience myself in all events in my life." This happens instantaneously in both psychedelic journeys and the death process.

Facing ourselves through the life-span review leads to a higher level of self-responsibility and spiritual maturity. We are confronted with our own karma and learn that, as another subject from the study above said, "I, alone, am in charge of my destiny." This is another theme from both near-death and entheogenic experiences. Mythologist Martin Shaw found the same lesson in fairy tales: "That's the point of the old vigils: to be broken open and shaken up by the great forces of the universe....Something has to be traded for this bounty. It's usually the child that you were."[24] Time to grow up. This level of existential responsibility for ourselves is precisely what Medridth referred to when she said, "We are responsible for our intentions and our choices. Responsible to ourselves and to humanity."

Existential psychotherapist Ernesto Spinelli described this higher level of responsibility: "Each of us is responsible for everything and to every being."[25] Underlying this perspective, as Thich Nhat Hanh liked to say, is the mutual connectedness or interbeing of all things human and nonhuman, living and nonliving.[26]

The final shared theme between the elder guides and those who recalled their death experience was the sense of mission or purpose. Medridth said, "I believe every single person presently here has a 'mission,' has opportunities to grow and learn and that we can alter our choices to better our own lives and the lives of the future generations."[27] This is our spiritual job — what are we exquisitely primed to contribute?

These themes, present in both entheogenic and recalled-death experiences, have a certain flow to them. By reviewing our lives in these expanded states, we reach a new level of honesty and sense of responsibility for what we create in our lives. From this self-confrontation we discover a higher purpose for our time in this world that paradoxically adds meaning to our lives and, at the same time, prepares us for death.

Trusting Intuition

People who recall their deaths and the psychedelic guides describe a wholly different way of knowing. A subject in the RED study said, "The thought was lucid and came through immediate knowing. It was a different way of thinking."[28] This is a definition of gnosis, which according to religion professor Jeffrey Kripal "is not the kind of knowledge that one can derive from the senses....It is not information. It is not data. You cannot Google it and 'get' it." Humanities professor Harold Bloom said it this way, "It is not a knowing about something. It is a kind of knowing by becoming that which one knows."[29]

The elders rely primarily on their intuition when guiding journeys. One could criticize that approach for not being evidence-based, but we have so little data about how to use the entheogens that experience-based intuition may be our best practice. Experience is the key. According to psychologist Allan Schore in *The Science of the Art of Psychotherapy*, therapists who have "experience-based, postreflective, well-educated intuition behave differently in the moment during a psychotherapy session.... They know what action would be effective and how to carry it out. Moreover, they have 'negative expertise' — they know what actions not to take in solving a problem and pay attention to intuitions that signal uncertainty."[30] Experienced therapists with well-educated intuition rely on, Schore says, "far more sophisticated unconscious deep and automatic knowledge that may have been painfully learned."

Schore credits intuitive clinical experience as the essence of the therapeutic alliance, which is the "major mechanism of therapeutic action" for psychotherapy in general.[31] This is an important variable for psychedelic psychotherapy as well.[32] As Schore says, "All technique sits atop these right brain implicit skills, which deepen and expand with clinical experience: the ability to receive and express nonverbal affective communications; clinical sensitivity; use of subjectivity/intersubjectivity; empathy; and affect regulation." Further, Schore writes, "Intuition is expressed not in literal language but is embodied in a gut feeling."[33]

Intuitive skills are learned via transmission, being at the elbow of a teacher. This is why apprenticeship is so important for becoming a guide. The learning is implicit, nonverbal. Cognitive scientist John Allman wrote, "We experience the intuitive process at a visceral level. Intuitive decision-making enables us to react quickly in situations that involve a high degree of uncertainty which commonly involve social interactions."[34] Exactly like an entheogenic journey.

I think the women elders had a strong sense of intuition earlier in their lives, even before they embarked on their entheogenic journeys. They were already receptive, fine-tuned to learn in these expanded states of consciousness. As they worked on their own healing and sat with others, their intuitive powers developed even further. And their relationships with unseen others or plant teachers also provided an additional source of information and guidance. However, this process of developing and refining their intuition took years to mature. The current psychedelic therapists are following a different path in their training and personal development. They don't have the luxury of time to ripen in experience. They are on a fast track to meet the cultural need for breakthrough therapies.

Experiencing an Ontic Shift

At this point, we part ways with the Western worldview, where reality is rooted in the physical, measurable dimension. After years of traveling in psychedelic realms, the women have a different sense of reality. We know that one psilocybin journey can transform an atheist into a mystic. Imagine how years of entheogenic experiences have transformed the psychedelic elders.

We do have one report from religious studies professor Christopher Bache, based on his seventy-three high-dose (500 to 600 micrograms) LSD journeys over a twenty-year period. Not as extensive a history of entheogenic traveling as the women elders, but still a relevant report. Bache noticed that his students, without any direct involvement from him beyond teaching, "often found themselves undergoing life-changing transformations without any encouragement from me to do so....Students began to have powerful spiritual openings...as though they were being activated....What was triggering these effects was not what I was *doing* but what I had *become* through my psychedelic practice."[35] Bache concluded that "states of consciousness are contagious."

His report stands as an affirmation of the concept of presence — who the guide is is critical, not what they do. Bache's report also confirms Schore's focus on "right-brain-to-right-brain communication within the therapeutic alliance" as the change mechanism of long-term psychotherapy.[36] The therapist heals, not the particular therapeutic technique.

Bache also concluded, "If I were to do it [the seventy-three trips] over again, I would take a gentler approach," meaning a lower dose that would make integration easier. He said, "It took me about ten years [after the journeys] to get fully grounded in life again."[37]

We know very little about how a person changes after years of working with entheogens, and what changes we do know about are very difficult to put into words. Radianthawk said matter-of-factly, "You get a mystical experience, but so what? You have to learn how to work with energy. If you don't shift your awareness, you'll never know how energy works."

I knew this was important when Radianthawk said it, but I can't explain exactly what she meant. Similarly, whenever Maureen used the word *nuance*, I would perk up, knowing this was an important teaching. But again, she was talking about subtle processes that I can't quite explain and can't find words for. These women are referring to something that is ineffable, not just a mystical experience, but a way of being that is distinct from consensus reality.

Ontology is the branch of metaphysics concerned with the nature of being, and an ontic shift describes when people feel a reality shift, a sense that they are no longer dealing with the world as it is ordinarily known, and this new state is fraught with significance.[38] Psychologist Peter Nelson described his personal ontic shift following a spontaneous mystical experience (not involving entheogens) in which his identity and sense of reality were deconstructed. He wrote, "There was no longer a 'me,' but somehow total awareness was still there, but it was not really clear exactly who was having this awareness."[39]

Nelson continued, "We live in a world of multiple realities…and as one moves from one reality to another, one experiences a kind of 'shock.'" He described this fundamental change in the perception of reality as "a leap across a worldview boundary…a shift from one experiential world to another…a leap into the sacred." And then, more than two decades before I began interviewing the women elders of the psychedelic underground, Nelson touched on something that is only recently emerging in our understanding of expanded states of consciousness: "The most important personality attribute associated with those who can make these ontic shifts appears to be Trait Absorption." This is what I discuss in chapter 4.

As I've mentioned, I score high on absorption but I lack the certainty that the elder guides have in their very bones. I never quite land my leap fully into the sacred. Nelson described my position well: "a profound unknowing that must be lived as an abiding existential ontological uncertainty." This position is a little like disembarking from a canoe with one foot remaining in the canoe and the other planted firmly on the grassy bank. A precarious position at best.

When Nelson uses the phrase "worldview boundary," that evokes a sense of concreteness to both concepts — worldview and boundary — making them seem more solid than they actually are. Ernesto Spinelli stated his critique, "This structural 'thing-ification' of our experience of being is expressed via the term *the worldview*." He proposed the term *worlding* "to signify that mode of existence which is always-becoming, ever-shifting, process-like, and linguistically-elusive."[40] This linguistic shift is reminiscent of the more accurate translation of the Lakota phrase *tanka wakan* from the Great Mystery to the Great Mysteriousing.

Spinelli wrote, "At a worlding level, our existence is a dynamic, continuous becoming. The experience of becoming cannot be entirely grasped and maintained at a worldview level." From this perspective, it's much easier to understand Radianthawk's admonition to shift your consciousness and learn how to work with energy. Everything is in the process of becoming, shifting, moving, swimming.

A Lifelong Journey

The women elders have worked with entheogens for decades, for their own healing and guidance, for spiritual practice, and in service to both the medicines and those who journey. They've nurtured their personal relationship to the medicines in general and most often to one or two particular ones that are "their medicine." This is quite a different model from the medicalization of psychedelics used primarily for symptom reduction and very brief clinical treatment.

If you win the trust of the psychedelic therapists and researchers on the study teams, you'll likely find that many of them are using the medicines, not as a medical prescription, but in the psychospiritual way of the elders. This is the good news. I know of no one indulging in the ways of Timothy Leary and his crew from the sixties. This time around there is a cultural respect for the power of these medicines and the entheogenic experience.

Entheogenic journeys become a part of life, not unlike the Mystery School at Eleusis where people retreated for ceremony once a year. With periodic ritual use, a relationship develops with an entheogen that calls, speaks, or touches you. Maybe you have visionary dreams of that medicine, the spirit of the medicine, or the plant teacher. An energetic connection is established and you receive teachings, insights, guidance, revelations, or downloads, as we now say. You learn how to dialogue with "your medicine." The relationship becomes more real and evolves over time. You learn how to enter into a reciprocal relationship with this unseen other, learn what this lifelong journey asks of you. Once again, this is quite a different model from the medical use of psychedelics.

Research studies have focused on mystical experience as the central mechanism of psychedelic healing using perhaps two to three journeys. But how does healing happen when the medicines are used periodically over a lifetime? The elder guides have worked with all the medicines and have concentrated on different ones at different times in their lives.

Perhaps the concept of learning within a relationship is a better fit for long-term, ritual use. Psychologist Benny Shanon referred to a school to describe his extended work with ayahuasca, complete with levels and graduations.[41]

The women guides have a passion, a longing for expanded states of consciousness. A number of them said they were more at home in these unseen worlds. They're committed to a lifelong process of learning and healing, following their own intuitive path. From a totally different perspective, philosopher Peter Kingsley described this process: "It demands tremendous courage. The journey…changes your body; it alters every cell.…The longing is what turns us inside out until we find the sun and the moon and the stars inside."[42]

Love the World

What's the purpose of all these entheogenic journeys if not to expand the heart and open with love for the world. And yes, with love for all humans and other-than-humans, living and nonliving. For rocks as Teilhard de Chardin saw them. For people we disagree with — the great mystics know "we are because they are" in the great interbeing and dependent co-arising. For transcending our personal histories and transforming our relationship to the life we are given, to the world we live in.

Even as he was dying, or perhaps because he was dying, Yongey Mingyur Rinpoche came to the realization that "when you love the world, the world loves you back."[43] This is the big healing that comes through the heart. Poet Raymond Carver, despite his tumultuous life, came to a similar realization in "Late Fragment" that is etched on his tombstone:[44]

> And did you get what
> you wanted from this life, even so?
> I did.
> And what did you want?
> To call myself beloved, to feel myself
> beloved on the earth.

To love and be loved leads to a shift in perspective in relation to the world or worlds. This shift in perspective allows for a deeper connection between the inner and outer worlds, through the heart. In a PBS documentary, Apache Bob Stevens described his relationship to the wild: "Being out here in the wild amongst this landscape. I feel the wind and the wind blows right through me, becomes the rhythm with my heart. Not only do I become the world around me but the world around me becomes me and we become one."[45]

Aboriginal elder David Mowaljarlai described his experience of being in the world:

> You have a feeling in your heart that you're going to
> feed your body this day, get more knowledge. You go
> out now, see animals moving, see trees, a river. You are

looking at nature and giving it your full attention, seeing all its beauty. Your vision has opened and you start learning now. When you touch them, all things talk to you, give you their story. It makes you really surprised. You feel you want to go deeper so you start moving around and stamp your feet — to come closer and to recognize what you are seeing. You understand that your mind has been opened to all those things because you are seeing them, because your presence and their presence meet together and you recognize each other. These things recognize you. They give their wisdom and their understanding to you when you come close to them. In the distance, you feel: 'Aaahh — I'm going to go there and have a closer look!' You know it is pulling you. When you recognize it, it gives strength — a new flow. You have life now."[46]

Trappist monk Thomas Merton intimately knew this connection between the inner and outer landscape. He wrote, "It was a strange awakening to find the sky inside you and beneath you and above you and all around you so that your spirit is one with the sky."[47] The individual dissolves into nature and upon return has a larger perspective for life.

As we journey, we become more permeable to the natural world, to the wild. Our energy bodies move through our boundaries into a much larger and more subtle world. We journey and learn other ways of knowing — we perceive the world by becoming one with the world. We develop an intimate relationship with nature, with a reciprocity that allows for balance and gratitude. We realize the transcendent is imminent.

More and more people are having numinous experiences with and without entheogens.[48] How do these experiences change us? What do we do differently? How do we live in an illuminated world?

What do these medicines want to teach us? How do they want to heal us? Why have they emerged once again into our modern world, some traveling out of the jungles, mountains, deserts, and chemistry labs? The women guides of the psychedelic underground have been in relationship with these medicines for decades, providing a sacred container for entheogenic journeys. We need to hear from them now more than ever.

ACKNOWLEDGMENTS

This book has been a journey for me on many levels, and I could not have completed the "trip" without the support and guidance of so many friends. My newest friends, from the list of underground women, spent countless hours with me, sharing and guiding me along the path. I am not who I was when I started this project, and it is primarily because of their presence in my life and in my psyche.

I have great appreciation for New World Library and the excellent care my books have received there — Jason Gardner who holds the vision, Jeff Campbell who edits with insight, and Kim Corbin who enthusiastically publicizes my books. And thanks to my agent, Barbara Moulton, who saw something in me I didn't fully recognize.

I have too many friends to thank who had faith in me when mine wavered. My beloved arch nemesis, Joe Tafur, always reminded me of the reality of the unseen world. Jerome Braun, a Jungian analyst in training with a Shipibo shaman, shared the wonder of our respective journeys. I was always grateful for a phone check-in with Bill Barnard, a lengthy text from Tony

Bossis, and love from Nelia and Carlos. Pluma and Lana are guiding lights in my world. My therapist, Jungian analyst Carolyn Bray, accompanied me along the way. Connie Grauds, who travels from the Western world to the jungle with ease, was a source of great clarification. Mark Brown, a self-described dreamy literary author, sent email support through the final chapter. My Berkeley sangha has been a home base for me, especially with support from David Presti. Kind thanks to my daily walkers on my island in Maine, Tom Guglielmo and Barbara Ternes, and others who join us along the way, Gerry Wurzburg and Grady Watts, Malcolm and Christine Woolen.

I am grateful to the Shipibo shamans who helped me after my major surgery and continue to sing healing *icaros* — Maestra Anita Perez Sinacay, Maestro Javier Vasquez Gomez, and Maestro Nelson Barbaran Gomez.

And finally, I am most grateful to the small island off the coast of Maine where I live seven months out of the year. When I'm not there, I long for the island's great beauty, dark nights, and silence.

ENDNOTES

Preface

1. Carl A. P. Ruck et al., "Entheogens," in *The Road to Eleusis: Unveiling the Secret of the Mysteries*, ed. R. Gordon Wasson, Albert Hofmann, and Carl A. P. Ruck (Berkeley, CA: North Atlantic Books, 2018), 139.

Chapter One: Out of the Silence

1. Amy Emerson, "Treating PTSD with MDMA-Assisted Psychotherapy," *MAPS Bulletin* 26 (winter 2016): 3, 27.
2. James Cowan, *Mysteries of the Dream-Time: The Spiritual Life of Australian Aborigines* (New York: Prism Press, 1993), 8.
3. Michael Pollan, *How to Change Your Mind: What the New Science of Psychedelics Teaches Us about Consciousness, Dying, Addictions, Depression and Transcendence* (New York: Penguin, 2018), 225.
4. Huston Smith and Jeffery Paine, *Tales of Wonder: Adventures Chasing the Divine* (New York: HarperCollins, 2009), 171.
5. Smith and Paine, *Tales of Wonder*, 172.
6. Rachel Harris and Lee Gurel, "A Study of Ayahuasca Use in North America," *Journal of Psychoactive Drugs* 44, no. 3 (July/August 2012): 213.
7. Brian C. Muraresku, *The Immortality Key: The Secret History of the Religion*

with No Name (New York: St. Martin's Publishing Group, 2020), 242; and Wasson et al., *Road to Eleusis*, 91.

8. Muraresku, *Immortality Key*, 242.

9. Barbara Ehrenreich and Deirdre English, *Witches, Midwives, and Nurses: A History of Women Healers* (New York: The Feminist Press at CUNY, 2010), 25; and Max Dashu, "Woman Shaman: Uncovering the Female Ecstatics," in *Psychedelic Mysteries of the Feminine*, ed. Maria Papaspyrou, Chiara Baldini, and David Luke (Rochester, VT: Park Street Press, 2019), 57.

10. Mariavittoria Mangini, "Unseen Women in Psychedelic History," *Journal of Humanistic Psychology* (July 2012): 12; "Historian Explains How Women Have Been Excluded from the Field of Psychedelic Science: Interview with Erika Dyck," Chacruna, October 16, 2018, https://chacruna.net/historian -explains-how-women-have-been-excluded-from-the-field-of-psychedelic -science; and Leia Friedwoman, "It's 2020 and White Men Still Dominate Psychedelic Conferences," *Lucid News*, July 15, 2020, https://www.lucid .news/men-still-dominate-psychedelic-conferences.

11. Monnica T. Williams et al., "Dr. Valentina Wasson: Questioning What We Think We Know about the Foundations of Psychedelic Science," *Journal of Psychedelic Studies* 4, no. 3 (2020): 146.

12. Richard Tarnas and Sean Kelly, *Psyche Unbound: Essays in Honor of Stanislav Grof* (Santa Fe, NM: Synergetic Press and MAPS), 2022.

13. George R. Greer and Requa Tolbert, "Subjective Reports of the Effects of MDMA in a Clinical Setting," *Journal of Psychoactive Drugs* 18, no. 4 (1986): 314.

14. George R. Greer and Requa Tolbert, "A Method of Conducting Therapeutic Sessions with MDMA," *Journal of Psychoactive Drugs* 30, no. 4 (1998): 371.

15. Requa Tolbert, "Gender and Psychedelic Medicines: Rebirthing Archetypes," *ReVision* 25, no. 3 (2003): 6.

16. Stanislav Grof and Christina Grof, *Holotropic Breathwork: A New Approach to Self-Exploration and Therapy* (Albany: State University of New York Press / Excelsior Editions, 2010), 177; and Ralph Metzner, *Alchemical Divination: Accessing Your Spiritual Intelligence for Healing and Guidance* (Berkeley, CA: Regent Press, 2009), 29.

17. Myron J. Stolaroff, *The Secret Chief Revealed* (Sarasota, FL: MAPS, 2004), xii.

18. Rosalind Watts, "Can Magic Mushrooms Unlock Depression? What I've Learned in the Five Years since My TEDx Talk," Medium, February 28, 2022, https://medium.com/@DrRosalindWatts/can-magic-mushrooms

-unlock-depression-what-ive-learned-in-the-5-years-since-my-tedx-talk
-767c83963134.

19. Wasson et al., *Road to Eleusis*, 46.

Chapter Two: Visions from Childhood

1.   Daniel J. Siegel, *The Mindful Therapist: A Clinician's Guide to Mindsight and Neural Integration* (New York: W.W. Norton, 2010), 244.

2.   Katherine A. MacLean, Matthew W. Johnson, and Roland R. Griffiths, "Mystical Experiences Occasioned by the Hallucinogen Psilocybin Lead to Increases in the Personality Domain of Openness," *Journal of Psychopharmacology* 25, no. 11 (November 2011): 11, https://www.researchgate.net /publication/51679019_Mystical_Experiences_Occasioned_by_the _Hallucinogen_Psilocybin_Lead_to_Increases_in_the_Personality _Domain_of_Openness.

3.   Ian Stevenson, *Children Who Remember Previous Lives: A Question of Reincarnation*, rev. ed. (Jefferson, NC: McFarland, 2001), 9.

4.   Tobin Hart and Catalin Ailoae, "Spiritual Touchstones: Childhood Spiritual Experience in the Development of Influential Historic and Contemporary Figures," *Imagination, Cognition and Personality* 26, no. 4 (2006–2007): 345–59, https://www2.westga.edu/share/documents/pubs /000471_107.pdf.

5.   John G. Neihardt, *Black Elk Speaks: Being the Life Story of a Holy Man of the Oglala Sioux* (Lincoln: University of Nebraska Press, 1988), 41.

6.   Kaisa Puhakka, "An Invitation to Authentic Knowing," in *Transpersonal Knowing: Exploring the Horizon of Consciousness*, ed. Tobin Hart, Peter L. Nelson, and Kaisa Puhakka (Albany: State University of New York Press, 2000), 11.

7.   Michael M. Piechowski, "Childhood Spirituality," *Journal of Transpersonal Psychology* 33, no. 1 (2001): 13, https://atpweb.org/jtparchive/trps-33-01 -01-001.pdf.

8.   Albert Hofmann, *LSD: My Problem Child: Reflections on Sacred Drugs, Mysticism and Science*, 4th ed. (Santa Cruz, CA: Multidisciplinary Association for Psychedelic Studies, 2017), 29.

9.   Hofmann, *LSD: My Problem Child*, 46.

10. Gordon W. Allport, *The Individual and His Religion: A Psychological Interpretation* (New York: Macmillan, 1950), 142.

11. Roland R. Griffiths et al., "Mystical-Type Experiences Occasioned by

Psilocybin Mediate the Attribution of Personal Meaning and Spiritual Significance 14 Months Later," *Journal of Psychopharmacology* 22, no. 6 (May 30, 2008): 623, https://journals.sagepub.com/doi/10.1177 /0269881108094300.

12. Peter L. Nelson and Tobin Hart, "A Survey of Recalled Childhood Spiritual and Non-ordinary Experiences: Age, Rate and Psychological Factors Associated with Their Occurrence," 2011, https://childspirit.org/wp -content/uploads/2011/09/Child-Spirit-Carrollton-Survey-childhood -exp.pdf.

13. Martin A. Lee and Bruce Shlain, *Acid Dreams: The Complete Social History of LSD: The CIA, the Sixties, and Beyond* (New York: Grove Press, 1994), 224.

14. Jay Stevens, *Storming Heaven: LSD and the American Dream* (New York: Grove Press, 1987), 47; and Aldous Huxley, *The Doors of Perception and Heaven and Hell* (New York: Harper Perennial, 2009), 14.

15. Pollan, *How to Change Your Mind*, 165.

16. Al Hubbard, interviewed by Oscar Janiger, 1978; transcribed by Connie Littlefield in 2018, shared with author in February 2019.

17. "Captain Al Hubbard," Vaults of Erowid, December 29, 2003, https:// erowid.org/culture/characters/hubbard_al/hubbard_al.shtml.

18. Todd Brendan Fahey, "Al Hubbard: The Original Captain Trips," *High Times*, November 1991, http://www.whale.to/a/fahey.html.

19. Al Hubbard, interviewed by Oscar Janiger.

20. Quote by Duncan Blewett from *Hofmann's Potion*, directed by Connie Littlefield (National Film Board of Canada, 2002), https://www.nfb.ca /film/hofmanns_potion.

21. W.V. Caldwell, *LSD Psychotherapy: An Exploration of Psychedelic and Psycholytic Therapy* (New York: Grove Press, 1968), 118.

22. Brad Holden, "Hubbard, Al (1901–1982)," History Link.org, August 26, 2019, https://www.historylink.org/file/20830.

23. Erika Dyck, *Psychedelic Psychiatry: LSD from Clinic to Campus* (Baltimore, MD: Johns Hopkins Press, 2008), 89.

24. John N. Sherwood, Myron J. Stolaroff, and Willis W. Harman, "The Psychedelic Experience: A New Concept in Psychotherapy," *Journal of Neuropsychiatry* 4, no. 2 (1962): 69, https://www.yumpu.com/en /document/read/15124495/the-psychedelic-experience-a-new-concept -in-psychotherapy.

25. Quote and details in this paragraph from Lee and Shlain, *Acid Dreams*, 46, 54.

26. G. Petri et al., "Homological Scaffolds of Brain Functional Networks," *Journal of Royal Society Interface* 11 (2014): 8, https://royalsociety publishing.org/doi/pdf/10.1098/rsif.2014.0873.

27. Lee and Shlain, *Acid Dreams*, 46.

28. Abraham Hoffer, "A Program for the Treatment of Alcoholism: LSD, Malvaria and Nicotinic Acid," in *The Use of LSD in Psychotherapy and Alcoholism*, ed. Harold A. Abramson (New York: Bobbs-Merrill, 1967): 364, https://www.samorini.it/doc1/alt_aut/ad/abramson-the-use-of-lsd -in-psychotherapy-and-alcoholism.pdf.

29. Caldwell, *LSD Psychotherapy*, 82.

30. Al Hubbard, interviewed by Oscar Janiger.

31. Al Hubbard, interviewed by Oscar Janiger.

32. James Fadiman, email with author, January 22, 2020.

33. James Fadiman, *The Psychedelic Explorer's Guide: Safe, Therapeutic, and Sacred Journeys* (Rochester, VT: Park Street Press, 2011), 231; and Al Hubbard, interviewed by Oscar Janiger.

34. Tania Manning, personal communication with author, February 18, 2020.

35. All Hubbard quotes from Al Hubbard, interviewed by Oscar Janiger.

36. Duncan B. Blewett and Nicholas Chwelos, "Handbook for the Therapeutic Use of Lysergic Acid Diethylamide-25: Individual and Group Procedures," 1959, https://maps.org/research-archive/ritesofpassage/lsd handbook.pdf.

37. *Hofmann's Potion*, Littlefield.

38. Ido Hartogsohn, "Constructing Drug Effects: A History of Set and Setting," *Drug Science, Policy and Law* 3 (January 1, 2017): 2, https:// journals.sagepub.com/doi/10.1177/2050324516683325; and Timothy Leary, "Drugs, Set & Suggestibility," paper presented at the annual meeting of the American Psychological Association, September 6, 1961.

39. Stevens, *Storming Heaven*, 56.

40. Huston Smith, introduction to *The Divine Within: Selected Writings on Enlightenment* by Aldous Huxley (New York: Harper Perennial Modern Classics, 2013), 2.

41. Fadiman, *Psychedelic Explorer's Guide*, 233.

42. Al Hubbard, interviewed by Oscar Janiger.

43. *Hofmann's Potion*, Littlefield.

44. Mac McClelland, "The Psychedelic Miracle," *Rolling Stone*, March 9, 2017.

45. María Sabina, *María Sabina: Selections Volume Two*, ed. Jerome Rothenberg (Berkeley: University of California Press, 2003), 75.

Chapter Three: Becoming a Psychedelic Guide

1. Stolaroff, *Secret Chief,* xii.

2. Jeremy Narby, Francis Huxley, and John Mohawk, "Shamans through Time: Tricksters, Healers, Voodoo Priests and Anthropologists," in *Visionary Plant Consciousness: The Shamanic Teachings of the Plant World*, ed. J.P. Harpignies (Rochester, VT: Park Street Press, 2007), 29.

3. All quotes are from Psychedelic-Assisted Therapies and Research certificate program, "Curricular Modules of Study," California Institute of Integral Studies, accessed January 2020, https://www.ciis.edu/research -centers/center-for-psychedelic-therapies-and-research/about-the -certificate-in-psychedelic-assisted-therapies-and-research/curriculum.

4. Christopher Alexander, *A Foreshadowing of 21st Century Art: The Color and Geometry of Very Early Turkish Carpets* (Oxford, UK: Oxford University Press, 1993), 24.

5. Connie Grauds, personal communication with author, 2019.

6. *Unmistaken Child*, directed by Nati Baratz (Samsara Films/Alma Films, 2008), https://vimeo.com/ondemand/unmistakenchild.

7. Quotes by Stolaroff and Zeff from Stolaroff, *Secret Chief,* 18, 30, 58.

8. Alexander Shulgin and Ann Shulgin, *Pihkal: A Chemical Love Story* (Berkeley, CA: Transform Press, 1991), 365.

9. Quotes by Shulgin and Zeff from Shulgin and Shulgin, *Pihkal*, 377, 378.

10. Stolaroff, *Secret Chief,* 64.

11. Stolaroff, *Secret Chief,* 64.

12. Stolaroff, *Secret Chief,* 68.

13. Private letter, October 2021.

14. "MAPS MDMA-Assisted Therapy Code of Ethics," *MAPS Bulletin* 29, no. 1 (spring 2019), https://maps.org/news/bulletin/maps-mdma-assisted -psychotherapy-code-of-ethics-spring-2019.

15. iO Tillett Wright and Lily Kay Ross, "Bad Hug," *The Cut* (podcast), *New*

York, December 21, 2021, https://www.thecut.com/2021/12/cover-story
-podcast-bad-hug.html.

16. Charles Stang, "The Psychedelic Moment, Part 1," *Voices of Esalen* (podcast), January 8, 2021, https://www.esalen.org/podcasts/the-psychedelic
-moment-pt-1-charles-stang-on-the-mystical-experience.

17. Stolaroff, *Secret Chief*, 60.

18. Stanislav Grof, *LSD Psychotherapy: The Healing Potential of Psychedelic Medicine*, 4th ed. (Santa Cruz, CA: MAPS, 2008), 87.

19. Pollan, *How to Change Your Mind*, 233.

20. Quotes by Stanislov Grof from Grof, *LSD Psychotherapy*, 89, 101.

21. Christopher Timmerman, Rosalind Watts, and David Dupuis, "Towards Psychedelic Apprenticeship: Developing a Gentle Touch for the Mediation and Validation of Psychedelic-Induced Insights and Revelations," *Transcultural Psychiatry* (December 2020).

22. Donald Kalsched, *Trauma and the Soul: A Psychospiritual Approach to Human Development and Its Interruption* (New York: Routledge, 2013), 4.

23. William Finnegan, "Finding a Way Up," *New Yorker*, November 29, 2021, 55.

24. Jamie Beachy, "Video: What Is Psychedelic Chaplaincy?," Harvard Divinity School Center for the Study of World Religions, March 8, 2021, https://cswr.hds.harvard.edu/news/2021/03/08/video-what-psychedelic
-chaplaincy.

25. Petra Rethmann, "On Presence," in *Extraordinary Anthropology: Transformations in the Field*, ed. Jean-Guy A. Goulet and Bruce Granville Miller (Lincoln: University of Nebraska Press, 2007), 50.

26. F. Bruce Lamb, *Wizard of the Upper Amazon: The Story of Manuel Córdova-Rios* (Berkeley, CA: North Atlantic Books, 1971), x, 165.

27. Maggy Anthony, *Salome's Embrace: The Jungian Women* (New York: Routledge, 2018), 31.

28. Sonu Shamdasani, "Toward a Visionary Science: Jung's Notebooks of Transformation," in *The Black Books*, by C. G. Jung (New York: W. W. Norton, 2020), 97.

29. Quotes in this paragraph from Nan Savage Healy, *Toni Wolff & Carl Jung: A Collaboration* (Los Angeles: Tiberius Press, 2017), 126, 135.

30. C.G. Jung, *The Red Book* (New York: W.W. Norton, 2009).
31. Jung and Shamdasani quotes are from Shamdasani, "Toward a Visionary Science," 31, 32.
32. Healy, *Toni Wolff*, 134.
33. St. Augustine, *Soliloquies and Immortality of the Soul*, ed. Gerard Watson (Warminster, UK: Aris & Phillips, 1990), 23.

Chapter Four: Guidance from Unseen Others

1. Jamy Faust and Peter Faust, *The Constellation Approach: Finding Peace through Your Family Lineage* (Berkeley, CA: Regent Press, 2015), 2.
2. James Hillman, *The Thought of the Heart and the Soul of the World* (Putnam, CT: Spring Publications, 2014), 9, 10, 11.
3. James Hillman, *Re-visioning Psychology* (New York: Harper & Row, 1975), 151.
4. Carl G. Jung, *Memories, Dreams, Reflections* (New York: Random House, 1961), 183.
5. Shamdasani, "Toward a Visionary Science," 24.
6. Quotes by Luke from David Luke, "Disembodied Eyes Revisited: An Investigation into the Ontology of Entheogenic Entity Encounters," in *Otherworlds: Psychedelic and Exceptional Human Experience*, ed. David Luke (London: Muswell Hill Press, 2017): 97, 102, 103.
7. Rick Strassman, *DMT: The Spirit Molecule: A Doctor's Revolutionary Research into the Biology of Near-Death and Mystical Experiences* (Rochester, VT: Park Street Press, 2001), 185.
8. Rick Strassman, *DMT and the Soul of Prophecy: A New Science of Spiritual Revelation in the Hebrew Bible* (Rochester, VT: Park Street Press, 2014).
9. Anna Lutkajtis, "Entity Encounters and the Therapeutic Effect of the Psychedelic Mystical Experience," *Journal of Psychedelic Studies* (2020): 3.
10. Alexander B. Belser et al., "Patient Experiences of Psilocybin-Assisted Psychotherapy: An Interpretative Phenomenological Analysis," *Journal of Humanistic Psychology* 57, no. 4 (2017): 365.
11. Roland R. Griffiths et al., "Survey of Subjective 'God Encounter Experiences': Comparisons among Naturally Occurring Experiences and Those Occasioned by the Classic Psychedelics Psilocybin, LSD, Ayahuasca, or DMT," *PLoS ONE* 14, no. 4 (April 23, 2019), https://journals.plos.org/plosone/article?id=10.1371/journal.pone.0214377; and Alan K. Davis

et al., "Survey of Entity Encounter Experiences Occasioned by Inhaled N,N-dimethyltryptamine: Phenomenology, Interpretation, and Enduring Effects," *Journal of Psychopharmacology* 34, no. 9 (2020): 1008.

12. "Video: Psilocybin and Mystical Experience: Implications for 'Healthy Psychological Functioning, Spirituality, and Religion," Harvard Divinity School Center for the Study of World Religions, September 29, 2020, https://cswr.hds.harvard.edu/news/2020/09/29/video-psilocybin-and -mystical-experience-implications-healthy-psychological.

13. Luis Eduardo Luna, "Indigenous and Mestizo Use of Ayahuasca: An Overview," in *The Ethnopharmacology of Ayahuasca*, ed. Rafael Guimarães dos Santos (Kerala, India: Transworld Research Network, 2011), 8.

14. Kathleen Harrison, University of California, Berkeley, talk at Botanical Garden, March 3, 2019.

15. Maestro Nelson Barbaran Gomez, Zoom conversation with author, February 19, 2021.

16. Stephen V. Beyer, "What Do the Spirits Want from Us?," *Journal of Shamanic Practice* 4, no. 2 (fall 2011): 12.

17. Jeremy Narby and Rafael Chanchari Pizuri, *Plant Teachers: Ayahuasca, Tobacco, and the Pursuit of Knowledge* (Novato, CA: New World Library, 2021), 32.

18. Quotes in this paragraph are from Narby and Chanchari, *Plant Teachers*, 32.

19. Jeremy Narby, conversation with author, Science and Non-duality Conference, Marin, CA, October 20, 2017.

20. Narby and Chanchari, *Plant Teachers*, 71.

21. Stephen V. Beyer, *Singing to the Plants: A Guide to Mestizo Shamanism in the Upper Amazon* (Albuquerque: University of New Mexico Press, 2010), 56, 61.

22. Maestro Nelson Barbaran Gomez, Zoom conversation with author, May 14, 2021.

23. Maestra Anita Perez Sinacay, Maestro Javier Vasquez Gomez, and Maestro Nelson Barbaran Gomez, Zoom conversation with author, December 2020.

24. Evgenia Fotiou, "Encounters with Sorcery: An Ethnographer's Account," *Anthropology and Humanism* 35, no. 2 (2010): 201.

25. Joe Tafur, *The Fellowship of the River: A Medical Doctor's Exploration into Traditional Amazonian Plant Medicine* (Phoenix, AZ: Joe Tafur Publisher, 2017).

26. Bonnie Glass-Coffin, "Anthropology, Shamanism, and Alternate Ways of Knowing-Being in the World: One Anthropologist's Journey of Discovery and Transformation," *Anthropology and Humanism* 35, no. 2 (2010): 206. In the same issue, see Edith Turner, "Discussion: Ethnography as a Transformative Experience," 220; and David J. Hufford, "Visionary Experiences in an Enchanted World," 142.

27. Michael Harner, *The Way of the Shaman* (San Francisco: Harper, 1980), 1.

28. Michael Harner, *Cave and Cosmos* (Berkeley, CA: North Atlantic Books, 2012), 3.

29. Kathleen Harrison, "The Leaves of the Shepherdess," in *Sisters of the Extreme: Women Writers on the Drug Experience*, ed. Cynthia Palmer and Michael Horowitz (Rochester, VT: Park Street Press, 1982), 304.

30. Monica Gaglianao, *Thus Spoke the Plant: A Remarkable Journey of Groundbreaking Scientific Discoveries and Personal Encounters with Plants* (Berkeley, CA: North Atlantic Books, 2018), 78.

31. Robin Carhart-Harris et al., "LSD Enhances Suggestibility in Health Volunteers," *Psychopharmacology* 232, no. 4 (2014): 791.

32. "Video: What Is Psychedelic Chaplaincy?"

33. Psychedelic Medicine," *Pharmacology and Translational Science* 4 (2021): 579.

34. If you're interested, see St. Petersburg Chamber Choir, "Alleluia, Behold the Bridegroom," https://www.youtube.com/watch?v=fqXQ-hn1TTc.

35. T.M. Luhrmann, *How God Becomes Real: Kindling the Presence of Invisible Others* (Princeton, NJ: Princeton University Press, 2020), xiii.

36. Auke Tellegen and Gilbert Atkinson, "Openness to Absorbing and Self-Altering Experiences ('Absorption'), A Trait Related to Hypnotic Susceptibility," *Journal of Abnormal Psychology* 83, no. 3 (1974): 271.

37. Michael Lifshitz, Michiel van Elk, and T.M. Luhrmann, "Absorption and Spiritual Experience: A Review of Evidence and Potential Mechanisms," *Consciousness and Cognition* 73 (2019): 3.

38. Eline C.H.M. Haijen et al., "Predicting Responses to Psychedelics: A Prospective Study," *Frontiers in Pharmacology* (2018): 15; and Erich Studerus et al., "Prediction of Psilocybin Response in Health Volunteers," *PlosOne* 7, no. 2 (2012): 7.

39. Michael A. Thalbourne and Peter S. Delin, "Transliminality: Its Relationship to Dream Life, Religiosity, and Mystical Experience," *International Journal for the Psychology of Religion* 9, no. 1 (1999): 46, 59.

40. St. Ignatius Loyola, *The Spiritual Exercises of St. Ignatius Loyola* (Chicago: Loyola University Press, 1951), 28.

41. Brother Lawrence, *The Practice of the Presence of God* (New York: Whitaker House, 1982), 42.

42. Henry Corbin, *Alone with the Alone: Creative Imagination in the Sufism of Ibn Arabi* (Princeton, NJ: Princeton University Press, 1969), 221, 251.

43. Farid ud-Din Attar, *The Conference of the Birds*, ed. Sholeh Wolpé (New York: W.W. Norton, 2017).

44. Annelise Kelly, "Mountain Girl Surveys the Psychedelic Renaissance," *Lucid News*, May 7, 2021, https://www.lucid.news/qa-with-psychedelic -pioneer-carolyn-garcia.

45. Myron J. Stolaroff, "Thanatos to Eros: 35 Years of Psychedelic Exploration," MAPS, 1994, https://maps.org/2014/11/19/thanatos-to-eros-35-years-of -psychedelic-exploration.

46. Marie-Louise von Franz, "Commentary to the Inward Gaze," in *Encounters with the Soul: Active Imagination as Developed by C. G. Jung*, by Barbara Hannah (Boston: Sigo Press, 1981), vii.

47. James Hillman and Sonu Shamdasani, *Lament of the Dead: Psychology after Jung's Red Book* (New York: W.W. Norton, 2013), 130.

48. Hannah, *Encounters with the Soul*, 3.

49. Sarah Wildman, "The Bat Mitzvah Question I Wasn't Expecting: 'Are We Safe at Synagogue?'" *New York Times*, January 23, 2022.

50. Shamdasani, "Toward a Visionary Science," 33.

51. Hillman and Shamdasani, *Lament of the Dead*, 1.

52. "Basic Information about Voices & Visions," Hearing Voices Network, accessed March 2021, https://www.hearing-voices.org/voices-visions.

53. Jeffrey Raff, *The Practice of Ally Work: Meeting and Partnering with Your Spirit Guide in the Imaginal World* (Berwick, ME: Nicholas Hays, 2006), 40.

54. Hillman and Shamdasani, *Lament of the Dead*, 40, 165.

55. Michael C. Mithoefer, "A Manual for MDMA-Assisted Psychotherapy in the Treatment of Posttraumatic Stress Disorder," MAPS (August 2015): 8, https://maps.org/research-archive/mdma/MDMA-Assisted -Psychotherapy-Treatment-Manual-Version7-19Aug15-FINAL.pdf.

56. Narby and Chanchari, *Plant Teachers*, 50.

57. Stolaroff, "Thanatos to Eros."

58. G. William Barnard, *Liquid Light: Ayahuasca Spirituality and the Santo Daime Tradition* (New York: Columbia University Press, 2022), 209.

59. Luis Eduardo Luna, "Some Observations on the Phenomenology of the Ayahuasca Experience," in *Ayahuasca Reader: Encounters with the Sacred Vine*, ed. Luis Eduardo Luna and Steven F. White (Santa Fe, NM: Synergistic Press, 2016), 277.

60. Chris Kilham, "Psychedelic La La Land — When Visions Go Wrong," Medicine Hunter, November 2013, https://www.medicinehunter.com /psychedelic-la-la-land-when-visions-go-wrong.

61. Narby and Chanchari, *Plant Teachers*, 69.

62. Tenzin Priyadarshi and Zara Houshmand, *Running toward Mystery: The Adventure of an Unconventional Life* (New York: Random House, 2020), 21, 63, 71.

63. Ruth Haley Barton, *Pursuing God's Will Together* (Downers Grove, IL: InterVarsity Press, 2012), 85.

64. Janet Adler, *Offering from the Conscious Body: The Discipline of Authentic Movement* (Rochester, VT: Inner Traditions, 2002), 151.

65. Llewellyn Vaughan-Lee, *The Circle of Love* (Inverness, CA: The Golden Sufi Center, 1999), 90.

Chapter Five: Visionary Realms

1. Aldous Huxley, *The Doors of Perception and Heaven and Hell* (New York: HarperCollins, 1954), 79.

2. Baba Hari Dass, *Path Unfolds: The Autobiography of Baba Hari Dass* (Santa Cruz, CA: Sri Rama Publishing, 2019), 146.

3. Mary Watkins, *Invisible Guests: Development of Imaginal Dialogues* (NJ: Lawrence Erlbaum, 1986), 4.

4. Henry Corbin, "Mundus Imaginalis or the Imaginary and the Imaginal," Spring 1972, 1. http://www.bahaistudies.net/asma/mundus_imaginalis .pdf.

5. Henry Corbin, "Towards a Chart of the Imaginal," *Spiritual Body and Celestial Earth* (Princeton, NJ: Princeton University Press, 1980), 7, http://philosophiaperennisetuniversalis.blogspot.com/2013/01/towards -chart-of-imaginal.html.

6. Carol Frenier and Lois Sekerak Hogan, "Engaging the Imaginal Realm: Doorway to Collective Wisdom," Collective Wisdom Initiative, 2, https://www.collectivewisdominitiative.com/papers/frenier_imaginal.htm.

7. Quotes from Corbin, "Mundus Imaginalis," 1, 5; and Corbin, "Towards a Chart of the Imaginal," 1.

8. Cynthia Bourgeault, *Eye of the Heart: A Spiritual Journey into the Imaginal Realm* (Boulder, CO: Shambhala Publications, 2020), 62.

9. Corbin, "Towards a Chart of the Imaginal," 3.

10. Hillman, *Thought of the Heart*, 71.

11. William C. Chittick, *The Sufi Path of Love: The Spiritual Teachings of Rumi* (Albany: State University of New York Press, 1983), 162.

12. Angela Voss and William Rowlandson, eds., *Daimonic Imagination: Uncanny Intelligence* (Cambridge, UK: Scholar Publishing, 2013), 3.

13. Corbin, "Mundus Imaginalis," 4.

14. Priyadarshi and Houshmand, *Running toward Mystery*, 132.

15. Jeffrey Mishlove, "Stanislav Grof, A New Paradigm of the Unconscious," Thinking Allowed TV, 2010, https://www.youtube.com/watch?v=vtwqZxjcgKc.

16. "Video: The Truth Shall Set Whom Free? A Conversation on Esoteric Knowledge, Alternative Spirituality, and Conspiracy Theories," Harvard Divinity School Center for the Study of World Religions, January 10, 2022, https://cswr.hds.harvard.edu/news/knowledge-spirituality-conspiracy/2021/12/8.

17. Tobin Hart, Peter L. Nelson, and Kaisa Puhakka, *Transpersonal Knowing: Exploring the Horizon of Consciousness* (Albany: State University of New York Press, 2000), 5.

18. Tom Cheetham, *Imaginal Love: The Meanings of Imagination in Henry Corbin and James Hillman* (Thompson, CT: Spring Publications, 2015), 80.

19. Hofmann, *LSD: My Problem Child*, 11.

20. "The Most Beautiful Death," Letters of Note, March 25, 2010, https://lettersofnote.com/2010/03/25/the-most-beautiful-death.

21. William Ernest Henley, "Invictus," *A Book of Verses* (London: David Nutt, 1888), 57, https://www.poetryfoundation.org/poems/51642/invictus.

22. Victor E. Frankl, *Man's Search for Meaning: An Introduction to Logotherapy* (Boston: Beacon Press, 1992), 75.

23. *Mission: Joy — Finding Happiness in Troubled Times*, directed by Louis Psihoyos and Peggy Callahan (Los Angeles: The Film Collaborative, 2022), https://missionjoy.org.

24. Hillman and Shamdasani, *Lament of the Dead*, 165.

25. Quotes by Shulgin from Ann Shulgin, "The New Psychotherapy: MDMA and the Shadow," *Eleusis*, no. 3 (1995), https://erowid.org /psychoactives/guides/guides_article1.shtml.

26. Robert N. Butler, "The Life Review: An Interpretation of Reminiscence in the Aged," *Psychiatry* 26 (1963): 68.

27. Charlotte Martial et al., "Neurochemical Models of Near-Death Experiences: A Large Scale Study Based on the Semantic Similarity of Written Reports," *Consciousness and Cognition* 69 (2019): 64.; and Christopher Timmermann et al., "DMT Models the Near-Death Experience," *Frontiers in Psychology* 9 (2018): 7.

28. Charlotte Martial et al., "Losing the Self in Near-Death Experiences: The Experience of Ego-Dissolution," *Brain Sciences* 11, no. 7 (2021): 937.

29. Stanislav Grof, *Beyond Death: The Gates of Consciousness (Art and Imagination)* (London: Thames and Hudson, 1980), 6.

30. Stanislav Grof and Joan Halifax, *Human Encounter with Death* (New York: E.P. Dutton, 1978), 59.

31. Shamdasani, "Toward a Visionary Science," 103.

32. WeCroak, https://www.wecroak.com.

33. *Hofmann's Potion*, Littlefield.

34. Stephen Jenkinson, *Die Wise: A Manifest for Sanity and Soul* (Berkeley, CA: North Atlantic Books, 2015), 203. For more on Jenkinson, visit Orphan Wisdom, https://orphanwisdom.com.

35. Eric Kast, "LSD and the Dying Patient," *Chicago Medical Society Quarterly* 26 (1966): 86.

36. Walter N. Pahnke et al., "Psychedelic Therapy (Utilizing LSD) with Cancer Patients," *Journal of Psychoactive Drugs* 3, no. 1 (1970): 74.

37. Charles S. Grob, Anthony P. Bossis, and Roland R. Griffiths, "Use of the Classic Hallucinogen Psilocybin for Treatment of Existential Distress Associated with Cancer," in *Psychological Aspects of Cancer*, ed. J.L. Steel and B.I. Carr (New York: Springer, 2022), 74, 79.

38. Anthony Bossis, "Psilocybin, Spirituality, and Palliative Care: Research and Implications," *Alternative and Complementary Therapies* 27, no. 1 (2021): 17.

39. Thomas C. Swift et al., "Cancer at the Dinner Table: Experiences of Psilocybin-Assisted Psychotherapy for the Treatment of Cancer-Related Distress," *Journal of Humanistic Psychology* 57, no. 5 (2017): 498.

40. Hazrat Inayat Khan, *The Complete Sayings* (Medford, OR: Omega Publications, 1990).

41. Max Ehrmann, "Desiderata," 1927, https://www.desiderata.com /desiderata.html.

42. Christopher Timmermann et al., "Psychedelics Alter Metaphysical Beliefs," *Scientific Reports* 11 (2021): 6.

Chapter Six: Somatic Sensing

1. Sigmund Freud, *The Ego and the Id* (New York: W.W. Norton, 1960), 20.

2. Bessel van der Kolk, *The Body Keeps the Score: Brain, Mind, and Body in the Healing of Trauma* (New York: Penguin Books, 2015), 95.

3. Phillipe Rochat and Tricia Striano, "Perceived Self in Infancy," *Infant Behavior and Development* 23 (2000): 516.

4. Christine Anzieu-Premmereur, "The Skin-Ego Sensuality, Trauma in Infancy and Adult Narcissistic Issues," *Psychoanalytic Review* 102, no. 5 (2015): 664.

5. Tiffany Field, Miguel Diego, and Maria Hernandez-Reid, "Preterm Infant Massage Therapy Research: A Review," *Infant Behavior and Development* 33, no. 2 (2009): 115.

6. Daniel N. Stern, *The Motherhood Constellation: A Unified View of Parent-Infant Psychotherapy* (New York: Routledge, 1998), 3.

7. Anzieu-Premmereur, "Skin-Ego Sensuality," 667.

8. Roland R. Griffiths et al., "Psilocybin Can Occasion Mystical-Type Experiences Having Substantial and Sustained Personal Meaning and Spiritual Significance," *Psychopharmacology* 187, no. 3 (2006): 12.

9. Frederick S. Barrett and Roland R. Griffiths, "Classic Hallucinogens and Mystical Experiences: Phenomenology and Neural Correlates," *Current Topics in Behavioral Neurosciences* 36 (2018): 405.

10. Jane Macnaughton, "Making Breath Visible: Reflections on Relations between Bodies, Breath, and World in the Critical Medical Humanities," *Body and Society* 26, no. 2 (April 27, 2020): 33.

11. Noga Arikha, "The Interoceptive Turn," *Aeon*, June 17, 2019, https://aeon .co/essays/the-interoceptive-turn-is-maturing-as-a-rich-science-of -selfhood.

12. Antonio Damasio, *Self Comes to Mind: Constructing the Conscious Brain* (New York: Random House, 2012), 17.

13. Van der Kolk, *Body Keeps the Score*, 95.

14. Wolf E. Mehling et al., "The Multidimensional Assessment of Interoceptive Awareness, Version 2 (MAIA-2)," *PLoS ONE* 13, no. 12 (2018): 4.

15. Beate M. Herbert and Olga Pollatos, "The Body in the Mind: On the Relationship between Interoception and Embodiment," *Topics in Cognitive Science* 4 (2012): 693.

16. Matthew Sanford, *Waking: A Memoir of Trauma and Transcendence* (Emmaus, PA: Rodale, 2006), 19, 292.

17. Drew Leder, "Inside Insights: A Phenomenology of Interoception," in *The Interoceptive Mind: From Homeostasis to Awareness*, ed. Manos Tsakiris and Helene DePreester (Oxford, UK: Oxford University Press, 2019), 314.

18. Charles V.W. Brooks, *Sensory Awareness: The Rediscovery of Experiencing* (New York: Viking, 1974), 16.

19. Krista Tippett, "Stephen Batchelor: Finding Ease in Aloneness," *On Being*, April 23, 2020, https://onbeing.org/programs/stephen-batchelor-finding-ease-in-aloneness.

20. Rosalind Watts, "Psilocybin for Depression: The ACE (Accept/Connect/Embody) Model Manual," Imperial College, 2021, 18, https://psyarxiv.com/5x2bu.

21. Quotes by Gendlin from Eugene T. Gendlin, *Focusing* (New York: Bantam, 1982) 82, 107, 121.

22. Anil Seth, "The Neuroscience of Reality," *Scientific American* 321, no. 3 (2019), https://www.scientificamerican.com/article/the-neuroscience-of-reality.

23. Damasio, *Self Comes to Mind*, 272.

24. Rich Simon, "An Interview with Peter Levine, Turning Psychotherapy Bottom Up," *Psychotherapy Networker*, March/April 2019, https://www.psychotherapynetworker.org/magazine/article/2347/an-interview-with-peter-levine.

25. Sharon Stanley, *Relational and Body-Centered Practices for Healing Trauma: Lifting the Burdens of the Past* (New York: Routledge, 2016), 63.

26. Marion Woodman, *Leaving My Father's House: A Journey to Conscious Femininity* (Boulder, CO: Shambhala, 1992), 15.

27. Alex Gearin, "An Amazonian Shamanic Brew in Australia: Ayahuasca Healing and Individualism," PhD Thesis, School of Social Science, the University of Queensland (2015), 103, doi: 10.14264/uql.2015.1038.

28. Rosalind Watts and Jason B. Luoma, "The Use of the Psychological

Flexibility Model to Support Psychedelic Assisted Therapy," *Journal of Contextual Behavioral Science* 15 (2020): 98.

29. Pedro Favaron, "Explicación de Los Cantos Medicinales Ikaros," You-Tube, posted March 18, 2019, https://www.youtube.com/watch?v=r5P1RqUkzws&t=1s.

30. Mohammed Rustom, "The Metaphysics of the Heart in the Sufi Doctrine of Rumi," *Studies in Religion* 37, no. 1 (2008): 4.

31. Kabir Helminski, *The Knowing Heart: A Sufi Path of Transformation* (Boulder, CO: Shambhala, 2000), 26.

32. Rustom, "Metaphysics of the Heart," 5.

33. John Perkins, *Touching the Jaguar: Transforming Fear into Action to Change Your Life and the World* (Oakland, CA: Berrett-Koehler Publishers, 2020), 99.

34. Christopher I. Roos et al., "Native American Fire Management at an Ancient Wildland–Urban Interface in the Southwest United States," *Proceedings of the National Academy of Sciences* 118, no. 4 (2021), https://www.pnas.org/doi/full/10.1073/pnas.2018733118.

35. Quotes by Sharrock from Dena Sharrock, "Smoky Boundaries; Permeable Selves: Exploring the Self in Relationship with the Amazonian Jungle Tobacco, Mapacho," *Anthropological Forum* 28, no. 2 (2018): 5, 7.

36. Lynne Hume, *Portals: Opening Doorways to Other Realities through the Senses* (New York: Oxford International Publishing, 2007), 22.

37. Masao Matsuhashi and Mark Hallett, "The Timing of the Conscious Intention to Move," *European Journal of Neuroscience* 28, no. 11 (2008): 2351, doi:10.1111/j.1460-9568.2008.06525.x.

38. Renate Oppikofer, "Tina Keller: Her Fascinating Life and Creative Work Inspired by the Psychology of C.G. Jung," *Jung Journal* 9, no. 1 (2015): 56.

39. Mary Whitehouse, "Physical Movement and Personality," paper presented at the Analytical Club of Los Angeles, 1963, 3.

40. Janet Adler, "Who Is the Witness?" *Contact Quarterly* 12, no. 1 (1987): 20–29.

41. Emilie Conrad, *Life on Land: The Story of Continuum, the World-Renowned Self-Discovery and Movement Method* (Berkeley, CA: North Atlantic Books, 2007), 384.

42. William A. Richards, "Mystical and Archetypal Experiences of Terminal Patients in DPT-Assisted Psychotherapy," *Journal of Religion and Health* 19, no. 2 (1978): 119.

43. Joan Chodorow, *Dance Therapy and Depth Psychology: The Moving Imagination* (New York: Routledge, 1991), 46.

44. Gia Kourias, "Joker: A Dance Critic Reviews Joaquin Phoenix's Moves," *New York Times*, October 11, 2019, https://www.nytimes.com/2019/10/11 /arts/dance/joaquin-phoenix-dancing-joker.html.

Chapter Seven: What the Hell Is Integration, Anyway?

1. Lee and Shlain, *Acid Dreams*, 46.

2. Lauren Lepow, Hirofumi Morishita, and Rachel Yehuda, "Critical Period Plasticity as a Framework for Psychedelic-Assisted Psychotherapy," *Frontiers in Neuroscience* 15 (2021): 4.

3. Ram Dass, "Little Schmoos," episode 16, *Here and Now* (podcast), Be Here Now Network, accessed February 2021, https://beherenownetwork .com/ram-dass-here-and-now-ep-16-little-shmoos.

4. Hannah, *Encounters with the Soul*, 7.

5. R. Gordon Wasson, "Seeking the Magic Mushroom," *Life*, May 13, 1957, 108.

6. Ahmed Kagil, "This Mexican Medicine Woman Hipped America to Magic Mushrooms, with the Help of a Bank Executive," Timeline, January 5, 2017, https://timeline.com/with-the-help-of-a-bank-executive -this-mexican-medicine-woman-hipped-america-to-magic-mushrooms -c41f866bbf37.

7. Robin L. Carhart-Harris and Guy M. Goodwin, "The Therapeutic Potential of Psychedelic Drugs: Past, Present, and Future," *Neuropsychopharmacology* 42 (2017): 2110.

8. Jordan Sloshower et al., "Psilocybin-Assisted Therapy of Major Depressive Disorder Using Acceptance and Commitment Therapy as a Therapeutic Frame," *Journal of Contextual Behavioral Science* 15 (2020): 15.

9. For more information on the suggested approaches to psychedelic integration, see the following articles: Watts, "Psilocybin for Depression"; Ingmar Gorman et al., "Psychedelic Harm Reduction and Integration: A Transtheoretical Model for Clinical Practice," *Frontiers in Psychology* 12 (2021): 5; Max Wolff et al., "Learning to Let Go: A Cognitive-Behavioral Model of How Psychedelic Therapy Promotes Acceptance," *Frontiers in Psychiatry* 11 (2020): 8; Alan K. Davis, Frederick S. Barrett, and Roland

R. Griffiths, "Psychological Flexibility Mediates the Relationship between Acute Psychedelic Effects and Subjective Decreases in Depression and Anxiety," *Journal of Contextual Behavioral Science* 15 (2020): 43; and Albert Garcia-Romeu and William A. Richards, "Current Perspectives on Psychedelic Therapy: Use of Serotonergic Hallucinogens in Clinical Interventions," *International Review of Psychiatry* 30, no. 4 (2018): 8.

10. Mithoefer, "Manual for MDMA-Assisted Psychotherapy."

11. Robin Lester Carhart-Harris et al., "Psychedelics and the Essential Importance of Context," *Journal of Psychopharmacology* 32, no. 7 (2018): 3.

12. Ari Brouwer and Robin Lester Carhart-Harris, "Pivotal Mental States," *Journal of Psychopharmacology* 35, no. 4 (2020): 322.

13. Bossis, "Psilocybin, Spirituality," 16.

14. Alan E. Kazden, "Mediators and Mechanisms of Change in Psychotherapy Research," *Annual Review of Clinical Psychology* 3 (2007): 6.

15. Ulrich Hoerni, Thomas Fischer, and Bettina Kaufmann, eds., *The Art of C. G. Jung* (New York: W.W. Norton, 2019), 14.

16. Fingal's Cave, https://www.atlasobscura.com/places/fingal-s-cave.

17. Elizabeth M. Nielson and Jeffrey Guss, "The Influence of Therapists' First-Hand Experience with Psychedelics on Psychedelic-Assisted Psychotherapy Research and Therapy Training," *Journal of Psychedelic Studies* 2, no. 2 (2018): 7.

18. Virginia Satir, "The Therapist's Story," in *The Use of Self in Therapy*, ed. Michele Baldwin (New York: Routledge, 2013), 20.

19. Carl G. Jung, "The Structure and Dynamics of the Psyche," *The Collected Works of C. G. Jung*, vol. 8, ed. Gerhard Adler (Princeton, NJ: Princeton University Press, 1960/1969), para. 558.

20. Shulgin, "New Psychotherapy," 5.

21. Murray Stein, *Jung's Map of the Soul* (Chicago: Open Court, 1998), 106.

22. Shulgin, "New Psychotherapy," 6.

23. For more on the relationship of mystical experience to therapeutic change, see the following: Griffiths, "Psilocybin Can Occasion Mystical-Type," 12; Garcia-Romeu and Richards, "Current Perspectives on Psychedelic Therapy," 13; and David E. Olson, "The Subjective Effects of Psychedelics May Not Be Necessary for Their Enduring Therapeutic Effects," *Pharmacology and Translational Science* 4 (2021): 564.

24. Leor Roseman, David J. Nutt, and Robin L. Carhart-Harris, "Quality of

Acute Psychedelic Experience Predicts Therapeutic Efficacy of Psilocybin for Treatment-Resistant Depression," *Frontiers in Pharmacology* 8 (2018).

25. See Alex Tzelnic, "The Dangerous Art of Depersonalization: What Psychedelics, Psychosis, and Mindfulness Can Teach Us about No-Self, and Why Set and Setting Play Such an Important Role in Ego Deconstruction," *Tricycle*, September 23, 2021, https://tricycle.org/trikedaily/depersonalization; and Gabrielle I. Agin-Liebes et al., "Long-Term Follow-Up of Psilocybin-Assisted Cancer," *Journal of Psychopharmacology* 34, no. 2 (2020): 10.

26. Shulgin, "New Psychotherapy," 8.

27. "Patients Who Took Psilocybin to Treat Depression and Anxiety Reflected on Their Experiences," YouTube, posted July 15, 2020, https://www.youtube.com/watch?v=L5CjgEmfnEs.

28. His Holiness the Dalai Lama, *The Four Noble Truths: Fundamentals of the Buddhist Teachings* (London: Thorsons, 1997), 38.

29. Yongey Mingyur Rinpoche, *In Love with the World* (New York: Spiegel & Grau, 2019), 372.

30. Shamdasani, "Toward a Visionary Science," 91.

31. For more on these topics, see Charlotte Martial et al., "Losing the Self in Near-Death Experiences: The Experience of Ego-Dissolution," *Brain Sciences* 7 (2021): 936; Megan Kirouac and Katie Witkiewitz, "Identifying 'Hitting Bottom' among Individuals with Alcohol Problems: Development and Evaluation of the Noteworthy Aspects of Drinking Important to Recovery (NADIR)," *Substance Use and Abuse* 52, no. 12 (2017): 3; and Janet C'de Baca and Paula Wilbourne, "Quantum Change: Ten Years Later," *Journal of Clinical Psychology* 60, no. 5 (May 2004): 532, http://thirdworld.nl /quantum-change-ten-years-later.

32. Shulgin, "New Psychotherapy," 5.

33. Jeffrey E. Young and Janet S. Klosko, *Reinventing Your Life: The Breakthrough Program to End Negative Behavior and Feel Great Again* (New York: Plume, 1994), 15; and Jeffrey E. Young, "Early Maladaptive Schemas," 2012, accessed February 12, 2016, http://www.schematherapy.com /id73.htm.

34. C'de Baca and Wilbourne, "Quantum Change."

35. C'de Baca and Wilbourne, "Quantum Change."

36. Stolaroff, "Thanatos to Eros."

Chapter Eight: Psychedelic Ways of Knowing

1. Mara Lynn Keller, "The Ritual Path of Initiation in the Eleusinian Mysteries," *Rosicrucian Digest* 2 (2009): 33.

2. William A. Richards, *Sacred Knowledge: Psychedelics and Religious Experiences* (New York: Columbia University Press, 2016), 144.

3. Gary Snyder, *The Practice of the Wild* (Berkeley, CA: Counterpoint, 1990), 25.

4. Ann Belford Ulanov, *The Psychoid, Soul and Psyche: Piercing Space-Time Barriers* (Einsiedeln, Switzerland: Daimon Verlag, 2017), 15.

5. Priyadarshi and Houshmand, *Running toward Mystery*, 190.

6. Simone Weil, *Gravity and Grace* (New York: Routledge, 2002), 35.

7. Jalaluddin Rumi, *Rumi: Selected Poems*, trans. Coleman Barks, with John Moynce, A.J. Arberry, and Reynold Nicholson (London: Penguin Books, 2004), 109.

8. Marc P. Bennett et al., "Decentering as a Core Component in the Psychological Treatment and Prevention of Youth Anxiety and Depression: A Narrative Review and Insight Report," *Translational Psychiatry* 11, no. 288 (2021): 2.

9. Jiddu Krishnamurti, *Krishnamurti's Notebook* (New York: HarperCollins, 1976), 214.

10. Hume, *Portals*, 21.

11. Tom Cheetham, *Imaginal Love: The Meanings of Imagination in Henry Corbin and James Hillman* (Thompson, CT: Spring Publications, 2015), 137.

12. Hillman, *Thought of the Heart*, 70.

13. David Herbert Lawrence, "Song of a Man Who Has Come Through," in *The Complete Poems of D. H. Lawrence* (London: Wordsworth Edition Limited, 1994), 195.

14. Kathleen Raine, "Unsolid Matter," in *The Oracle in the Heart and Other Poems* (Dublin, Ireland: Dolman Press, 1980), 13.

15. Quotes by Teilhard de Chardin from Pierre Teihard de Chardin, *The Heart of the Matter* (New York: Harvest Book, 1979), 15, 17, 27, 50.

16. Shamdasani, "Toward a Visionary Science," 99.

17. Jung, *Memories, Dreams, Reflections*, 4.

18. Anthony Bossis, personal communication with author, June 11, 2022.

19. Muraresku, *Immortality Key*, 30.

20. Alice Clinch, "Ecstasy and Initiation in the Eleusinian Mysteries," in *The*

Routledge Companion to Ecstatic Experience in the Ancient World, ed. Diana Stein, Sarah Kielt, and Karen Pollinger Foster (New York: Routledge, 2022), 315.

21. Jalaluddin Rumi, "If you could get rid," in *Essential Sufism*, ed. James Fadiman and Robert Frager (San Francisco: HarperSanFrancisco, 1997), 244.

22. Christopher Timmermann et al., "DMT Models the Near-Death Experience," *Frontiers in Psychology* 15 (August 2018): 2.

23. Sam Parnia et al., "Guidelines and Standards for the Study of Death and Recalled Experiences of Death — A Multidisciplinary Consensus Statement and Proposed Future Directions," *Annals of the New York Academy of Sciences* 1511, no. 1 (May 2022): 6.

24. Martin Shaw, *Courting the Wild Twin* (White River Junction, VT: Chelsea Green Publishing, 2020), 24.

25. Ernesto Spinelli, "Relatedness — Contextualising Being and Doing in Existential Therapy," *Existential Analysis* 27, no. 2 (July 2016): 23.

26. Thich Nhat Hanh, *Heart of Understanding: Commentaries on the Prajñaparamita Heart Sutra* (Berkeley, CA: Parallax Press, 1988), 17.

27. Parnia et al., "Guidelines and Standards," 8.

28. Parnia et al., "Guidelines and Standards," 5.

29. Elizabeth G. Krohn and Jeffrey J. Kripal, *Changed in a Flash: One Woman's Near-Death Experience and Why a Scholar Thinks It Empowers Us All* (Berkeley, CA: North Atlantic Books, 2018), 328; and Harold Bloom, *Omens of Millennium: The Gnosis of Angels, Dreams, and Resurrection* (New York: Riverhead Books, 1996), 138.

30. Allan N. Schore, *The Science of the Art of Psychotherapy* (New York: W.W. Norton & Company, 2012), 133.

31. Schore, *Science of the Art*, 13.

32. Roberta Murphy et al., "Therapeutic Alliance and Rapport Modulate Responses to Psilocybin Assisted Therapy for Depression," *Frontiers in Pharmacology* 12 (2022): 11.

33. Schore, *Science of the Art*, 42, 134.

34. John M. Allman et al., "Intuition and Autism: A Possible Role for Von Economo Neurons," *Trends in Cognitive Sciences* 9 (2005): 370.

35. Christopher Bache, "The Challenges of Integrating an Extreme Psychedelic Journey," in *Psychedelics and Psychotherapy: The Healing Potential of*

Expanded States, ed. Tim Read and Maria Papaspyrou (Rochester, VT: Park Street Press, 2021), 308, 309.

36. Schore, *Science of the Art*, 7.

37. Bache, "Challenges of Integrating," 301, 312.

38. Julia D. Howell, "The Social Sciences and Mystical Experience," in *Exploring the Paranormal*, ed. George K. Zollschan, John F. Schumaker, and Greg F. Walsh (Dorset, UK: Prism Press, 1989), 86.

39. All quotes from Peter L. Nelson, "Mystical Experience and Radical Deconstruction through the Ontological Looking Glass," in *Transpersonal Knowing*, ed. Tobin Hart, Peter L. Nelson, and Kaisa Puhakka, 61, 69, 70, 72, 75.

40. Quotes from Spinelli, "Relatedness — Contextualising Being," 15, 16.

41. Benny Shanon, *The Antipodes of the Mind: Charting the Phenomenology of the Ayahuasca Experience* (New York: Oxford University Press, 2002), 8.

42. Peter Kingsley, *In the Dark Places of Wisdom* (Point Reyes Station, CA: The Golden Sufi Center, 1999), 65, 67.

43. Yongey Mingyur, *In Love*, 510.

44. Raymond Carver, "Late Fragment," in *All of Us: The Collected Poems* (New York: Vintage Contemporaries, 1996), 616.

45. *First Peoples*, episode 1, "Americas," directed by Nicolas Brown, aired on June 24, 2015, PBS, https://www.pbs.org/show/first-peoples.

46. David Mowaljarlai and Jutta Malnic, *Yorro Yorro: Everything Standing Up Alive* (Broome, Australia: Magabala Books Aboriginal Corporation, 2001), 53.

47. Thomas Merton, *When the Trees Say Nothing* (Notre Dame, IN: Sorin Books, 2003), 340.

48. Pew Research Center Report, "Many Americans Mix Multiple Faiths," December 9, 2009, https://www.pewresearch.org/religion/2009/12/09/many-americans-mix-multiple-faiths/#6.

INDEX

ABOUT THE AUTHOR

Psychologist Rachel Harris, PhD, has been in private practice for thirty-five years. She has received a National Institutes of Health New Investigator's Award, published more than forty scientific studies in peer-reviewed journals, and worked as a psychological consultant to Fortune 500 companies. She is the author of *Listening to Ayahuasca: New Hope for Depression, Addiction, PTSD, and Anxiety* and *Twenty Minute Retreats: Revive Your Spirit in Just Minutes a Day with Simple, Self-Led Practices*. She lives on an island off the coast of Maine and in the San Francisco Bay Area.

ListeningToAyahuasca.com